DIFFERENCE AND DIVERSITY IN COUNSELLING

CONTEMPORARY PSYCHODYNAMIC PERSPECTIVES

DIFFERENCE AND DIVERSITY IN COUNSELLING

CONTEMPORARY PSYCHODYNAMIC PERSPECTIVES

Difference and Diversity in Counselling

Contemporary Psychodynamic Perspectives

Edited by

Sue Wheeler

palgrave
macmillan

First published 2006 by
PALGRAVE MACMILLAN
Houndmills, Basingstoke, Hampshire RG21 6XS and
175 Fifth Avenue, New York, N.Y. 10010
Companies and representatives throughout the world.

PALGRAVE MACMILLAN is the global academic imprint of the Palgrave
Macmillan division of St. Martin's Press, LLC and of Palgrave Macmillan Ltd.
Macmillan® is a registered trademark in the United States, United Kingdom
and other countries. Palgrave is a registered trademark in the European
Union and other countries.

ISBN-13: 978–1–4039–4327–9
ISBN-10: 1–4039–4327–3

This book is printed on paper suitable for recycling and made from fully
managed and sustained forest sources.

A catalogue record for this book is available from the British Library.

Library of Congress Cataloging-in-Publication Data
    Difference and diversity in counselling : contemporary psychodynamic
perspectives / edited by Sue Wheeler.
        p. cm.
    Includes bibliographical references and index.
    ISBN 1–4039–4327–3 (cloth)
        1. Cross-cultural counseling. 2. Psychotherapy. I. Wheeler, Sue, 1948–
BF637.C6D537 2006
158′.3—dc22   2006043230

10 9 8 7 6 5 4 3 2 1
15 14 13 12 11 10 09 08 07 06

Printed in China

Contents

List of Figures and Tables

Figure

Tables

Notes on the Contributors

Sue Wheeler is Professor of Counselling and Psychotherapy and Director of the Counselling and Psychotherapy programme at the University of Leicester. She is a BACP accredited counsellor and UKCP registered psychotherapist and Fellow of BACP. She is the author of many papers on counsellor training, supervision and the professional development of therapists. Her books include *Training Counsellors: the Assessment of Competence* (Cassell, 1996) and, with David King, *Supervising Counsellors: Issues of Responsibility* (Sage, 2001).

Mariette Clare has a professional background in adult and community education with a special interest in widening participation and inclusive learning. She is a part-time lecturer in psychodynamic counselling at the University of Leicester. In addition she is Chair of the Leicester Counselling Centre, which offers low cost, long term counselling. She also works there as assessor, counsellor and supervisor, besides having a small private practice. Her research interests arise from the intersection of clinical practice with the field of contemporary cultural studies and she has a particular interest in questions about narrative, identity and what it is that lies outside discourse.

Nicola Barden is Head of Counselling Services at the University of Portsmouth, a UKCP registered psychoanalytic psychotherapist and a BACP accredited practitioner. She is currently Chair of BACP. She is the editor, with Susannah Izzard, of *Rethinking Gender and Therapy* (Open University Press, 2001).

David Mair is a BACP registered practitioner, and a UKRC accredited counsellor. He works as a counsellor and supervisor at the University of Birmingham and in private practice. He has published several articles in counselling journals informed both by the outcomes of his research into gay men's experiences of counselling as well as by his own experience as a gay man. He trains counsellors to be aware of the impact of sexual orientation within the therapeutic relationship for university courses and for organisations such as RELATE. He is currently writing a book for gay and lesbian clients on ways to handle the coming out process.

Fiona Aitken is a UKCP registered psychotherapist and BACP accredited counsellor and supervisor in private practice with 20 years' experience. She initiated a sexual abuse project at Nottingham Counselling Centre and has trained many counsellors and professionals in the helping agencies in working with sexual abuse as well as facilitating therapeutic groups for adult survivors of sexual abuse. She has designed and taught a 'Counselling Men' module for a counsellor training course and is currently a member of the Integrative Psychotherapy training team at the Sherwood Institute, Nottingham.

Aileen Coupe has been a counsellor, UKCP registered psychotherapist and supervisor for the last 15 years, having trained as a psychodynamic counsellor at the University of Leicester. She has an MA in Integrative Psychotherapy. She has worked with a voluntary counselling service and two University student counselling services in the past. She currently works for several employee assistance programmes, in two GP practices, and in her own private practice.

Julia Segal has worked as a counsellor for people with Multiple Sclerosis for the past 20 years. She trains counsellors and other professionals working with illness and disability. Her two main interests are the application of the ideas of Melanie Klein and her followers to everyday life, and illness and disability in the family. As well as writing numerous articles and book chapters, her books include *Phantasy in Everyday Life: a Kleinian Approach to Understanding Ourselves* (Pelican, 1985, and reprinted several times); *Melanie Klein*, in the Key Figures in Counselling and Psychotherapy series (Sage, 1992); and, with John Simkins, *Helping Children with Ill or Disabled Parents: a Guide for Professionals* (Jessica Kingsley, 1996).

Shula Wilson is a UKCP registered therapist and BACP accredited counsellor and the founder and Clinical Director of SKYLARK, Counselling Service for People Affected by Disability. She is the school counsellor at Centre Academy, a school for students with special educational needs. She teaches at the School of Psychotherapy and Counselling at Regent's College. As an immigrant, she is interested in the experience of 'being an outsider' and in particular the issue of communication. She was a founder member and a chairperson of the European Society for Communicative Psychotherapy (ESCP). Currently she is a committee member of the Multi Lingual Psychotherapy Centre (MLPC) and a trustee and a training committee member of the Institute for Psychotherapy and Disability (IPD). She is the author of *Disability, Counselling and Psychotherapy – Challenges and Opportunities* (Palgrave Macmillan, 2003).

Hilary Wellington managed day care services for Age Concern Leicester, and established a carers' support service for the Alzheimer's Disease Society, before training as a counsellor. She has taught mental health issues, death and dying, and social gerontology for the Open University. Her MA research in Women's Studies explored motivations and experiences of daughters caring for frail elderly mothers. She has experience of counselling in a number of voluntary settings, including Leicester Counselling Centre, Farm Crisis Network and the Anglican Diocese of Leicester. Currently she works as an organising tutor for the Counselling and Psychotherapy training programme at the University of Leicester and as a counsellor in private practice.

Gill Tuckwell is a counsellor, supervisor and trainer who currently works in private practice. Her interest in cultural and racial issues dates back over many years to her former career in teaching in central Birmingham. For several years she worked with a multicultural development unit. Recognising the need for greater racial and cultural awareness in the counselling profession, her doctorate focused on the influence of race and culture on the counselling process. She has contributed several articles to counselling journals, and is author of *Racial Identity, White Counsellors and Therapists* (Open University Press, 2002).

Miriam Isaac is Senior Lecturer in Health and Social Welfare at University College Worcester. She has been a counsellor and trainer in the statutory and voluntary sectors and is currently in private practice. Her interest in class dates back over many years and is related to her first discipline of Sociology, lecturing in Social Welfare, and her experiences in counselling. She is currently studying for a PhD, researching the topic of counselling and class.

Alistair Ross has been a Minister of Religion and counsellor in several settings over the last 20 years. He has trained counsellors and pastoral counsellors through St John's College, Nottingham and the Institute of Pastoral Counselling, Nottingham. He is currently the academic team leader for counselling at the University of Birmingham. Alistair is also a research fellow and personal tutor at the Queen's Foundation for Ecumenical Theological Training, Birmingham. He is the author of many articles and chapters on counselling and pastoral counselling. His books include: *Evangelicals in Exile: Wrestling with Theology and the Unconscious* (DLT, 1997) and *Counselling Skills for Church and Faith Community Workers* (Open University Press, 2005).

Acknowledgements

Many people have contributed to the development and production of this book. The idea arose when redesigning a Diploma course in Counselling with Aileen Coupe and Angela MacLeod at the University of Leicester. We wanted to update the course to include recognition of the diversity of culture, race, religion, and sexual orientation that is prevalent in Britain in the 21st century. We designed the course and then came to the reading list. There were a few useful texts on race, sexual orientation and so on, but we had to search harder to find anything written from a psychodynamic perspective. Hence the decision to edit this book. My thanks go to Aileen and Angela for their ideas and enthusiasm for the project.

Many authors have contributed to this book and my thanks go to them for working so hard, sticking to deadlines and being gracious with my editing suggestions. Several colleagues have read various draft chapters and offered valuable comments, including Jenny Kidd (while on her honeymoon) and Henry Miller. Kathryn Noble has provided invaluable secretarial assistance. Two reviewers and Catherine Gray at Palgrave Macmillan read and commented on the first draft of this book. Their feedback was constructive and informative and served to improve the book considerably.

One of the joys of putting this book together is that I have learned so much myself, particularly about politics, economics and sociology. From being sceptical, because of my ignorance, I am now convinced that sociology should be part of the curriculum for all counselling and psychotherapy courses. The stimulus for much of that learning has come from conversations, debates and even mini lectures from my partner Henry Miller, whose depth of knowledge, and ability to communicate it clearly to others, never ceases to impress me. For his teaching, patience, support and love, I thank him.

Introduction

Sue Wheeler

Psychodynamic counselling is rooted in psychoanalytic theory and practice. It is taught throughout Britain and other countries worldwide on counselling and psychotherapy training courses. It draws on the work of Freud, Jung, Klein, Winnicott, Kohut, Erickson, Guntrip and many others, a rich wealth of material that helps us to understand the functioning of the human psyche, the stages of human development, intimate relationships and mental health. The theory provides us with the potential for insight and understanding in working therapeutically with individuals, couples, groups or organisations when things go wrong or when expectations are not fulfilled.

In fact there is such a wealth of theory to refer to that for a counsellor training course of limited duration, it is a major task to decide what is essential to the curriculum and what must be left out. There is also the problem of distinguishing between what is appropriate for five times weekly analysis, compared with brief psychodynamic therapy in a GP practice. The diverse schools of psychoanalytic thinking also challenge the trainer, particularly when no particular body of knowledge is favoured and an integration of theory is attempted.

We are also compelled to take account of the modern world in which diversity abounds. Searching classical psychoanalytic literature for references to race, culture or disability is not always rewarded. Searching classical psychoanalytic literature for references to gender identity, sexual orientation and the emancipation of women reveals plenty, but much of which is not acceptable in a world that embraces diversity and seeks to afford equality for all. It is possible to find reference to some aspects of religion and certainly to psychotherapy with older people, but in the context of the modern world, in multi faith societies and with life expectancy ever increasing, there is room for more contemporary ideas. Indeed, the social context of the twenty first century, that provides the backdrop for the hopes, fears and aspirations of our clients, warrants attention, as people and organisations are shaped by the social systems that prevail.

The intention of this book is to re-examine various topics that might be valuable to the counsellor in practice, when faced with someone who is in some way 'different' in the consulting room, from a psychoanalytic perspective. The intention is to fill in some of the gaps left by other psychoanalytic writers, by providing some thoughts about how psychoanalytic ideas can be applied to counselling that meet the demands of the modern world.

This book should be essential reading for all counsellors and psychotherapists in training and for experienced practitioners who need to ensure that they are up to speed in thinking about issues of difference that affect their practice. It is only in the past decade that equal opportunities legislation and the need to be proactive in thinking about diversity have begun to make their mark on counselling and psychotherapy training. Many experienced therapists will not have been introduced to the kind of issues discussed in this book. Complacency is no longer acceptable and this book will provide good continuing professional development material, to bring the reader up to date.

PART I

Social Context and Society

Thinking Psychodynamically about Diversity

Sue Wheeler

Counsellors and psychotherapists are usually liberal minded people. Such a career is chosen because we care about people, embrace altruism, and strive to make some contribution towards righting the ills of this world. At the same time we are powerfully and often unconsciously influenced by the culture and society in which we live. While wanting to help others, we also need to look after ourselves and fit in with the families, communities and organisations in which we live and work, and that can create conflicts in our value and belief systems. Diversity in society can be considered at many levels. Signing up to an equal opportunities policy is easily done; understanding some of the more complex implications and implementing it is not so simple. Engaging with difference and diversity at a deep level is challenging and leaves no assumptions undisturbed, no values and beliefs unchanged. It can be profoundly disturbing.

Some years ago while visiting Egypt I took a felucca across the Nile. Our sailor was a handsome young man called Abdul, aged about 20 years. His boat was the first in a line of feluccas on the shore offering their services for the short crossing. He spoke excellent English and was clearly articulate and intelligent. We chatted happily about numerous topics and then I asked Abdul what he was going to do with his life. He replied, 'I am going to sail a felucca.' Somewhat surprised I asked what he did during the summer months when there were fewer tourists around. He replied, 'I will swim and wait for the winter.' I have pondered on that conversation for many years, trying to reconcile my expectations of life, education, good job, promotion, pension, nice home, social status, with his experience and expectations. He was satisfied with his life and was in no hurry to change anything. He radiated a peace and tranquillity that was most attractive. As a psychotherapist, it made me question whether my cultural norms and expectations inhibit my clients exploring theirs or whether I collude in a blinkered way with the status quo.

Affluent Western societies may be advanced in many ways, but pressures to achieve and consume lead to stress and mental health problems abound. Such societies produce contradictions that echo personal moral dilemmas. The planet is being rapidly destroyed by carbon emissions and depletion of resources but it is hard to give up cars or foreign travel. Religion is encouraged as long as it does not lead to fundamentalist fanaticism. Gay relationships can be tolerated but not legalised in marriage. Intolerance and oppression are rife throughout the world and the counselling room is one place in which individuals should be able to explore their values and beliefs, but how open can the therapist be to the client when their own value system is challenged?

Counselling and psychotherapy is a strange activity, often presented as concerned with intrapsychic and interpersonal processes. Some psychoanalytic theories metaphorically place the mother and child in a bubble and map human development as if nothing outside the bubble matters, or influences that intimate relationship and the growth that ensues. The therapist works in the rarefied atmosphere of the consulting room devoid of personal accoutrements in order to preserve the power of the transference. However, there is turbulence everywhere, not just related to the psychic equilibrium of the client, but also in the therapist and most powerfully in the world outside that room. World events, whether it be the invasion of a country, terrorist attacks, natural disasters or the continued erosion of the ozone layer and the ensuing climate change permeate the therapy room one way or another. Therapists and clients, including those who are black, disabled, Muslim, lesbian or gay, rich or poor, old or young, carry not just their personal family history but also their social and political history. In the words of Juliet Mitchell (1974), 'the personal is political and the political is personal'; therapists take a political stance as an integral part of their role.

The Western world in the 21st century hosts a diverse society; many countries have legislation written and enforced to foster inclusive societies, covering topics such as equal opportunities, discrimination with respect to religious beliefs, age, sexual orientation, gender or disability. There is often other legislation that is not so generous; immigration, particularly for asylum seekers for example, is ever more tightly monitored and controlled. Counselling and psychotherapy services proliferate in English speaking countries, but are not widely used by some sections of society. Indeed, assessment for psychotherapy will render some disadvantaged groups unsuitable because of a lack of psychological mindedness (being able to construe some of life's difficulties as being related to the self and not all externally driven) (Coltart, 1988) or an inability to articulate needs clearly and make appropriate demands. The individualistic worldview that counselling promotes will serve to alienate cultural groups that value family and community above individual responsibility. If older people, particularly those in institutions have access to counselling, they are in a minority; Freud's assertion that psychotherapy has little to offer those over the age of 50 has not helped the development of services in this sector.

Training to be a psychodynamic counsellor or therapist is challenging for both student and teacher; the curriculum always demands more time than is available. A multitude of theories have evolved from the work of Freud that warrant attention: human growth and development must be understood, psychoanalytic technique must be practised, the interface with psychiatry needs to be appreciated, and the numerous ways in which therapy can be practised, briefly, in groups, families, over the internet, studied. While various client groups and presenting problems are a legitimate focus for study, the role and function of society as a powerful influence on individuals and groups, particularly minorities or other overtly disadvantaged groups, tends to be relegated to the study of sociology that does not quite make the tight agenda of a training course. The stretched curriculum promotes tokenism. A seminar on cross-cultural counselling focuses on the client who is in some cultural sense different, in the protected space of the consulting room rather than the less tangible context of wider society. The educational background of counsellors and therapists is wide ranging. Ideally, a suitable foundation for psychotherapy training would be the social sciences: history, politics, economics, sociology, anthropology and philosophy, that would provide a matrix of background knowledge to aid understanding of the client in his/her social, economic and political context. Regrettably the pull towards psychotherapy training is an urgent need to make sense of self and others through the fascinating and all consuming study of intra and interpersonal processes. Such a process is adequately supported by a rich fund of psychoanalytic literature to fuel the intellect on such a quest, and a dearth of psychoanalytic literature that makes the social, historical and political context of the therapeutic relationship a priority. Young (1994) describes his quest to find psychoanalytic literature on racism: 'Never, never before have I come up with so little, and much of what I have found isn't much use … it's pathetic' (p. 100).

This book aims to fill in some of the gaps traditionally found in psychoanalytic literature by bringing world history, sociology, politics and religion into the consulting room in the service of understanding clients who might be labelled as 'different', recognising that we are all involved in the labelling process and the alienation it creates. It aims to bring the political in its broadest sense into the frame of therapy, in order to give all involved in the therapeutic endeavour a broader view of the emotional stresses and strains of civilisation and their impact on humanity as well as on the individual.

Elliot (2002) analyses the links 'between the psyche and the contemporary social world' (p. 11) to conclude that the development of self is inevitably and inextricably influenced not just by current culture and society but also by historical events that have shaped that society. 'The cultural and institutional processes of modernisation which have launched the West upon a dazzling path of global expansion are said to have reached into the heart of selfhood and created new forms of personal identity' (p. 11). Particularly pertinent to this argument is the concept of transference in its widest sense. Often understood as a response to a person that is rooted and shaped by early life experiences with significant others, usually authority figures and parents, a broader interpretation evident in the work of Freud is a transference response to social relationships and the cultural realm beyond the family. The development of self is a complex process that can be explained by numerous psychoanalytic theories, but introjection is acknowledged to play its part, whether the introjection of the mother's smiles and love symbolised by the breast in Kleinian theory or self objects as defined by Kohut (Siegel, 1996). If we acknowledge the transference relationship with culture and society, the implications for the development of self and identify in a hostile or prejudicial society are frightening. For members of an oppressed minority group, whether black, disabled, without good language or communication ability, internalising the negative reaction of the external world will inevitably have a damaging impact on their identity and sense of self. The elderly, while not a minority group in any sense, will have absorbed the impact of challenging world events, as well as a rapidly changing culture that, added to the anxiety created by physical decline in later years, gives them good cause for psychotherapeutic attention.

The social context of the 20th century within which psychoanalysis, psychotherapy and counselling have developed since Freud's day has been marked by conflict and cooperation, differentiation and integration, often in dialectical movements. The ambivalence inherent in personal relationships is apparent on a global stage. Political and economic events affect the everyday lives of ordinary people, their work, lifestyle, relationships, habits and consciousness as well as spawning theories about the nature of society and human nature. Freud (2001) recognised three sources of human suffering: 'the superior power of nature, the feebleness of our own bodies and the inadequacy of the regulations which adjust the mutual relationships of human beings in the family, the state and society' (p. 86). About the first two there is a limit to what can be done, although pollution and global warming are making strides towards the deterioration of the environment and medical science continues to make advances in prolonging life, but such progress is not without an impact on the organisation of society. Given that human beings organise their social systems and institutions to support their way of life for their own comfort and satisfaction, we have been spectacularly successful in creating wealth in the Western world but less successful in promoting health, well being and the relief of suffering. Given these man-made systems, the conclusion must be that 'a piece of unconquerable nature may lie behind – this time a piece of our own psychical constitution' (Freud 2001, p. 86), not least human aggression.

Unbridled human aggression is evident throughout the Western world even in the early years of the 21st century. Some groups of people bond with some common sense of identity and then proceed to persecute and slaughter another group that may be identified as being different because of their race, culture, language or religion. 'Anyone who calls to mind the atrocities committed during the racial migrations (Greeks and Turks) or the invasions of the Huns ... or at the capture of Jerusalem by the pious Crusaders or even indeed the horrors of the recent world war [First World War] ... anyone who calls these things to mind will have to bow humbly before the truth of this view' (Freud 2001, p. 112). Certainly the slaughter of the First World War (1914–18) had a profound effect on Freud's writing, influencing his works *Beyond the Pleasure Principle* and *Civilisation and its Discontents* (both in Freud 2001). The recrudescence of anti-Semitism and the rise of the Nazis prompted Freud's flight to England.

At the time of his death, the extent of the massacre of millions of Jews, gays, communists and gypsies in concentration camps was unknown, but such events fit with his predictions and his pessimistic analysis of the human psyche. Freud (2001) states, 'It is always possible to bind together a considerable number of people in love so long as there are other people left over to receive the manifestations of their aggressiveness' (p. 114).

Other events of the 20th century have had a powerful impact on the organisation of society, such as the economic slump of the inter war years and the Second World War, which have weakened beliefs in notions of progress and liberal democracy. The collapse of the Austro-Hungarian, Ottoman and Russian empires after the First World War and of the British Empire after the Second World War, as well as of the Soviet Union and Communism in Eastern Europe (1988 to 1992), marked the replacement of multi-ethnic empires ruled by metropolitan authoritarian governments from London, Paris, Berlin, Istanbul or Moscow, by nation states based in large measure on ethnic identity.

Wars and revolutions have changed the political map of the world. World Wars I and II, the Cold War, Korean War, anti-colonial, materialist and socialist revolutions in China, Vietnam, Algeria and Cuba claimed many lives and changed cultures. For a time, at the end of the Cold War, there was a sense of triumphalism and a boost to the notion of the liberal capitalist market and democracy, but this was short-lived. The relatively peaceful revolutions that led to the overthrow of Soviet Communist power in Russia and Eastern Europe (East Germany, Poland, Czechoslovakia, Romania and Bulgaria) are set in contrast with the violent conflict in the former Yugoslavia. Ethnic cleansing provides a horrible illustration of the intolerance of difference and the barbaric way in which aggression against men, women and children, including sexual violence, was unleashed when the institutions that governed and ordered society broke down. States have been established according to religious and ethnic identity (such as Israel, Serbia, Croatia, Pakistan), which has led to the expulsion, torture or death of others who were identified as different, for whom there was no place and no mercy.

In South and Central America – Chile, Argentina, Brazil, Venezuela and Nicaragua – conflicts raged between a variety of popular/radical/socialist revolutionary movements and authoritarian military rule, often backed by multi-national corporations and the US government. At the same time these conflicts have testified to the potential for cooperation and solidarity across different groups and nations; workers, peasants and intellectuals have found common cause, as in the case of Zapatistas from Mexico linking in dialogue with French farmers.

There have also been some triumphs for civilisation in the 20th century, shaping people's behaviour and consciousness, that are relevant to this book: the emancipation of women and the growth of feminism in the Western world and the abolition of Apartheid in South Africa, to name just two. Starting with their achievement of the vote, women have united to challenge institutional and familial oppression, to create opportunities for choice of role in the home, organisations and society as a whole. The process and progress of liberation continues, but much has already been achieved. In South Africa, the pressure from within the country and outside, not least the anti-Apartheid movement, finally yielded a liberation that was long overdue. In the words of Nelson Mandela (1995), it was a 'Long walk to freedom'. That society still struggles to empower, support and protect all its citizens, but it is work in progress.

For a generation reaching maturity in the 1950s and 60s there was an ever present threat of nuclear war. This sometimes reached a climax: as during the time of the Russian suppression of the Hungarian uprising in 1956, the Anglo–French–Israeli Suez crisis in 1956 and the Cuban missile crisis in 1962. In 1968, besides the uprising in Prague, there were democratic demonstrations on North American university campuses and in European cities (London, Paris, Rome and Berlin), with students and sometimes workers revolting against US government involvement in the Vietnam war as well as more generally against the alienation and exploitation of consumer capitalism. The effects of these events led to changes in consciousness and involvement in political activity spread into a wide range of movements. Feminism, ecology, human rights and identity politics fuelled political activity and political engagement changed personal identities.

One of features of the world scene that has become increasingly apparent in the last 20 years is globalisation, particularly the power of transnational corporations such as Microsoft, BP, General Motors, Wal-Mart, Tesco, where economic power is greater than in many middle sized states. In shopping centres throughout Europe and the USA, the same shops will be evident, as giant businesses establish dominance over smaller traders. Balancing that to some extent has been the growth of international agencies that promote peace and cooperation: the League of Nations (1919), United Nations (1945), and associated agencies like UNESCO. In addition there are economic regulating agencies like the World Trade Organisation, the International Monetary Fund, the World Bank, all of which attempt to regulate and mediate conflict, albeit often in the interests of large corporations, dominant Western states or markets. Regional associations such as the European Union attempt to regulate economic, political, social and cultural activity. Meanwhile non-governmental agencies, relief agencies and pressure groups with a world brief like Oxfam, Greenpeace, Amnesty International and Médicins sans Frontières address issues related to the environment, famine, war, torture and disease. Moreover, disillusionment with conventional social democratic policy has been parallelled in Britain with involvement in specific issue campaigns such as opposition to the Iraq war and legislation affecting education and gay rights. These are some of the many examples of ways in which the individual can now attempt to influence institutions that govern society, by uniting and applying group pressure.

That globalisation in political, economic, cultural and technological arenas has had a profound effect on individuals as well as societies is epitomised by the dominance of some consumer brands and symbols like Coca-Cola, Nike or McDonald's, all of which now rival the Cross as images that are most widely recognised. At the same time the dominance of Western culture has led to an increasing recognition, if not acceptance, of the diversity of religion, ethnicity, gender, and sexual orientation. Anti-globalisation movements such as the European Social Forum challenge market capitalism and US imperialism, reasserting the value of the welfare state and socialist and democratic ideals.

Furthermore the development of communication and transport, in all its forms, had a profound effect on relationships, institutions and society in the 20th century. Advanced transport and communication systems facilitate movement and migration of labour across countries and continents: some are economic migrants and others flee oppression. Whatever the reason for migration, the impact on families, communities and individuals is not to be underestimated.

The proliferation of print publications and means of instantaneous oral and visual communication has brought the whole world and even the universe into our everyday lives. Radio, television, mobile phones and computers monitor world events as they happen (at least in countries where censorship is limited). The scale of human suffering is increasingly apparent and has an impact on the consciousness of people in the developed world. TV images of civilian casualties in Iraq or Palestine, as well as the sight of famine victims in the Sudan can lead to a loss of belief in progress. The social impact of instant communication through email and text messaging is yet to be measured, but may prove to have a substantial impact on the quantity as well as the quality of personal relationships.

As we begin the 21st century the words of Freud still ring true: 'In spite of every effort, these endeavors of civilisation have not so far achieved very much (2001, p. 112). The gaps between rich and poor, upper class and working class, employed and unemployed have increased in our sophisticated, technological, advanced, developed world. The gap between the richest and poorest nations and peoples has also widened on a world scale. Aggression is condoned in unilateral action to wage war, but condemned in terrorist wars and when acted out by alienated individuals committing crimes. Splitting is rife between the good guys and the bad guys, and whole societies are induced to collude with perceptions often propagated to sustain economic and political power. However, with roots going back at least to the Enlightenment, the assertion of ethnic identity, religious freedom and the struggle for recognition and rights for women, the disabled, gay, lesbian, the elderly and children, can all be seen as different aspects of the human rights movement for political and civil emancipation; it proceeds despite all the setbacks.

This brief overview of some of the events in world history and of some of the movements that have emerged to promote equality and alleviate suffering, puts the practice of psychotherapy in a historical context. Encouraged by Samuels (2001) the political consciousness of psychotherapists is being raised both in the therapy room and in society. The recognition that a myriad familial, community, national and world influences reside in the unconscious of each individual will enhance communication and understanding. Object relations theory (Winnicott, 1986) tells us that individual identity is created and embellished through the process of fantasy by the internalisation of part objects, aspects of people, who are in turn influenced by systems, societies and cultures. Social and political movements affect society and social structures in turn affect the nature of the self. 'In this connection the nature of social transformations this century [is] palpable. Modernity – with its global economic mechanisms, its restructuring of time and space, its capitalist commoditisation, its phantasmagoria of mass media – brings into existence new forms of personal and social identity' (Elliot, 2002, p. 22).

In Britain and elsewhere counselling and psychotherapy services are booming. There is demand for psychotherapeutic treatment that is variously supplied, throughout the National Health Service, companies, colleges and universities, as well as in voluntary agencies and private practice. A well trodden route towards training is through the experience of being a client. Motivation for becoming a therapist has many origins, but an element of narcissism can usually be recognised, as the drive towards helping others inevitably reflects on self-image and self-esteem. Projection also plays its part, as engaging with the powerless, suffering client provides a vehicle for harnessing power and wellbeing, as unwanted aspects of the self are projected into the other. Psychotherapy can provide a satisfying existence for the therapist since their shadow side and all its vicissitudes are not only expressed by, but also processed by, the client. Guggenbuhl-Craig (1971) notes that: 'All those active in the social professions who work to "help humanity", have highly ambiguous psychological motives for their actions. In his own consciousness and to the world at large, the social worker feels obliged to regard the desire to help as his prime motivation. But in the depths of his soul the opposite is simultaneously constellated – not the desire to help but lust for power and joy in depotentiating the "client" ' (p. 8).

Furedi (2003) condemns the counselling and psychotherapy profession for its role in pathologising individuals, fostering dependency and not questioning the function of globalisation, capitalism, bureaucracy, terrorism, consumerism and so forth, in creating personal suffering. Allwood (in Parker et al. 1995) has noted how depression, a common mental health problem in contemporary society, serves a number of societal functions: urging people to see the events of life as a matter of the psyche rather than of the public domain, encouraging self-regulation, particularly of women, and as a potentially damaging form of liberal humanist therapeutic theory, which emphasises personal responsibility rather than a need for social change (p. 47).

To some extent it is to the shadow side of the therapist that this book is addressed. It invites the therapist to look beyond their well meaning and empathic capacities, their fascination with the misfortunes of others, to their collusion with the inequalities in society, not least as manifest through the power relationship with clients that perhaps makes some contribution, albeit unconsciously, to the perpetuation of the status quo. As part of a process to explore racism, Young (1994) reflects on some of his own thoughts and fantasies: 'I have at one time or another – almost always silently in my adult years – despised 'Japs', hated Germans ... thought of Arabs as fanatics, and noticed the smells of other cultural groups and found them alien' (p. 116). He goes on the say that 'My point is that it is second nature, and there's the rub. Second nature is history, culture and personal experience disguised as first nature or biology' (p. 116). There is nothing easy about living and working with people who are different to ourselves and one of the most painful aspects is being confronted and shamed by our inevitable prejudices. Young refers to Freud's pessimism, noting that 'the psychotic and rapacious parts of human nature are kept at bay only by constant effort and they are omnipresent in phantasy and ever ready to erupt if sublimation and guilt fail in their work' (p. 117). There are no formulaic solutions for managing envious, hateful and destructive feelings towards others, but it behoves the therapist to keep them in mind and under control. It is all too easy to use the mask of toleration to mask intolerance (Bauman, 1991).

Clarke uses the phrase 'new racism' (2003) to describe the way in which: 'we, the British nation are tolerant, we open our arms to you, but in doing so the "we" marginalises "you". "You" cannot be like "us" because you are not like "us". We make reparation to you but in doing so we are unable to cope with the anxiety that we feel, the guilt of treating you the way we have' (p. 143). This is similar to the impossible position, argued by Guggenbuhl-Craig (1971), that all therapists find themselves in when attempting to help others. The client invests power in the therapist as the archetypal healer. While not consciously seeking power, if the therapist identifies with the archetype, they distance themselves from the client. The more the therapist's conscious efforts are directed towards being helpful to others, the more their shadow absorbs their less altruistic, selfish, aggressive and destructive tendencies. As a result the therapist becomes more grandiose and self-righteous, hence less in touch with her or his own inner world. If the therapist invests too much in her or his position of power, the client cannot be healed as they become the recipient of the vulnerable parts of the therapist as well as their own.

Kleinian theory, and particularly the effect of splitting, helps to explain racism (Clarke, 2003). In order to make sense of our good and bad experience of others (symbolised by the presence and absence of the breast/mother) the good is introjected and the bad projected onto others. Persecutory anxiety ensues from the feared, bad 'other', and resolution is achieved in the depressive position, when one person, 'the other', is seen as containing both good and bad and the self is acknowledged as having both good and bad tendencies. Anxiety is then generated by the recognition of the capacity for destructiveness. Guilt, shame and the need to make reparation ensue, which may be so powerful that paranoid schizoid defences are redeployed. In the explanation of racism, anxiety is not created by acceptance and celebration of difference; rather it is the doubt on the part of the individual of their ability to do so that leads to the employment of paranoid schizoid defences. If this works for racism, then it also holds true for dealing with any other 'difference' between self and other. There is considerable capacity for reflection on relationships between a majority or minority group, between more and less powerful groups, and where understanding of the experience and world view of the other requires a substantial suspension and/or questioning of currently held views, beliefs and experiences. This will be discussed in more detail by Tuckwell in Chapter 9.

The issues of difference that have been chosen for exploration in this book are by no means exhaustive. Many other topics could have been chosen. The choice was partly fortuitous in that I was acquainted with the work, interests and expertise of all of the authors. The social context of counselling was included because it is universally missing from counselling and psychotherapy literature and underpins all that follows. The choice was also informed by a literature search that highlighted some social factors or groups that have been largely ignored in other psychotherapeutic writing, such as class differences and the elderly. Some chapters present research recently conducted by the authors (race and culture, religion) and others provide new insight into therapy with people with physical and language disabilities. The chapter on religion, written from the perspective of a Christian minister, has been included because religious differences are so prominent in our contemporary world and fuel so much misunderstanding and vilification. The two chapters on gender and sexual orientation were commissioned because I knew that the authors had some interesting ideas that would challenge current thinking.

The book is organised in four parts: social context and society; gender and sexuality; disability and old age; and race, culture and beliefs. This chapter is the first of Part I, to be followed by a chapter on the social context of counselling which looks critically at aspects of the social environment that are influencing the inevitable and rapidly advancing professionalisation of counselling and psychotherapy. Mariette Clare (Chapter 2) discusses the concepts of power and knowledge encapsulated in professionalism that have the potential to alienate the client. She draws on the work of Foucault to discuss ways in which the individual and society are inextricably linked and how personal difficulties are in themselves a mirror of the dynamics played out in the external world. Professional knowledge has a history of adding to the oppressive regulation of clients or 'service users' (a contemporary NHS term used to try to counteract disempowerment), through its claim to be able to distinguish reliably between 'normal' and 'pathological'. At the same time, professionalisation itself will police both the practice of counselling and those who are accredited to practise it. To these perspectives needs to be added the increasing pressure to produce quantifiable results for the sake of justifying expenditure. That the therapist has a political, social and psychological role is anathema to many, who believe that their focus should be entirely on the relief of suffering of the client, generated from their internal world and immediate environment. But modern society is economically stratified as well as marked by differences of age, gender, sexuality, disability and ethnicity. In these circumstances, the provision of counselling to help heal the casualties of injustice feeds social control: those in power can relax in the knowledge that the needy are receiving attention and that the status quo can be retained.

Part II, on gender and sexuality, has three chapters. Nicola Barden's chapter (Chapter 3) tracks the psychoanalytic theories about the development of gender identity from Freud to the present day. It looks at Freud's positioning of the male as normative, and the consequent limitations for the understanding of female development. Through Klein, the emphasis is moved from the role of the father to the role of the mother, and from what a girl lacks to what she has. Jung's unique contribution on the contrasexuality of the individual is considered through his development of the concepts of the anima and animus as archetypal animations of gender, with both their liberating and their conservative implications.

Freud's view of the feminine has been the subject of much criticism, some of which will be discussed together with new thinking on the development of male identity stimulated by the work of Frosh and Samuels. The final section of Chapter 3 follows the move away from the 'grand theory' approach to women as a group towards understanding the web of difference that is part of individual gendered identities. Gender as a binary construct is challenged, and implications for the counselling relationship outlined. In accordance with the theme that runs throughout the book, the chapter addresses the cultural and social context that has informed these theories, a perspective that has previously been largely ignored.

The next chapter, by David Mair (Chapter 4) follows on from the discussion of gender differentiation. It provides a brief overview of psychoanalytic thinking about homosexuality. The implications of an 'Oedipus-complex resolution' model of psychosexual development are controversial for working with gay clients. The notion that homosexuals are a homogenous, easily defined sub-group of the population is challenged. As is appropriate to contemporary therapy, an alternative understanding of how to work with gay clients is offered. With reference to Kohut and Jacobs, the dilemma of neutrality versus affirmation of homosexuality (including the issue of therapist authenticity) is addressed. Homophobic views held by therapist and client, and the internalisation of societal prejudices, have to be fully appreciated when working with gay clients as they lead to a debilitating 'false-self' defence structure against internalised homophobia within the client. 'Coming-out', the process of both internal and external acknowledgement of homosexuality, is a major life transition and a critical appraisal of the process is presented. Mair considers the way in which psychodynamic counsellors can use their theoretical understanding of human development and therapeutic technique, alongside their desire to be fully present with the gay client. As in many of the other chapters, transference and countertransference, as means of understanding the intrapsychic processes of the client, are prominently featured. Stress is also laid on how important it is for therapists to work through their own homophobia if they are to be able to use countertransference appropriately.

Chapter 5, written by Aileen Coupe and Fiona Aitken, opens up the therapeutic relationship between women and men, in which the woman holds the power as the therapist. Although men are less likely to seek counselling and psychotherapy than women they often choose a female therapist. The many changes in the social, cultural and political roles of men and women in the last century have profoundly affected both sexes. It could be argued that (some) women have wrested power from (some) men in the workplace and the home. Masculinity is described by Clare (2000) as being in crisis. Patriarchy has been threatened, and intimate relationships have provided both the battleground and the casualty station for the conflict between men and women. This can be echoed in the therapy room if the female counsellor insensitively trumpets too loudly, too quickly the need for emotional expression on the part of the male client, creating an environment that may echo the conflict of other relationships, leading to alienation and withdrawal from the process. Managing the power dynamic in a female–male therapeutic relationship, particularly through the countertransference, is vital. The female therapist's history of relationships with men, both intimately and through historical and social associations, will impact on her ability to withstand the heat of her aggressive and retaliatory tendencies, especially when her identification with the female partners of her clients prompts her to protect them. The chapter also examines the therapeutic space needed for men to allow their vulnerability to emerge, with particular reference to class, race, and sexuality, demonstrating how psychodynamic thinking can help or hinder the therapeutic relationship.

Part III, on disability and old age, has three chapters. Julia Segal writes about illness and disability in Chapter 6, stressing the significant affect such afflictions have on the way people feel about themselves and how others feel about them. Each individual has a unique experience depending on their beliefs and fantasies (conscious and unconscious) about themselves and the response of society, family and friends. Not all clients perceive their illness or disability to be a problem, while others present it as their primary concern. The illness or disability of a loved one has serious implications for the lives of some people. Counsellors with limited experience of working with disabled clients are inhibited by their anxiety. Since no two disabilities (and no two people) are the same, this applies even if they have a disability themselves. Julia Segal draws on her Kleinian insight and understanding to illuminate the complex dynamics of the counselling relationship when one party is disabled. She is pragmatic and encourages therapists to be respectful but bold and look beyond and behind the disability to the person within, as well as promoting optimism that individuals can lead fulfilling lives despite the obstacles they face.

Chapter 7 picks up some of the themes of disability raised in the previous chapter but with specific reference to communication difficulties through speech impediment. Shula Wilson presents the dilemmas and dynamics of working with an interpreter, whether human or computer assisted, when conducting therapy with such clients. Controversially she links the onset of speech impediments with regression and a process that is akin to the developmental stages of adolescence. She presents the uncomfortable notion of the client feeling like an 'outsider', alienated from others through the inability to communicate clearly. She notes how hard it can be to be independent when treated by others as immature and incapable of managing adult relationships. As in most other chapters, the author draws attention to the therapist's reactions, such as frustration, lack of confidence, irritation, or paternalism that are evoked by the client with distorted or absent language, that warrant careful monitoring if the client is to be truly engaged.

The third chapter in Part III concerns therapeutic work with older people. Older people past retirement age account for a substantial and increasing percentage of the population. Hilary Wellington (Chapter 8) reviews relevant literature and uses her personal experience as well as her own qualitative research to consider the relevance of psychodynamic counselling for older adults. She evaluates the significance of dependency and attachment theory, both in terms of the problems older people bring to counselling, and in the therapeutic relationship and counselling process. She appraises various views on the efficacy of counselling older people, and the specific opportunities and challenges for working therapeutically with older clients.

In the final part of the book, on race, culture and beliefs, Gill Tuckwell (Chapter 9) explores race and culture, and traces the development of the psychodynamic interpretations of racism and prejudice. Recognising that race and culture have often been viewed synonymously, the chapter delineates clearly between these terms by drawing attention to significant historical and sociopolitical forces that have been instrumental in shaping them. Particular consideration is given to the collective experiences of black people and white people as the oppressed and the oppressor in world-changing events such as slavery and colonisation. Power dynamics are thus discussed, and attention is given to the influence of racial and cultural phenomena in determining social status and access to authority in society. The psychodynamic frame is examined for its relevance and effectiveness in working with race and culture. Concepts such as transference and countertransference, and defence mechanisms such as projection and projective identification, are discussed in relation to racial and cultural phenomena arising in counselling dyads. While it is argued that some psychodynamic principles are theoretically inconsistent with the needs of a diverse client population, Tuckwell concludes that the emphasis on unconscious material and the influence of the past on the present offer great potential for understanding complex racial and cultural dynamics in the counselling process.

Social class in counselling and therapy is the focus of Chapter 10, in which Miriam Isaac considers class to be a fundamental component of identity. She uses a Marxist analysis to explain how class differences combined with the power of the counselling relationship can obscure the transference and impede progress for the client. One complication arises from personal definitions. People are identified by their gender or ethnicity, but when it comes to class, the personal definition is confused by misconceptions, ambivalence and status. She argues that class is similar to 'race' – a cultural and political idiom related to the underlying structure of society. If class differences are ignored in the spirit of treating all human beings as equals, and to preserve the comfort zone of the therapist, a fundamental aspect of human experience, that might encompass alienation, deprivation or humiliation, can be missed. Powerlessness is debilitating. Powerlessness can be pathologised by blaming the poor and uneducated for their impoverished circumstances. Such thinking creates a chasm in the therapeutic relationship. The link is made between Marxist and object relations theories to the effect that people interrelate inextricably with their social context, which impacts on the outer and inner world of the client and therapist.

The final chapter (Chapter 11), written by Alistair Ross, offers a psychoanalytic perspective on religion as it affects the therapeutic relationship. Historically, psychoanalysis and religion have been antipathetic. Freud saw the overthrow of 'heathen religions' by Christianity as part of the demise of civilisation and declared that the commandment of 'Love thy neighbour as thy self' runs contrary to the nature of humankind. In recent years, the maturation of psychoanalysis and the willingness of some to revisit traditional theories have led to a rapprochement. Pioneering figures in this resumption of friendly relations include analysts such as Neville Symington, who describes psychoanalysis as a 'mature religion'; Matte Blanco, who understands the unconscious to possess a symmetrical logic that allows for eternity, infinity and transcendence to exist; James Jones, who, writing from an American context, uses transference as a key way of understanding and working with clients' religious and spiritual experiences; and Nina Coltart's warm appreciation of, and accessible writing about, psychoanalysis and Buddhism.

As psychoanalysis and religion can now be mentioned in the same sentence, distinctions are made between religion and spirituality, with the recognition that spirituality is found inside and outside of religion. As a consequence the notion of spirituality-apart-from-religion has emerged. Thorne (1998) has mined this rich vein from a person-centred perspective, whilst Rowan, Wilber and other humanistic practitioners have been exploring such themes for the last 20 years. Alistair Ross acknowledges the potential for religion to be used as a defence, but suggests ways in which therapists can both be empathic with the need for specific beliefs and also challenging of them when they impede personal growth.

Psychodynamic counselling, as it has emerged in the last 20 years, has taken many rich and useful concepts from psychoanalytic writing and applied them in a broad range of different contexts, including those in which psychoanalysis would find it difficult to operate. Counselling as a discipline has been part of the wider post-modern trend to redefine, revalue and reassess previous modernist understandings and connections. Contemporary psychodynamic counsellors are in a unique position to respond to the changes in society and to embrace diversity. They have the potential to enhance the experience of the client regardless of their age, class, gender, sexual orientation, race or religion in new and life-changing ways. Counsellors and therapists are now reaching out into all corners of society and engaging with anyone who seeks help. They need to be equipped and prepared to see the world from the client's often differing perspectives. The chapters in this book present a pluralistic, or even integrative interpretation of psychoanalytic ideas, as the authors have seen fit to apply them to particular circumstances or client groups. Throughout the book the objects relations school informs most chapters as authors acknowledge nature, nurture and social context. However, many other ideas are incorporated from attachment theory to self-psychology and from Kleinian theory to Marxist theory. When considering difference and diversity, one size does not always fit all, and theoretical diversity can enrich the conceptualisation of human problems.

Another concept that links all the chapters is reflexivity and self-awareness on the part of the therapist. Faced with diversity, countertransference responses can be overwhelming and provoke hostility or defensiveness, shame or denial. Such feelings must be acknowledged and processed for the benefit of the therapeutic relationship. Prejudices and preconceived stereotypical ideas serve to inhibit communication and need to be aired appropriately. The power invested in the therapist threatens to sabotage the work by accentuating the powerlessness of the client. The therapeutic frame serves to contain the relationship, but may be perceived as another manifestation of control. There are no easy solutions, but many tensions that can and must be used to enrich therapeutic work. Hopefully this book will make a substantial contribution to the capacity to understand and communicate just that little bit better, for all who read it.

REFERENCES

Bauman, Z. (1991). *Modernity and Ambivalence*. Cambridge: Polity Press.

Clare, A. (2000). *On Men: Masculinity in Crisis*. London: Chatto and Windus.

Clarke, S. (2003). *Social Theory, Psychoanalysis and Racism*. Basingstoke: Palgrave Macmillan.

Coltart, N. (1988). 'The assessment of psychological mindedness in the diagnostic interview'. *British Journal of Psychiatry*, 153: 818–20.

Elliot, A. (2002). *Psychoanalytic Theory: An Introduction*. Basingstoke: Palgrave Macmillan.

Freud, S. (2001). *Civilisation and its Discontents* [1930] in *The Standard Edition of the Complete Works of Sigmund Freud, Volume XXI*, London: Vintage.

Furedi, F. (2003). *Therapy Culture: Cultivating Vulnerability in An Age of Uncertainty*. London: Routledge.

Guggenbuhl-Craig, A. (1971). *Power in the Helping Professions*. Putnam, CT: Spring.

Mandela, N. (1995). *A Long Walk to Freedom: The Autobiography of Nelson Mandela*. London: Abacus.

Mitchell, J. (1974). *Psychoanalysis and Feminism*. London: Allen Lane.

Parker, I., Georgaca, E., Harper, D., McLaughlin, T. & Stowell-Smith, M. (1995). *Deconstructing Psychopathology*. London: Sage.

Samuels, A. (2001). *Politics on the Couch: Citizenship and the Internal Life*. New York: Other Press.

Siegel, A. (1996). *Heinz Kohut and the Psychology of the Self*. Hove: Brunner-Routledge.

Thorne, B. (1998) *Person-centred Counselling and Christian Spirituality*. London: Whurr.

Winnicott, D. (1986). *Home Is Where We Start From*. Harmondsworth: Penguin.

Young, R. M. (1994). *Mental Space*. London: Process Press.

Psychodynamic Counselling, Knowledge and the Social Context

Mariette Clare

For counsellors, and I include myself, it often feels as if the heart of the matter is the experience of being with a client in a room: a fantasy of the therapeutic couple, uncontaminated by any other political or social reality. This chapter challenges this comfortable and familiar perspective. It draws together theoretical perspectives on society from disciplinary fields other than counselling and psychotherapy, and uses them to evaluate what social and political ends psychodynamic counselling may unwittingly be serving. In particular it looks at the place of professionalism within Western societies and its links with knowledge and power. In no sense is the social context simply out there, separate from me. One of the many ways it enters into me is through the forms of knowledge that I have made my own, which shape how I feel and think as well as how I view the world. For example, my choice of theoretical concepts produces not only a view of the external world, but also consolidates or makes uneasy my own sense of identity within that world.

The need for illusions

It should come as no surprise to psychodynamic counsellors that counselling may have, in Winnicott's term, an 'illusory' aspect. Illusion is not for Winnicott a negative category: he does not denigrate illusion as false or as compensatory wish fulfilment, but uses it to think about the inevitable conditions of social – and therefore individual – life. Winnicott's work can be seen as an effort to theorise how human beings can first of all come into subjective being; then how we come to inhabit the external world; and what it is we need for the 'perpetual human task of keeping inner and outer reality separate yet inter-related' (1975, p. 230).

Winnicott suggests that religion and art have a similar function in the life of adults to the formative processes of illusion and disillusion in the development of infants. They are the essential means by which individuals come to be able to combine the experience of other and self, without denying either (Phillips, 1988). We live through a process of creating illusions from the found materials of a culture and of dealing with the subsequent disillusion, with the inevitable partiality and failure of our ideas, beliefs and attachments. This is a process of loss and grief but at the same time it is the only available means to the realisation and renewal of the self. One aspect of this, as Winnicott says, is the way 'we may collect together and form a group on the basis of the similarity of our illusory experiences' (Winnicott, 1975, p. 231). This links with the need as counsellors to develop 'epistemological loyalties' (Pilgrim, 1997, p. 111). Our work involves a decision to use one particular framework in order to know the world, with both the clarifications and limitations that entails. Then the unconscious processes of identification and disavowal set to work, shaping each of us as a part of communities that share the same beliefs, making the beliefs a part of us. It is easy to see, for example, adolescents' need for a peer group, marked by ways of dressing, speaking or behaving that are obviously 'different' but which can help them to secure a sense of belonging and identity. So counsellors can cling to a theory that creates a world of 'us and them', with its subsequent gains and losses. Similarly, counsellors can use a belief such as 'we're all just people' in a way that prevents us from thinking about difficult questions of difference, of power and of injustice and the ways in which they are entrenched in society, culture and our very selves.

Knowledge and the reproduction of society

The 'social context' of the UK in the first years of the 21st century is exceedingly complex; conflicting interests struggle for dominance across a variety of economic, political and cultural fields, both public and private. One key concern that informs my argument is the shift in the political ground in both the UK and the USA since the late 1970s and 1980s. This can broadly be seen as the widespread acceptance that market forces are the best measure of what is of value. Hall describes how this is

> ... the rise of the new *individualism* and the hegemony of the neo-liberal free-market ideas. (2003, p. 11; my emphasis)

As counsellors, there is an ethical need to ponder over this identification of individualism as a central element in these changes and to examine how our work may contribute to a worldview that is inimical to other human values.

The last decade has seen the deepening of economic inequality in the UK (IPPR, 2004; Levitas, 2004), despite the election of a Labour government that would traditionally have been in favour of a more egalitarian distribution of wealth. The anodyne term 'modernisation', with its emphasis on 'efficiency' and flexible working practices, is intensifying labour so that not only are working hours in the UK longer, but the rate and pressure of working are increased (Bunting, 2004). A report commissioned by the Joseph Rowntree Foundation (Burchell, 2004) showed that these pressures result in stress related ill health and tense family relationships. The report recognised that productivity might be improved by gains in efficiency, but it also identified worrying implications for the health of Britain's social environment. Another aspect of the shift to a market economy is that buying and selling is increasingly represented as a paradigm for all human relationships.

This commoditisation of social life is expanding into areas such as education, medicine and even marriage, which formerly were understood within a variety of different frameworks (Needham, 2004; Rustin, 1999, 2000). If counselling trainees, for example, see their role primarily as being consumers of a course, then they may fail to anticipate the struggle needed to understand difficult new ideas; they may have only an impoverished way of regarding the disappointments and losses associated with intense learning; they may be unable to enjoy and benefit from the demanding but protected status of being an apprentice, of being allowed to get things wrong; and in their anxiety to get their money's worth, they may not notice the more subtle invitation to become part of an ongoing dialogue in which they would be contributors, not mere purchasers.

Where counsellors work, as many do, in the public sector, they are, together with other state professionals, becoming subject to ever more intense forms of managerial regulation that are hostile to the practice and ideals of psychodynamic counselling. For in the pursuit of profit, market forces bring a particular type of rationality into play:

> The imposition of the disciplines of measurement, conformity, performance, reward and punishment on so many public sector activities ... elaborates a regime, virtually a way of life, on spheres which used to define themselves as committed to values opposed in many ways to those of the market. (Rustin, 2000, p. 124)

This social environment makes it hard to defend a space for working with unconscious processes, for what may be a long-term and unpredictable period of time. The market is driven by short-term considerations. Within its regimes there is little space for a serious focus on what human beings need to live a good life, consonant with promoting economic justice and peace and protecting our deteriorating environment. Counselling is entangled with these shifts in a variety of ways which are hard to disentangle and even harder to evaluate.

The social unconscious

Our dependence on the social environment means that what we are able to know, think and feel depends as much on what is externally available to us as on what goes on inside us. As with individual identity, social formations have to work at maintaining a semblance of cohesion. Just as individuals preserve themselves through the unconscious processes of repression, disavowal, disassociation or splitting, so societies deal with ideas or experiences that subvert the status quo by marginalising, denying or misrepresenting them. This can be seen as producing a kind of social unconscious (Dalal, 1998).

There is little reason to suppose that either counselling practice or theory are immune to these processes, although they are probably far from a counsellor's mind as s/he greets a new client. It is not easy from within the confines of a practice based view to think consciously about how it is that this rather odd form of encounter between two strangers has become so natural and taken for granted. Yet it is as important to understand the social, economic and philosophical history of counselling as it is to grasp the influence of an individual's past on their present life: both have determining effects which may not be immediately obvious.

Psychodynamic counselling traces its ancestry back to classic psychoanalytic theory but also to counselling, with its roots in the 'caring professions' and the voluntary sector. This is a divided inheritance in more than one way. At one level there are the questions as to whether counsellors know more about clients' unconscious processes and therefore about their lives than do clients; or whether they are companions on a voyage of discovery where neither can claim superiority, where shared humanity or bearing witness is at the core. At another level, there is the controversy as to whether psychoanalysis itself is an art or a science. This is the fundamental issue about the scientific status of psychodynamic or psychoanalytical knowledge, and behind that debate lie centuries of thinking about epistemology, about the nature of knowledge. Freud was a medical doctor who aspired to a level of objective certainty for his theories and hoped to be able to demonstrate their truth through the experimental methods of empirical science, in which he included clinical 'observation'. Yet paradoxically what he sought to prove, that human beings are basically irrational creatures, driven by unconscious forces, was to contribute to a growing scepticism about the nature of science and its role in human lives (Horrocks, 2001). This is not an abstract academic concern (Gomez, 2005; Samuels, 1993). Understanding the roots of human destructiveness and hatred is an urgent need in a politically divided and dangerous world. However, we also live in the middle of a real clash over knowledge and power.

Arguments about how we know what we know and who is allowed to say so affect everyone's lives. For example, the composition of the feedstuffs for cattle that produced the BSE crisis was the outcome of considerable scientific and technical skill. It was no doubt effective at encouraging growth in animals and efficient in using otherwise wasted parts of carcasses and could therefore be considered a rational development. However, the rationality that drove such a development was very narrow and could not take into account ethical issues about the welfare of animals; nor could it be neutral in assessing the risk of such practices spreading disease, especially where profits might be put at risk. Similarly, it is not reassuring to hear the assertion that the UK government will take decisions on the acceptability of GM crops based 'on the science'. Unfortunately science cannot evaluate the role played by the transnational companies in deciding upon the direction of this research and how it is moved by their drive for profits and control of global markets. Decisions about biodiversity, ownership of strains of plants, unheeded environmental consequences and the social and health implications of GM crops are necessarily political: they require the application of ethical principles and cannot be 'objectively' answered. So, central to these struggles is the status of objective, scientific thought, the heritage of the Enlightenment.

Such empiricism serves now not only the maximisation of profit but the claim to scientific certainty that forms the basis of most professions. So there is something contradictory and paradoxical about psychodynamic counselling's pursuit of professionalisation. At a conscious level, the argument for professionalisation seems incontrovertible: only trained and accredited people would be eligible to practice; it would therefore protect clients; and it would provide status, authority and financial gain for practitioners. So in theory everyone would benefit. Its very rationality, however, may prove to be part of the problem, ignoring as it does some deeply problematic aspects of the current social context, and of the unconscious role of professions within it. It is also at odds with its psychoanalytic inheritance (Frosh, 2002). To believe that human activity is always imbued with, if not driven by, unconscious processes is radically to part company with instrumental reason.

A further paradox is that while there is now a widespread intellectual critique of the limits of objective, scientific knowing, there is an increased use of such methods in planning and management. In most workplaces, the setting of targets, audit trails, and systems of appraisal or control are all now commonplace. Subjecting themselves to such scrutiny, it is all too easy for counsellors to have anxieties about what cannot be controlled, such as a fear of litigation, for example. Thus professionalisation, by encouraging phantasies of omniscience and control, may affect, for example, the way case notes are written and how clients' difficulties may be conceptualised. Management also draws on such kindred professions to counselling as Human Resource Development and life coaching, and on such concepts as 'emotional literacy' (Smith, L. S., 1999; Smith, P., 1999). These are frameworks which promise that the unruliness of feelings may also be brought into line with the rational objectives of management. Hancock and Tyler pose the essential question about such developments:

> Do modes of organizing based on the values of flexibility, multi-skilling, employee-friendly cultures and the like, represent anything other than redefined instrumental technologies designed to extract greater levels of labour from employees than the modern or Fordist practices they are supposed to have supplanted? (2001, p. 60)

Such apparently benign practices may prove to be subtle attempts to colonise the hearts and minds of employees, spaces previously left free from the rationality of capital.

This links with the criticisms of the whole idea of a dispassionate observer, impartially seeking truth. In the fields of academic study interested in questions of identity, including psychoanalysis, feminists (Benjamin, 1990; Campbell, 2000; Flax, 1990; Seu and Heenan, 1998), post-colonial writers (Said, 1994; Spivak, 1990) and gay and queer theorists (Butler, 1999; O'Connor and Ryan, 1993; Plummer, 1995) have all made plain that the ideal, neutral, rational mind was always part of a human body, usually male, white, and ambitious to be part of the dominant social classes. Coming from social groups who have historically been seen as the 'Other', as objects of study rather than producers of knowledge – women, colonised peoples, the working class, gays and lesbians – the point they make is that knowing about human beings is a very different project from knowing about the non-human world (Bauman, 2000). This is not an argument that therefore nothing is true, but an acknowledgement that truths are always plural: real but limited, and produced within, about and from a particular social perspective. As Haraway (1991, p. 189) argues, there is no 'god-trick of seeing everything from nowhere'. This is as true of psychodynamic counselling as of any other body of knowledge. Knowledge about human beings and human society is always replete with values and human purpose, even – perhaps especially – when it claims to be professional and objective. It is uncomfortable but necessary to weigh up the way in which all such knowledge, and counselling not least, is political: it is deeply implicated in relations of power and in either challenging or reproducing them.

The notion of a rational, centred subject, capable of objectivity and producing certain, value free knowledge underpins science and technology (Stanley and Wise, 1983); it is assumed by theories of consumer choice and drives managerial calculations. The subjective or the personal are seen as sources of error. For these reasons much of psychology and psychiatry has historically disdained the concept of unconscious processes and maintained the view that emotional involvement disqualifies a researcher from producing reliable knowledge.

Yet many counsellors come to be practitioners because of their emotional experience of its value and their sense of its ethical purposes. Certainly in the past it was felt to be impossible to reconcile such diverse stances. Shuttleworth (2000) writes about the impact of psychoanalytically influenced ideas on social policy and practice in the UK since the 1920s. He remarks on this absolute divide between what he describes as the 'interpreters' and the 'correlators', roughly speaking the difference between a therapeutic search for the individual meaningfulness in human experience, and science's search for what is replicable and quantifiable.

The professionalisation of counselling has to resolve these oppositional ways of knowing. It challenges settled epistemological loyalty. The therapeutic commitment to openness, to relationship and to a kind of deliberate not-knowing has to find a way of resisting the lure of certainty and ameliorating the demand to plan, to set targets, to monitor and to adopt an intellectual stance which over-values what can be known through empiricist enquiry. There are important debates to pursue about what sort of knowledge is needed for what purpose; about who defines the purpose and who generates the knowledge and how all these questions encode relationships of power. It may be time to give up some illusions.

The rise and fall of the professions

Professionals are inevitably a part of the social processes through which these issues are fought over and resolved. Professions are gatekeepers: only those they admit may lay claim to the 'competent speech' that carries power. The means by which professionalisation secures its advantages, however limited they may currently be, need to be carefully considered. It is easy to erase any historical perspective and to overlook the ways in which all mental health professions find it hard not to pathologise certain individuals, creating and maintaining social hierarchies in both their own interests and in those of the dominant classes. Also, by mystifying ordinary human feelings professionalisation deskills people, and robs them of local and grounded ways of solving their own problems by creating an artificial dependency on 'experts'.

The production and control of 'expert' knowledge is a particular issue for counsellors. It raises questions about just what it is psychodynamic theory claims to know and what relationship this knowledge has to clients' own views of themselves and their lives. The way in which psychodynamic theory presents its case histories, for example, is usually of socially decontextualised individuals whose troubles are ascribed mainly to the operation of internal forces of which the clients/patients are unaware. There is a real risk that clients' existing views and values may be considered only as evidence of the pathology of their inner world, rather than as the outcome of a never ending dynamic between unconscious processes of different sorts, culturally available ideas, idiosyncratic autobiographical experience and the impact of social forces.

The perspective of a predominantly white, female and middle class group is bound to be limited (Hannon et al., 2001; Pointon, 2004). Yet new recruits to the professions are subject to selection and assessment by established practitioners, and dissenting voices can easily be silenced or expelled. Clearly, criticism of trainers and accrediting bodies can all too easily be attributed to difficulties in trainees themselves. Substantive issues can be avoided and alternative perspectives can be reduced to personal pathology. The historical judgements of psychoanalysis towards gay men or lesbians wishing to train as analysts is a dramatic instance of entrenched professional attitudes, and one which still has some influence in the heterosexist bias of versions of the Oedipus complex (Campbell, 2000; Domenici and Lesser, 1995). The *Journal of the British Association of Counselling and Psychotherapy* carries articles and letters about the difficulties faced by, for example, working class or disabled individuals in successfully accessing training and accreditation and the impact of differences of social identities within therapy (Alleyne, 2004; Batmanghelidjh, 2004; Hayes, 2004; Laungani, 2004; Livingstone, 2004; Pointon, 2004; Rose, 2004; Shivanath et al., 2004) and issues of race and gender are attracting attention (Lago and Smith, 2003; Tuckwell, 2002). Professionalisation, by formalising training practices and making them conform to the demands of institutions of Further and Higher Education, is extremely likely to narrow the field of recruits (House, 2003).

Professionalisation is often presented as an unproblematic way of gaining respect, yet an inherent aspect of it is the struggle with other professions for the right to define clients' problems and to establish a dominant place in the hierarchy of helping professions. In a perhaps not wholly intentional way, the psychoanalysts, Bollas and Sundelson, reveal the inevitable rivalry between differing professional standpoints, the mudslinging and the competition to hold the final and universal truth:

> DSM-IV demands that all clinicians fit their patients into categories that experienced analysts know to be spurious. Very few patients really exist within the simplistic con-fines of the labels in this book. Happily, people are more complex than that ... With every new diagnostic term comes yet another group who publish books, proclaim their expertise, and enjoy their profit. In any city of the US one can find experts on PDD, MPD, and now ADHD. The dulling effect of these acronyms reflects the intellectual retardation occasioned by such thinking. (1995, pp. 134–5)

It is hard not to sympathise with the critique of ever proliferating syndromes, manualised treatment regimes and their rigid claims to truth, but psychoanalysts too 'publish books, proclaim their expertise, enjoy their profit'. What seems striking about this quotation is the lack of self-reflection, the paradoxical mirror-ing of the certainties that are despised in DSM-IV and the desire to aggrandise psychoanalytic knowledge as the only truth.

A structuralist view: counselling as control

Psychodynamic counselling cannot avoid operating on this deeply contested professional terrain. However, it is not only practitioners who have an interest in the outcomes. Professions are of interest to the state because one of its functions is to maintain social order. Through its legislation as well as its rhetoric the UK government has clearly signalled its idea of the ideal citizen: self-reliant (student loans; private pensions; individual savings); autonomous (the idea of a meritocracy where anyone can succeed); and a wage earner (the drive to get mothers to work; childcare paid for when provided by professionals but not family members). And above all, of course, responsible (exercising rational choice over their supplier of utilities; volunteering to be mentors, school governors and so on) and well behaved (anti-social behaviour orders; identity cards). Nevertheless, in a demo-cratic system any government has to win consent to its programme, especially the notion that the system is basically just and that lack of success is due to personal deficiencies. To the possible causes of failure there has now been added the notion of whole groups of people who lack 'emotional literacy'. So while the call to 'bring in the counsellors' in the wake of a disaster may in one way be an encouraging sign of the increased awareness of the impact of emotional trauma, it may also signal a belief that survivors necessarily lack resources among them-selves and within their communities.

Seen in this light, occupations such as counselling and therapy act in contra-dictory ways. I have no doubt that therapy can act to relieve individual suffering. However, at the same time, it may have at least two unintended consequences. One is that what are seen as acceptable or normal responses to life's difficulties become ever more narrowly drawn and policed (Furedi, 2004). The other is that, as radical psychiatrists have argued in the past (Illich, 1973; Laing, 1965) and continue to argue today in such publications as the *Journal of Critical Psychology, Counselling and Psychotherapy*, it reconciles people to the oppressive conditions of life, which may have created the fragmentation and pain in the first place. In this sense counselling also plays an ideological role. Ideology is a vastly contested concept (see for example Schwarz, 1978), but I am using it here to mean dominant and widespread ideas about how society works and what people are like. To be ideological, such ideas must, in some way, conceal the operation of power, help to win consent to the status quo and disorganise, denigrate or silence social criticism. As Althusser (1970) argues, ideology is not merely about ideas but also depends on the familiar material practices of everyday life, backed up by the coercive agencies of the state. Counselling might be implicated, for example, through a prisoner being obliged to attend a therapeutic course to address offending behaviour; or divorcing couples might be directed to seek mediation; or 'problem' teenage drinkers might be referred for counselling as part of a probation order.

The ideology of counselling; counselling as ideology

Consciously, psychodynamic counselling has nothing to do with ideology. Training focuses on the awareness of ubiquitous unconscious processes, understood in a developmental framework and presented as universal. The counsellor seeks to bring into conscious thought and experience that which has previously been hidden and unbearable, so as to enable people to free themselves of compulsively repeating old ways of doing and being. Understanding the relationship, real and transferential, within the boundaries of the therapeutic frame is part of the process of healing. It is an intense, perplexing and rewarding occupation.

Yet in this daily absorption with individual clients social processes are relegated to the unconscious. Counsellors are not innocent when they enter the consulting room. Our training and theory predispose us to see certain patterns and to interpret them in particular ways, which, given the nature of what counsellors offer, is a tendency to locate both problems and solutions within the individual. And it is this that is ideological. The question is not simply whether what counsellors do 'works', whether it succeeds in helping individuals feel 'better', but how its ideas about what this means fit in with wider ideological forces. If, in the counsellor's eyes, unconscious intrapsychic forces are the main or only underlying forces at work in their clients' lives, then already at work are ideologies of individual responsibility. Such ideas deny the significance of economic forces on the shape of individual lives and suffering, and also skate over cultural and political determinations.

Ideologies are understood as being (usually) subtle and unnoticed, although those of the past may be glaringly obvious when viewed from the present. Freud's case study of Dora, for example, has been subject to review by feminist scholars who argue that Freud's patriarchal position led him to ignore Dora's real subordination to the complex social and sexual demands of far more powerful male figures (Bernheimer and Kahane, 1985). Ideology in this sense can be often seen in what is left out, what is not focused on as well as what is selected to exemplify particular points. In order to demonstrate how this might manifest itself in counselling theory and practice, I have chosen an example from a recent textbook published in 2004: *An Introduction to Psychodynamic Counselling* by Spurling. In the section in question, Spurling is making an important point about the nature of therapeutic attention. However, the point of dominant ideologies is precisely that they operate unconsciously behind our backs. In this case, learning about psychodynamic counselling can also be seen to reinforce problematic ideologies.

In Chapter 1 Spurling gives two fictional examples of an interaction between a mother and a child who has woken up with a nightmare. One scenario is used to show the significant difference made by the mother when she is able to 'put her own feelings (of wanting to go downstairs and watch TV) aside ... This frees her to get in touch with her love for her daughter and her feelings' (p. 7). She can then listen to the child patiently, allay her fears and settle her back to sleep. By contrast, in the other version, the mother is imagined as comforting and assuring the child that there's nothing really wrong but also as asserting herself: ' ... she is sure the daughter will get back to sleep, all she needs to do is lie down and close her eyes, and anyway she is going back to watch TV' (p. 6). And then the commentary suggests that harm and difficulty will ensue: ' ... a vicious cycle of misunderstanding and battle for control can develop'. If this is thought about simply in its own terms, as an example of a micro-interaction that reveals interpersonal dynamics, it is quite unexceptionable. There is no doubt that the act of trying to see how the world looks and feels to another person needs a temporary suspension of commitment to our own views and emotions. However, this example bears significant traces of more ideological assumptions.

The writer's choice of words leave little doubt as to which course of action is to be preferred. One mother is *patient, listens carefully, takes the dream seriously, expresses curiosity and interest, experiences pleasure and satisfaction.* By contrast the other mother is *impatient, irritated, not sensitive to her daughter's state of mind,* and *her child does not feel very supported by her mother, may have further bad dreams about a wicked witch.* So the scenario makes moral judgements, creates its own version of 'good' and 'bad' mothers, and in doing so reinforces the ideology that women's role and duty in life is to serve others and subordinate their own needs and wishes. Further, by giving no social context whatsoever to this mother/daughter pair, the scenario can only show the impatience and irritation as arising from within the mother, frustrated by not being able to watch her favourite TV programme. Implicitly therefore the mother is shown as responsible for the inadequacy or otherwise of her response: the ideology of individualism is in play. It would have been as easy to construct a vignette which showed a mother overburdened by holding down two part-time jobs on the minimum wage, trying to pack tomorrow's lunches and get the washing done. The same point about therapeutic attention could have been made, but at the same time it would have suggested that interpersonal exchanges are deeply affected by outside social and economic forces and are not simply a matter of individual choice. In fact it might well be suggested that for some people the way society is organised forecloses – through tiredness, money worries, lack of time, absence of friendly support – on their chances of being able to be easily available to each other (Smail, 1996).

Seen from this perspective the main task of professionals is to promote the sort of people that ideology declares as exemplary: rational, hard working consumers. Then the major institutions of society will run smoothly: emotionally literate employees will boost profits; schools and universities will be filled with hard working students, achieving qualifications for the world of work; the NHS will benefit from health conscious individuals who watch their weight and moderate their intake of alcohol. Those who fail in such tasks may be denied access to collective provision and pathologised or condemned in other ways. Indeed, the right of access to NHS resources by heavy smokers or people considered seriously obese is already being challenged (Peck, 2004). Thus ideology helps to reproduce social inequalities. What is socially and politically constructed becomes seen as natural common sense and it seems irrational even to question it. Because as counsellors we work as individuals with other individuals we are particularly susceptible to taking for granted the ideologies of individualism which saturate Western society.

The empirical: the epidemiology of mental health

Empiricism does not acknowledge the issues of value or purpose that inevitably frame the specific questions which it asks. It can, however, provide particular sorts of evidence to support the view that we live in an unequal society. Demographic studies make plain the truth that social difference is also always about privilege and deprivation. The incidence of mental health problems, the most common of which are the anxiety and depression experienced by clients of counselling, is not randomly distributed across the population. The Office of National Statistics publication *Social Trends 34* (HMSO, 2004) states quite baldly:

> As with many other illnesses, mental health problems are associated with socioeconomic disadvantage. Results from the 2000 Psychiatric Morbidity Survey of people living in private households in Great Britain found that, among those aged 60 to 74, the likelihood of neurotic disorder increased in both sexes as household income fell. Among women in this age group, the prevalence of neurotic disorder, such as anxiety or depression, was around three times as common among those with a weekly household income of under £200 (16 to 18 per cent) as it was among those women with a weekly household income of £500 or more (6 per cent).

Such evidence should give all counsellors pause for thought since it shows how social and economic inequalities play themselves out in personal suffering. Pilgrim (1997) sets out further evidence of the differences in mental health associated with gender, age, 'race' and sexual orientation. Smail (1996) argues that

> What caused people distress was not so much their own mistakes, inadequacies and illnesses as the powers and influences that bore down upon them from the world beyond their skin. (p. 12)

In short, there is abundant evidence that the external world plays a significant role in creating emotional distress, that the roots of psychological distress are neither simply within our minds nor purely individual problems. Models of how to help repair damage and lessen suffering may be more adequate if they do not split off unconscious processes from social resources. Personal autonomy, so dear to counsellors' hearts, is far from an individually achieved virtue. It is, paradoxically, highly dependent on a measure of prosperity and security and flourishes in a context of social and political justice. The plight of victims of torture is an extreme case that clearly demonstrates this (Bahri, 2004; Papadopoulos, 2002) but it is on a continuum with the situation of many people whose lives have been burdened by poverty and discrimination.

From macro to micro

Counselling could take up the task of tracing out the effects of such macro-structures on the fabric of individual lives. While the ideological, economic and political forces of class, 'race', gender, sexuality and so on bear down on all of us, their precise impact cannot be taken as read. Although quantifiable forms of research may be useful for demonstrating the impact of social forces, the particularity and complexity of autobiographical experience can be flattened and distorted in the process. Other ways of knowing are needed for this: more interpretive, more socially located, more aware that the goals, assumptions and methods of the observer, the practitioner or researcher will profoundly affect what comes to be known. This is a problem only if psychodynamic theory is taken as providing a universal and incontrovertible knowledge, some kind of equivalent to the laws of gravity. In fact, psychodynamic theories give a range of different accounts about the nature of the self and its processes, not all of which can be literally true. Schafer (1992) is one of the psychoanalytic writers who takes this to its logical conclusion when he says:

> I do not regard the self as an entity found in nature and available for detached study by non-participative observers. Selves are told through dialogue, in words, images and enactments, and they are retold by observers whose narrative preferences and strategies express specific aims, values and competencies. (p. xvi)

In other words analysis, therapy and counselling are among the many means by which selves are brought into being. If this is so, then counsellors cannot escape the duty to think about what sort of 'selves' their techniques, theories and practices are consciously and unconsciously promoting.

The belief that the individual self is the source of all authenticity is a foundational one for Western societies. It is common for counsellors to envisage their task as putting clients in touch with their pre-existing 'real' selves. This belief provides a particular sort of 'technology of the self'. The expression is drawn from the work of Foucault (1971, 1975, 1990) who uses it to convey the productive nature of power. He was particularly interested, through investigating the history of madness and of sexuality, in the changing ways in which individuals are socially disciplined into being human, and in the changing definitions of what it is to be human. According to his view, professionals are part of 'regimes of truth' that define these matters. Although this idea is similar in some ways to ideology, there is a crucial difference in the way such systems are understood as operating. It is not about imposing unwanted limitations or definitions on an unwilling subject, with counsellors as unwitting agents of the state. Instead, counselling can be understood as making desirable particular sorts of identity, particular sorts of personhood. Through both its practices and its theory it offers to people resources through which they can not only make sense of their lives, but actually construct themselves. This is also the sense in which there can be no separation between counselling and social context: they are fundamentally inextricable at every turn. A young male client, for example, may work hard to understand the painful experiences that underlie his problematic use of drugs, and he may be serious about wishing to deal with his difficulties in another way. However, while he still lives in an area where many of his friends are drug users and where drug dealing is widespread, it will be very hard for him to change himself and his life without changing his social context. Less obviously, the ideologies he has absorbed within his social group about what it is to be male will also be exerting an influence. If he strays too far away from those particular definitions of masculinity he will undoubtedly lose social acceptability too.

This Foucauldian view recognises that individuals do not somehow exist outside language and culture. Selves may be founded on the unique history of a particular body, but they are also made out of social relationships and language. Indeed, if this were not so, it is hard to see how counselling could have any effect. In fact much psychodynamic theory suggests that far from being grandly isolated individuals, our very selves are built up from internalisations and introjections from the external world and are preserved through the expulsion and projection of what cannot be tolerated. This raises a crucial issue about what sort of personhood the practice of counselling promotes and how it does so, both at the level of the individual counsellor/client and in the way it produces, uses and spreads knowledge.

It is hard to step outside our culturally taken for granted ideas about what it is to be a human being, the socially sanctioned illusions which address some of our deepest anxieties. The ideal Western personality is highly autonomous, self-directed and orientated to individual choice and control (Rose, 2003). Of course this would have appeared extremely strange throughout much of history and indeed in many non-Western societies today, as an asylum seeker points out:

> There, where you [the asylum seeker] came from, nobody had their 'personal space', there are no boundaries. Everybody steps over each other's boundaries all the time. They call it warmth, caring. You used to, as well. (Bahri, 2004, p. 8)

In other times and places the defining characteristics of a person might be their social place or familial loyalties, and an acceptance of fate rather than an heroic individual rebellion against destiny is more the norm.

It is also no accident that the individualistic way of being human produces exactly the sort of people needed by a consumerist and market led society, as Cushman (1995) among others has explored. However, the nature of human being is shaped by human cultures, and professionals have considerable power to determine what counts as cultural truth. Counselling undoubtedly has played a significant part in the increasing acceptance and normalisation of this intense individualism – despite some evidence that the higher the degree of individualism in a society the higher the suicide rate (Scott et al., 2003). Psychotherapeutic theories and practices are part of the defining paradigm of Western culture: the sense of freedom found in the idea that 'we are called upon to invent our own identity and live in our own way and be true to ourselves' (Rutherford, 2004, p. 14). It is less clear that that psychodynamic counselling has developed a view on the counter-balancing human need for security and for the existence of others; on our equal need for 'public discourses and spaces that can orchestrate, enable and symbolise commonalities which are the necessary framework for creating social cohesion and individual identity' (ibid., p. 14). Without this contrasting ethical emphasis, individualism is reduced to the impoverished version of 'economic man', basing all choices on a calculus of financial self-interest rather than on collective values such as solidarity with a community, love for another, public health or justice.

Conclusion

Like all truths, representations of ideal human beings and psychodynamic theories exist only in a whole network of language and images, interactions with others and relationships of power. While we cannot escape them, as they constitute who we are, we are able to reflect on them and the purposes they serve. Above all we cannot separate psychodynamic counselling from the social context in which it inescapably plays a part. Understanding contemporary critiques that undermine an unthinking belief in the certainty of knowledge can help psychodynamic counsellors to evaluate their practice in a difficult and contradictory time. Only by attending to different illusions can we hope to clarify values and purposes and to develop theory and practice in ways that are respectful of both unconscious processes and social structures, of both the individual self and the power of the environment.

REFERENCES

Alleyne, A. (2004). 'The internal oppressor and Black identity'. *Counselling and Psychotherapy Journal*, 15: 8, 21–4.

Althusser, L. (1970). *Reading Capital*. London: New Left Books.

Bahri, H. (2004). *'Strange case'. The Supporter*, 28 (May). London: Medical Foundation for the Care of Victims of Torture.

Batmanghelidjh, C. (2004). 'Life on the edge'. *Counselling and Psychotherapy Journal*, 15: 8, 24–7.

Bauman, Z. (2000). 'Sociological enlightenment – for whom, about what?'. *Theory, Culture and Society*, 172, 71–82.

Benjamin, J. (1990). *The Bonds of Love: Psychoanalysis, Feminism and the Problem of Domination*. London: Virago.

Bernheimer, C. and Kahane, C. (1985). *In Dora's Case: Freud – Hysteria – Feminism*. New York: Columbia University Press.

Bollas, C. and Sundelson, D. (1995). *The New Informants*. London: Karnac.

Bunting, M. (2004). *How the Overwork Culture is Ruling Our Lives*. London: HarperCollins.

Burchell, B. J. (2004). *Job Insecurity and Work Intensification*. London: Joseph Rowntree Foundation. www.jrf.org.uk/knowledge/findings/socialpolicy/849.asp, accessed 10 November 2004.

Butler, J. (1999). *Gender Trouble*. New York and London: Routledge.

Campbell, J. (2000). *Arguing with the Phallus: Feminist, Queer and Postcolonial Theory: A Psychoanalytic Contribution*. London: Zed.

Cushman, P. (1995). *Constructing the Self, Constructing America*. New York: Da Capo.

Dalal, F. (1998). *Taking the Group Seriously*. London: Jessica Kingsley.

Domenici, T. and Lesser, R. C. (eds) (1995). *Disorienting Sexuality*. New York: Routledge.

Flax, J. (1990). *Thinking Fragments: Psychoanalysis, Feminism and Postmodernism*. Berkeley, CA: University of California Press.

Foucault, M. (1971). *Madness and Civilisation: A History of Insanity in the Age of Reason*. London: Tavistock.

Foucault, M. (1975). *The Birth of the Clinic*. London: Tavistock.

Foucault, M. (1990). *The History of Sexuality, Volume 3: The Care of the Self*. London: Penguin.

Frosh, S. (2002). *Afterwords, the Personal in Gender, Culture and Psychotherapy*. London: Palgrave Macmillan.

Furedi, F. (2004). *Therapy Culture*. London: Routledge.

Gomez, L. (2005). *The Freud Wars*. London: Routledge.

Hall, S. (2003). 'New Labour's double-shuffle'. *Soundings*, 24: Autumn, 10–24.

Hancock, P. and Tyler, M. (2001). *Work, Postmodernism and Organization: A Critical Introduction*. London: Sage.

Hannon, J. W., Ritchie, M. and Rye D. R. (2001). 'Class: the missing discourse in counselling and counsellor education in the United States of America'. *Journal of Critical Psychology, Counselling and Psychotherapy*, 1: 3, 139–54.

Haraway, D. J. (1991). *Simians, Cyborgs, and Women: The Reinvention of Nature*. London: Free Association.

Hayes, K. (2004). 'Serious mental illness and the black community'. *Counselling and Psychotherapy Journal*, 15: 2, 28.

HMSO (2004). *Social Trends 34*. London: HMSO. www.statistics.gov.uk/statbase/Product.arp?vlnk, accessed 10 November 2004.

Horrocks, R. (2001). *Freud Revisited*. New York: Palgrave Macmillan.

House, R. (2003). *Therapy beyond Modernity: Deconstructing and Transcending Profession-Centred Therapy*. London: Karnac.

Illich, I. (1973). *Celebration of Awareness*. Harmondsworth: Penguin.

Institute of Public Policy Research (IPPR) (2004). *State of the Nation – An audit of injustice in the UK*. London: IPPR. www.ippr.org.uk/press/index.php?release=332, accessed 10 November 2004.

Lago C. and Smith, B. (2003). *Anti-Discriminatory Counselling Practice*. London: Sage.

Laing, R. D. (1965). *The Divided Self: An Existential Study into Sanity and Madness*. Harmondsworth: Penguin.

Laungani, P. (2004). 'East meets West'. *Counselling and Psychotherapy Journal*, 15: 8, 21–3.

Levitas, R. (2004). 'Shuffling back to equality?'. *Soundings*, 26: Spring, 59–72.

Livingstone, T. (2004). 'Otherwise human beings'. *Counselling and Psychotherapy Journal*, 15: 8, 13–15.

Needham, C. (2004). 'Customer-focused government'. *Soundings*, 26: Spring, 73–85.

O'Connor, N. and Ryan, J. (1993). *Wild Desires and Mistaken Identities: Lesbianism and Psychoanalysis*. London: Virago.

Papadopoulos, R. (2002). *Therapeutic Care for Refugees: No Place like Home*. London: Karnac.

Peck, E. (2004). 'Force for good'. *Guardian*, 25 August 2004, Society section, 2.

Phillips, A. (1988). *Winnicott*. London: Fontana.

Pilgrim, D. (1997). *Psychotherapy and Society*. London: Sage.

Plummer, K. (1995). *Telling Sexual Stories: Power, Change and Social Worlds*. London: Routledge.

Pointon, C. (2004). 'Does our training embrace difference and diversity?'. *Counselling and Psychotherapy Journal*, 15: 8, 5–9.

Rose, C. (2004). 'Class matters'. *Counselling and Psychotherapy Journal*, 15: 8, 10–12.

Rose, N. (1990). *Governing the Soul*. London: Routledge.

Rose, N. (2003). *Power and Psychological Techniques: Ethically Challenged Professions*. Ross-on-Wye: PCCS.

Rustin, M. (1999).'Editorial: Where are we now?'. *Soundings*, 14: Spring, 7–10.

Rustin, M. (2000).'The New Labour ethic and the spirit of capitalism'. *Soundings*, 14: Spring, 111–26.

Rutherford, J. (2004).'Commentary: Common life'. *Soundings*, 26: Spring, 11–17.

Said, E. (1994). *Culture and Imperialism*. London: Vintage.

Samuels, A. (1993). *The Political Psyche*. London: Routledge.

Schafer, R. (1992). *Retelling a Life: Narration and Dialogue in Psychoanalysis*. New York: Perseus.

Schwarz, B. (ed.) (1978). *On Ideology*. London: Hutchinson.

Scott, G., Ciarrochi, J. and Deane, F. (2003).'The increasing incidence of suicide: Economic development. individualism and social integration'. *International Scope Review*, 5: 9. www.socialcapital.foundation.org/journal//volume%202003/issue%pdf/1_scott & al. pdf, accessed 4 December 2004.

Seu, I. B. and Heenan, M. C. (eds) (1998). *Feminism and Psychotherapy: Reflections on Contemporary Theories and Practice*. London: Sage.

Shivanath, S., Sills, C. and Miniken, A. (2004).'Will you read this – if it's about race and culture?'. *Counselling and Psychotherapy Journal*, 15: 3 (April), 32 –4.

Shuttleworth, A. (2000).'Psychoanalysis, its connections and change'. *Soundings*, 15: Summer, 104–17.

Smail, D. (1996). *How to Survive without Psychotherapy*. London: Constable.

Smith, L. S. (1999).'Arlie Hochschild – Soft-spoken conservationist of emotions'. *Soundings*, 11: Spring, 120–7.

Smith, P. (1999).'Emotional Labour'. *Soundings*, 11: Spring, 114–19.

Spence, D. P. (1982). *Narrative Truth and Historical Truth*. New York: Norton.

Spivak, G. (1990). *The Post-Colonial Critic: Interviews, Strategies and Dialogues*. London and New York: Routledge.

Spurling, L. (2004). *An Introduction to Psychodynamic Counselling*. New York and Basingstoke: Palgrave Macmillan.

Stanley, L. and Wise, S. (1983). *Breaking Out: Feminist Consciousness and Feminist Research*. London: Routledge and Kegan Paul.

Tuckwell, G. (2002). *Racial Identity, White Counsellors and Therapists*. Buckingham: Open University Press.

Winnicott, D. W. (1975). *Transitional Objects and Transitional Phenomena: Through Paediatrics to Psychoanalysis*. London: Karnac.

PART II

Gender and Sexuality

Psychodynamic Counselling and Gender

Nicola Barden

Introduction

Freud presented a plan for the development of gender identity that reads a little like an assault course. There is a direction to aim for, obstacles to be overcome, and the journey is character building. At the end the girl has a feminine identity, the boy a masculine one – or perhaps not, but there is room for deviation and difference. It is a radical plan as it goes far beyond the essentialist route of saying that gender just *is*. The vision is wide open. Yet it is also conservative in detail, reflecting the patriarchal society in which Freud lived. It may be that all discussions about gender are the same – imbued with the culture of the moment, so the decentred, multiple identities of the 21st century will later be critiqued as no more than a reflection of a post-modern era – and of course this may be true, and a good reason to treat the past with generosity. However, information increases, knowledge grows and thinking develops, and psychodynamic understandings of gender deserve re-examining in the light of this. The purpose is not so much to settle the question of gender as to keep it open: ' ... gender oppositions are so central to the history of psychoanalysis as a discourse that even when they figure as obstacles and omissions we are continually required to return to them' (Benjamin, 1995, p. 12).

Starting with the father: beginnings with Freud

Freud took the little boy as his starting point, initially thinking that the girl would have an equal and opposite development. It became clear to him that this was not the case, and later papers outlined differing pathways for boys and girls (Freud, 1932).

The boy's mother is his first love object. He wishes to be everything to the mother, to have her babies and to marry her. However, the father is an obstacle in his way, and the boy develops hostility to the father as to a rival for love. Around this point the little boy becomes aware of the absence of a penis in the female sex, through observations of mother, or sisters, or others in the family. A consequent fear is that he too could lose his penis, and that such a loss would be occasioned by incurring the wrath of the father. The father is now a feared rival, and the boy accommodates this by identifying with him rather than competing with him. This enables him to give up the mother as the aim of his desire, and eventually to replace her with another woman, who is often derived from or similar to her. Because the boy has such a fear of the father he is able to internalise him as a robust super-ego that enables him to control his desires, or id, to avoid the threat of castration. The boy may, in this sequence of events, develop a disparaging attitude towards his mother – and therefore towards women – as already, in effect, being castrated. Whether or not hostility is present, it remains an important task for the boy to continue differentiating himself from being a girl, and to model himself increasingly on his father and other men. To become a man he must repress his feminine identification (Minsky, 1996).

The girl, too, starts with her mother as her first love object, and sees the father as a rival for the mother's love. The difference is that when the girl understands that she too does not have a penis, and therefore is not able to give her mother the love and the babies that the father has given, she realises that she cannot continue to compete on an equal footing with the father for the mother. This creates a number of potential scenarios:

(a) The girl may become repulsed by the whole area of sexuality, being dissatisfied with her clitoris as an inferior penis, and therefore giving up phallic activity – including sexual activity – completely.

(b) She may cling stubbornly to her belief that she possesses a penis, refusing to acknowledge her inferior position in this respect, and continue to hope for the arrival of the penis that she holds in her psyche. This pathway may lead to the development of homosexuality.

(c) The girl will give up hope of keeping the mother and will instead take up the father, first in identification, and then as her love object. Underneath this attitude may lie resentment at the mother for denying her a penis in the first place, while at the same time awakening her libidinal desires, and for not wanting her complete devotion – evidenced by the mother's interest in the father and in other children. The girl's envy of the penis is transformed into a wish for a baby by the father, which she then replaces with a wish to have a baby with a male father-replacement, as the boy settles for a female mother-replacement. To become a woman, she must repress her homosexuality and make the transition from a 'masculine' (clitoral based) to a 'feminine' (vaginal based) sexual life.

Both sexes have in this fashion found a way to separate from the mother and gain an independent position of their own. Freud compared the girl's more complicated journey as being not unlike a second marriage, entered into in more certain knowledge of the undertaking, and with a better chance of success than first love.

Freud's account of the development of gender identity through the Oedipus complex seems very outdated these days. It is best approached with an appreciation of his own starting point and context – as the originator of psychoanalysis, theorising from his own small sample population of patients within Viennese culture. Women were second class citizens whose lives were shaped by biological destiny: there was no adequate contraception, and economic survival was dependent on marriage. Knowledge about the human body was rudimentary at best; knowledge about sexuality was worse. Concepts like those of gender and sexual identity were not yet meaningful. Sexuality focused on the body, so sodomy existed as a category but homosexuality as a concept of identity was only just appearing.[1] Relations between men and women had become the focus for morality in Western thought, although the emphasis had moved from the ethics of pleasure to those of desire (Foucault, 1992), a move which was captured in Freud's thinking about the Oedipal situation. For Freud, 'perversions' were in childhood a normal expression of sexuality, overcome on the journey to adulthood through engagement with culturally prescribed taboos, notably on incest and homosexuality. He was at pains to separate perversions and neurosis (Freud, 1905), already linked by the medical establishment. His preference for a 'normal' heterosexual identity was tempered by an acceptance of alternative outcomes, although this did not prevent him from viewing homosexuality as a sign of arrested development. He argued that 'homosexuals' should not be debarred from training as analysts – an argument that was not sustained by analytic institutes subsequently established in his name.

In this context Freud, for all his culture bound notions of gender and sexuality, was a radical thinker. He insisted that identity formation was precarious, and that identities themselves were unstable. Innately bisexual, children could potentially identify equally well with both genders and could take either as the object of their desires (Freud, 1923). It was only through a series of developmental stages centring on the Oedipus complex that this flexible beginning resulted in a more fixed outcome.

Freud had vigorous supporters and detractors of his theories of gender even as he was developing them. Analytic trainings were open to women, who were quick to identify the failings in his views on female development. Perhaps in response to his starting point that girls were in effect little boys until they evolved through the Oedipal conflict (Freud, 1932), some tried to reclaim a sense of essential femininity for women, something innate that was simply different to men. This has been rather a strong line of debate ever since, and not just in Freudian circles.

Karen Horney was one of the first to challenge Freud on his concept of penis envy. While agreeing that it existed, she disputed its significance. For her, the girl naturally left behind her envy of such a visible organ as her pleasure in her own sexual organs became established, leading to a comparatively straightforward turning to the father with a desire for his penis as a part of her own pleasure, rather than to replace a lack. The identification stayed with the mother, never having been seriously removed from her. Horney also argued that men could envy women, that the strength of their envy of childbirth and motherhood was greatly underestimated, and that women's envy of the penis was constituted in part by the penis as a phallic representation of the greater power available to men in society – something that Freud did not take into account. 'Men are evidently under greater necessity to depreciate women than vice-versa' (Horney, 1926, p. 12).

There was however a traditional and conservative side to Horney's argument that rested on a belief that girls were born 'feminine', with innate heterosexual tendencies. Helene Deutsch, a contemporary and close supporter of Freud's, went further in this respect, insisting that motherhood too was a primeval female desire, and that narcissism, masochism and passivity were essential traits of femininity (Wright, 1992, p. 68), that rested on identification with the mother's painful lot of labour and menstruation and the dependency on an active penis to awaken the receptive vagina. Nevertheless, despite her strong support for his work, Deutsch too rejected Freud's emphasis on penis envy as a clinical phenomenon, believing that as society became more accepting of women there was correspondingly less to envy; like Horney, interpreting the penis symbolically and from within a social context. This is increasingly how it has come to be thought of, socially as well as sexually, as representative of man's place in the world, so that penis envy is attached more to that interpretation, and less literally to the sexual organ.

Moving towards the mother: Melanie Klein

These criticisms of penis envy and the classic Oedipal complex were strongly supported by Melanie Klein, whose ideas moved away from the overriding significance of the father, towards the child's early relationship with the mother. Klein observed the baby forming a viable, stable sense of self during the first two years of life. She thought that a rudimentary ego was present in the infant from birth, already influenced by intra-uterine experiences. Thus unconscious phantasies and instincts were immediately active in response, as Klein saw it, to the innate life and death instincts. The ego makes use of phantasy to create an internal world that enables psychic survival and interprets external experience according to this aim. Warmth and fullness produce phantasies of wellbeing related to the life instinct; cold and hunger produce phantasies of persecution and rejection related to the death instinct. In addition to external stimuli, the infant has to deal with their own destructive fantasies – wanting to tear apart the breast that will not provide food, being overwhelmed by a destructiveness that could harm the loved as well as the hated object. The world outside is full of inexplicable monsters; the world inside contains unmanageable feelings. If the external reality is sufficiently nurturing and reassuring, it is gradually internalised until anxieties can be managed from within. It then becomes possible for the monstrous part objects to become ambivalent whole objects, and the infant can make good their destructive impulses, so that they are no longer experienced as the loss of everything good. It is therefore the early relationship with the caregiver – whom Klein invariably saw as the mother – that is of most significance in the development of a sense of self. Although Klein placed great importance on the Oedipal conflict, she put this at a much earlier stage of the child's life. Moving away from the breast in search of a less frustrating object of gratification, the child moves on to desiring the father's penis, which is eventually integrated with the breast, corresponding to actual observation of the parental couple.

Up to this point, the sex of the infant is not relevant to development – the early sense of self is not gendered. This is consistent with Vas Dias's observations that 'The development of this sense of self … is the primary developmental task of the infant from 0–2 years irrespective of sex and gender and is accomplished with little or no awareness of them' (2001, p. 31). Yet Klein did have a belief in some innate aspects of gender. She saw children of both sexes as having an 'inherent unconscious knowledge of the existence of the penis as well as of the vagina' (Klein in Weininger, 1992, p. 104), so the girl's sexuality is not organised primarily around a lack, as there is also a strong sense of presence. To the child the mother's body contains everything within it – penis, womb, breast, and baby. In this sense the father can be said to originate within the mother's body. In the paranoid/schizoid position of the part-object infant world, the penis acts as a block to access to the mother as it represents the father's union with her, and in this phantasy it is harsh and repressive; the same harshness makes it a solid safeguard of the mother against the infant's attacks and so it provides safety and lessens anxiety. When the depressive position is reached the penis-father is a new object to explore, away from the intensity of the relation with the mother. At this point both boy and girl turn away with some relief from the mother towards the father, adopting what Klein calls the 'feminine attitude'. In these constructs it is possible to see inherent father/mother male/female characteristics that are not altogether dissimilar to those in Freud's thinking. For Klein, however, because initially all of these states are experienced in phantasy and at a part-object level, they are available without their gender attribution, which comes at a later and more conscious level. As part objects they are available in either parent – and therefore in either gender, leaving open the capacity for both genders to be experienced as aspects of the self.

Two in one: the contrasexual archetype of Carl Jung

With her emphasis on the role of internal objects in the formation of the ego, Klein was an important figure for the object relations theorists who followed. The other significant figure contributing to the future of psychotherapy, though not specifically to object relations, was Carl Jung. Neither Jung nor Klein settled comfortably into the mainstream of psychoanalysis, Jung so much so that his work became better known as analytical psychology.

Jung was for some years a close confidant of Freud's. They separated over a number of fundamental disagreements, particularly Jung's interest in the spiritual dimension of life, which clashed with Freud's rational, scientific self, and Freud's emphasis on the sexual drive, or libido, which Jung could only accept as part of the picture.[2] Jung's emphasis on the spiritual has continued to cast him as a controversial figure, although he made clear his essentially psychological interest in the non-material aspect of life. He stressed the importance of bringing spirit back into a conscious relationship with matter (Samuels et al., 1986) through thinking about out-of-ego experiences rather than dismissing them. He had little interest in the early years of life, assuming that children had no psychology of their own until they developed an ego around the age of four; prior to this they largely reflected the egos of their parents. This was not the same as the character of a child, which he believed to be present from birth, ready to meet and be formed in relation to the outside world.

Jung's interest in the second half of life, in the task of becoming a whole person, and his interest in philosophy, religion and the search for meaning, led him to develop his theory of the collective unconscious which, together with the personal unconscious, is part of the whole human psyche. While the personal unconscious consists of all that happens in an individual's life, the collective unconscious consists of non-personal matter. The personal unconscious was at one point known, but has been forgotten or repressed; the collective unconscious has never been known, but is inherited, universal and impersonal. Its contents are archetypal, that is, contain a disposition to ordering experience which can be recognised by the groupings and 'images' common to all humanity – a 'blueprint' for the gathering together of thought and experience, a 'deposit of the constantly repeated experiences of humanity' (Jung, 1917, p. 68). Archetypes are discovered in the imagery that represents them. They are not images themselves, and the images connected with them change depending on culture and context; it is the underlying theme that is the same, and which indicates the presence of the archetype. Collective images are often found in myth and legend. In this way the idea of God is an archetype; each culture will have its own representation of its gods, but there is no culture without some such representation.

Gender has a place in the collective unconscious through the contrasexual images of anima and animus, or the 'fundamental forms which underlie the "feminine" aspects of man and the "masculine" aspects of woman' (Samuels et al., 1986). Jung believed that men and women carried within them, biologically and psychologically, traits of the 'other' gender. These traits have an active existence in the psyche and, if not acknowledged, are projected onto actual men and women, usually in an idealised or devalued form. For Jung, male and female formed two parts of a whole, and the expectation of the other is present from the start (Jung, 1917).

This is consistent with Jung's vision of a psyche based on polarities, in which transformation is found in 'the *union of opposites through the middle path*' (Jung, 1917, p. 203, emphasis in original). In some ways his approach was liberating. Freud's Oedipal pathway requires renunciation of identification with the opposite gender if a mature adult position is to be achieved. The boy must be freed from the constraints of love for the mother. He might maintain a connection with the 'feminine' in himself through possession of a woman as his object choice, that is, by replacing mother with wife he can still be in relationship with the feminine – but it is no longer inside himself. The girl must give up false hopes of possessing a penis, refocus on a vaginal sexuality, and align herself with her feminine disposition through identification with the mother and desire for the father. Jung saw masculine and feminine as a lively part of the inner world of both genders, and placed a value on the man being in relationship with his 'feminine' and the woman with her 'masculine' aspect. However, this was also a rather essentialist view, complicated by the fact that Jung's versions of masculine and feminine were far from free of the gender stereotypes of the day, while being entirely free of any recognition of that fact. His descriptions of anima and animus traits are permeated with normative gender expectations:

> The conscious attitude of woman is in general far more exclusively personal than that of man. Her world is made up of fathers and mothers, brothers and sisters, husbands and children ... The man's world is the nation, the state, business concerns, etc ... The general means more to him than the personal ... whereas [the woman's] world, outside her husband, terminates in a sort of cosmic mist. (Jung, 1917, p. 208)

While possibly an accurate reflection of the constraints on the lives of many men and women, this is used by Jung, not as a description of an external reality, but as evidence of natural internal gender dispositions. On this is built his characterisation of the contrasexual archetype, so that the man's anima makes him moody, timid, effeminate, while the woman's animus makes her opinionated, disputatious and inflexible. Jung felt that women, by virtue of their greater involvement in the personal side of life, were more in touch with the unconscious world. In a good partnership the woman provided a bridge for the man into the otherwise alarming areas of intuition and feeling. Without this bridge, and lacking a conscious relationship with the feminine within himself, the man would exhibit the negative anima tendencies outlined above, while perhaps projecting idealised features onto other women who will inevitably, in the end, disappoint him. The woman, without her inner masculine being given life through good connection with her husband, will show the negative animus traits which relate to her exclusion from the worldly side of life, resulting in an overly dogmatic and defensive position. If she is able to get into relationship with her inner masculine, then it need not come out in these extreme forms, but can be integrated with the feminine to form a whole person incorporating both aspects.

This position can be freeing for both sexes in being able to value and express a broader range of gender positions, and is in tune with Jung's concept of individuation, or becoming 'whole, indivisible and distinct from other people or collective psychology' – although still in relation to them (Samuels et al., 1986, p. 76). Jung's psychology creates a clear separation between the archetypal predisposition for imaging contrasexuality, and the images themselves. The readiness to perceive male and female was one thing; the perception itself was another, and would be expected to change across time and culture. Yet Jung contradicts his own thinking on this point by conflating these two things (Wehr, 1988). His description of the anima and animus was bound by his own ideals of women and men, but he speaks about them as if these ideals were in fact the ageless truths of the archetype. The effect of this is greater than just an out of date image. As an archetype is universal it gathers to itself an authority beyond the personal; when this authority is misplaced onto the culture bound image rather than the archetype itself, the image is given an extra legitimacy. So Jung's assertion of dogmatism in women and timidity in men as archetypal images come across instead as definitions of an almost divine order. Conversely, in this guise animus and anima are constraining rather than liberating forces in the full expression of a gendered self.

Taking it forward: object relations

In Britain and America the work of the object relations theorists and ego psychologists acted in parallel to gradually move questions of gender identity away from the central role of the father on the Oedipal stage. They emphasised rather, as had Klein, the significance of the mother in infant development. Put simply, the relationship with the mother was the arena for the infant's development of a sense of self; the role of the father was to protect the mother/infant space, and then to provide a pathway from this exclusive love into the wider world.

In this formulation there was again the use of societal norms without acknowledging them as such. Object relations developed in a conservative era. Men were not closely involved in the intimate care of young children, who spent their earliest years usually in the care of mothers or female relatives or nannies. It was in this atmosphere that influential thinkers like Winnicott and Bowlby gained the clinical practice that led to their theories of child development. The relationship of the infant to these 'primary caregivers' became the focus of attention, rather than the satisfaction of instinctual life. Maternal power was seen as the most significant factor in the emotional health of the young child in its early stages of dependency. The economic and social power of men in the world was construed as irrelevant at this stage, as if the whole family existed within the baby's encapsulated world. The concentration on the mother as constituting the relational world of the infant lost perspective on the mother as a person outside of the mother/infant dyad. Winnicott's famous injunction that there was no such thing as a baby, only a mother and a baby, is not to say that the same is true in reverse. Mothers may have periods of intense involvement with the world of the infant, but this is continually brought into relief by relationships with other adults, children, the outside world. The mother can and must exist independently of the baby, indeed must psychically and physically be able to be separate from it in order to be able to tolerate and embrace the demands for oneness when they arise. The mother's experiences are complex and to sentimentalise motherhood is the other side of denigrating it. Maternity is no longer – if it ever was – the 'hub of a woman's identity' (Raphael-Leff, 2001, p. 181). A woman brings into her mothering the rest of her life experience, and so to some extent this is the infant's experience too.

The achievement of object relations theory was to progress from an individuality based on autonomy and separateness to a relational individualism. The mother reflected back the infant's experience of itself in relationship with her as a self-experience, thus beginning the construction of a world of inner objects that led the infant to an eventual recognition of itself, and then others, as subjects. The profound attachment of both the little girl and the little boy to the mother was obvious in this framework. Feminist therapists began to look more closely at the possibility that a mother related differently to her male and female children, in a sense passing down remnants of her journey with her own mother. As a girl she identified with her mother; as a mother she identified more with her daughter than her son. This identification was ambivalent, containing the unconscious need to prepare her daughter for a world in which she must manage the emotional life of both genders and the meeting of others' needs before her own. This is exemplified in the role of motherhood itself, while also raising in the mother all the feelings of unmet need from her own mothering that may then be projected onto the little girl in the unrealisable hope of having them met, in effect, by proxy (Eichenbaum and Orbach, 1983). The girl's identity would therefore be formed around this complicated relational framework, with a consequent struggle to achieve the level of separation necessary for autonomy while maintaining the sense of connectedness that was core to her experience. There is no such parallel identification from the mother to the son; there is greater consciousness of the boy as 'other' from the start. However, his early intimacy with the mother leaves him with some uncertainty about a basic gender identity that needs to be continually proved to be different to that of the mother. The girl's first identification is with a woman and stays there; the boy must clarify his position in relation to gender identification, and so clear demarcations between masculine and feminine become important, even when the only available option requires devaluing woman and forming a defensive, compensatory attitude to masculinity (Chodorow, 1989).

The meaning of gender

As the intricacies of mother/father/daughter/son relationships were mapped out, it was harder to maintain a view of 'women' and 'men' as universal categories with common characteristics. The pre-feminist debate had been over questions of nature versus nurture – were women born or made? These were feminist debates too, but they continued alongside an increasing awareness of the other components to be considered in the formation of gender identity. Race, ethnicity, class, sexuality, and culture – all were determinants in the shaping of lived gender realities. Worldwide ethnographic studies on gender show two consistent findings. One is that gender difference is an issue in every society. All societies have markers to distinguish between male and female, with institutionalised gender roles that are used as a basis for self-esteem, the male role being ascribed more value than the female (Gilmore, 1997). The other is that there is little consistency in the *content* of these roles, and it is impossible to give any but the broadest of generalisations regarding 'traditional' male and female functions. The person of the researcher began to be acknowledged as a significant factor in the interpretation of the roles as having universal application, as Western observers unconsciously assumed the Western male model as a norm (Ehrenberg, 1997).[3] In similar fashion, analytic theory has started to acknowledge its debt to social context and move from constructing a variety of routes resulting in a single gender identity to a more plural position of understanding pathways towards gendered *identities*. The analytic view of gender came out of a comparatively narrow range of clinical experience that was shaped by class, race and culture as much as by gender – but without acknowledgement or even awareness of this. Global economies and mass communication systems, immigration and multiculturalism, feminism and gay rights, have all brought broader perspectives into focus that have begun to feed the psychodynamic understanding of gender. This may be at an early stage in the field as a whole, but in some areas at least values are less often being taken as facts (Gilligan, 1993, p. xv).

Studies of adolescent girls' voices (Taylor et al., 1995) focused on listening to what girls were actually saying about themselves, rather than what it was expected that they should say. Taylor traced the contours of ethnicity in these studies, drawing parallels between the silencing of women's voices in a dominant male culture and the silencing of black voices in a dominant white culture. Along with Baker Miller (1978), she reframed the 'problem' of girls achieving separation and autonomy from their mothers as instead a struggle to maintain connection. In doing this she challenged the orthodoxy that autonomy was the goal of development, seeing it rather as a description of the pattern of male development that had become a model for, rather than an account of, growth. She argued that 'civilisation', with its colonialist overtones, created a structure in which women and men were bound into false relationships with themselves and each other, and that psychoanalysis has spoken with the voice of civilisation to the detriment of real understanding – 'the lie in psychological theories which have taken men as representing all humans, and the lie in women's psychological development in which girls and women alter their voices to fit themselves into images of relationship and goodness carried by false feminine voices' (Gilligan, 1993, p. xxvi).

The impetus for gender studies in the field of psychoanalysis came from women needing to articulate their place in a theory that struggled to move away from the 'Adam's rib' approach to women's psychology; therefore much of the discussion was about developing a psychodynamic theory relevant to women. Achievements in this area have revealed failings in the development of men's psychology too. In a study not dissimilar to Gilligan's, Frosh embarked on structured conversations with male adolescents with conscious comment on the ways in which other factors came into the building of their masculinity – 'masculinities are constructed out of a complex network of identity factors, including "race", ethnicity, social class and sexuality' (Frosh et al., 2002, p. 258). Common factors that threatened a sense of masculinity were any alignment with homosexuality, femininity and girls, and the boys were at pains to dissociate themselves from all three. This set up some contradictions, as sexual relationships with girls, or at least interest in these, were also important markers of maleness; therefore any such relationship would have to contain within itself clear gender demarcations and the boy would have to behave 'as a boy' in order not to compromise his masculine identity. Fear of homosexuality was profound – it would have been impossible to survive and admit to gay feelings. The factors that boys thought made other boys popular were: not being like girls; being hard, evidenced in sporting prowess, coolness, dominance and not being serious about school; and class and racial factors. Black African Caribbean boys were most popular in these terms, congruent with the dominant view of black culture as very masculine, that is, sporty, cool and tough, unlike, say, Asian culture with its emphasis on educational achievement and religion. It is immediately apparent from these generalisations that identification with a culture will profoundly affect the way in which views are formed about what is 'appropriate' in gender identity, both within the individual and from the observer's standpoint. Asian boys, who do not rate highly as masculine at school, may nevertheless rate very highly in the Asian community, where the precise markers will be altered to meet that particular context. Black boys growing up gay may have to cope with enormous internal dissonance as a result of having to meet the high demand on their 'masculinity'; at the same time they must attempt to preserve a part of their sexual identity which threatens to undermine the very same sense of maleness because of the prohibition on homosexuality.

In this way boys, and men, have had to wear masks in order to preserve a gender identity. This has perhaps been longer recognised for women, and the critique of femininity as a mask has been a subversive theme throughout analytic writing. Joan Riviere wrote of the difficulty that achievement presents to a woman, placing her in competition with the father, and therefore forcing an appeasing attitude in order to divert aggression away from herself. She describes womanliness in this context as a 'masquerade', and further asserts that there is no real difference between the mask and the femininity underneath it – 'whether radical or superficial, they are the same thing' (Saguaro, 2000, p. 73). Kaplan talked of stereotypical femininity being a disguise for forbidden masculine strivings. As girls have to give up those aspects of themselves ascribed to the 'masculine' sphere in order to achieve a recognisable female identity, femininity itself becomes a half-truth. Womanly self-sacrifice is displayed to cover greedy ambition; worldly weakness is cultivated to detract from the frustrated ruthlessness that finds outlet in the domestic sphere. Unless social conditions allow women to experience themselves as they truly are, they must accommodate prescribed femininity through a form of bondage to it, cultivating 'a masquerade of denigrated, submissive femininity that hides a woman's forbidden and dangerous "masculine" ambitions' (Kaplan, 1993, p. 184).

Perhaps the time is coming when masculinity will also be open to reconstruction. Such a process is difficult though – as Baker Miller points out, the group with the power has an investment in maintaining the conditions of dominance at the same time as it hold the tools for the dismantling of those conditions. Internally, this may link with fear of a return to the state of complete dependency upon the mother. As the route out of this has been defined as separation from the mother and the development of an autonomous self, there is little room for negotiating a more relational approach that would allow for connection with the discarded 'feminine' without a concomitant threat to a gendered identity. Male values are dominated by concepts related to potency (Jukes, 1993) that must be continually demonstrated. Desire for the mother, experienced as a simple need for intimacy, is feminine, or for a boy, 'girly', therefore to be feared and hated. Women's independence is likewise threatening, and independent women have failed in their feminine role. To be gay is thus the ultimate failure of masculinity; to be lesbian, the ultimate failure of femininity. A challenge for men is how to relinquish power without the experience of psychological castration. Men may of course already have some understanding of this through, say, their class or ethnicity.

To be added to the recognition that there is no such thing as a unified category of gender is the argument that there is not even a unified experience of sex. There has been a habitual usage of the term 'sex' to denote a biological category, indicated by sexed genes, hormones and bodies, and the term 'gender' to denote the characteristics ascribed to each sex, whether informed by 'nature' or by 'nurture'. Thus psychoanalysts have been able to consider the development of gender subsequent to the assignment of a biological sex. Although this chapter has noted that understandings of gender have been culturally influenced without necessarily being aware of that fact, it is also true to say that theorists were not always completely unaware. Even Freud contradicted himself, on the one hand building concepts based on the active masculine and passive feminine aim and ideal, and on the other acknowledging that 'all human individuals ... combine in themselves both masculine and feminine characteristics, so that pure masculinity and femininity remain theoretical constructs of uncertain content' (Freud, 1925, p. 258). The search to categorise gender in some definitive way has never reached a conclusion.

General agreement has it that a basic gender identity is fixed by the age of three (Stoller, 1968) as a result of internal and external processes from birth onwards. This is congruent with the age at which children start to evince consistent awareness of gender differences applying to themselves and other, and are able to identify boys and girls, men and women, rather than trousers and skirts, guns and ribbons, daddies and mummies. Establishing a gendered sense of identity is crucial in the world – there are no comfortable words for those whose gender is not clear cut, and a medical response is usually to make a gender assignment shortly after birth based on the appearance of the genitals. One renowned case at the Johns Hopkins Medical School, a centre of gender research, assigned a female gender to an infant boy of 18 months whose penis had been removed as a result of a circumcision that had gone wrong. The team were certain that if raised as a girl, the boy would have no trouble identifying as one. What is extraordinary about this is both the attachment of so much significance to the penis as the marker of the baby's sex – without a penis, he still had testicles, male hormones and all the body mapping required for a male puberty; and the simplicity of the assumption that being treated like a girl would make him respond as one, which would be an alarming assumption at birth let alone after 18 months of being in the world as a boy. This was a reduction of the nature/nurture debate – never a helpful split – to the point of absurdity.[4] A route out of this stale debate is to explore what lies behind it – the emphasis on the binary gender divide (Izzard and Barden, 2001).

Binary splits: language and gender

The drive to order and separate does not apply to gender alone. It is a human trait to order activity to create a liveable life. Yet a boundary immediately forms an inside and an outside, and this is available for uses other than survival and safety; it can equally be used for power and dominance, arguably extensions of the need for security. It can also become rigid, preventing the fertile confusion that needs to be present for change to occur. Both order and disorder are required – 'So levity is important, but no one can, in the end, escape gravity' (Tatham, 1992, p. 171). Ordering gender has acquired many of these secondary purposes, analogous with the hegemonic ordering of race and class. Gender has become a dualistic ordering principle. The wish to disorder it, to bring some creative chaos back in, connects with the strand of analytic thinking that questions the existence of gendered subjects at all, exemplified by the school of French feminists following on from Lacan, for whom language created gender, and without which gender has no existence.

Lacan differentiated between need in the infant, which is transformed into a demand that can be answered by food and warmth, for example, and desire, which cannot be met because it is ultimate: longing to possess the mother entirely, to be the only one for her, the best baby ever. Because it can never be fully met it always exists, and the residue of loss is always present. The signifier for this ineradicable desire is the phallus – which Lacan carefully described as *not* the penis, nor even a phantasy of the penis, but as something that was not there – the castrated penis – inherently false, and gender neutral. Lacan emphasised the lack in both male and female development: women lack an actual penis; men believe they have a phallus but it is only a penis; women try to be the phallus for the man by fulfilling his desire, but inevitably fail at this impossible task (as desire is inherently unfulfillable); men neither receive the phallus from a woman nor from themselves, no matter how much the penis is fetishised in an attempt to gain it as a phallus. Both sexes lose something in gaining a gendered identity, as the price is an acknowledgement that identity gathers around a lack of something. Lacan asserts a difference between the sexes, while finding no words to adequately describe it. Masculinity is vulnerable to exposure as essentially bogus, and women take on the cultural representation of the 'lack', projected onto them by men. Gender is therefore a precarious identity in Lacan as well as in Freud, compared to the more stable identity posited by object relations theorists, unless undermined by neurosis.

Putting gender on the edge in this way, connecting identity with loss, is a position through which Lacan enables others to question the symbolic meaning of gender, and its construction through discourse – is gender described by language or formed by it? Could gender exist without language? Even the so-called obvious about gender is questionable. The assumption of two sexes rests on a squeezing out of legitimate space for bodies not sexed in this way, which enter a zone of 'intersex', ascribed a sex, re-sexed. The existence of language gives a shape to these bodies that may not be their own shape, and so the assumed naturalness of male and female may also be more constructed than is imagined. A woman with cropped hair, wearing jeans and a leather jacket, boots, studs, walks down the road. 'That's not a woman', remarks an observer, scornfully. Of course she is a woman. Yet also she is not, by the laws that enforce the category of womanliness. The laws are the result of endless discourses that shape and reshape expectations and definitions of gender. From this perspective, no woman is there before the language to describe her is present, whatever body she inhabits. All existence is social in that it is lived in relation to others; the midwife's cry of 'It's a girl!', or 'It's a boy!' is cried to someone and about someone. It is a cry that emerges from what existed before it, namely an array of meanings about what it is to be a girl or boy. The naming comes from this array, and in this way the body is named for what it is already perceived, socially, to be (Salih, 2002). By inhabiting these perceptions the possessor of the body confirms themselves as girl or boy. This is what Butler (1990) refers to as gender 'performativity'. To find recognition as a subject, as a person whom others can relate to, a woman or man must submit himself or herself to the appropriate discourse. Language, according to Butler, determines gender, is no mere descriptor of it. The girl performs her gender according to the ways in which gender performance pre-exists her. This is the place of gender performativity (Butler, 1990) – to find recognition as a subject, a woman, or man, must submit herself or himself to the appropriate discourse. The submission need not be meek, and the performance can be subversive of the discourses, but must connect with them in order to exist. The performance predates the performer. Butler emphasises that the assumption of a heterosexual norm is integral to gender discourses.[5] This assumption adds confusion rather than clarity to the debate as it creates a false link between gender and sexuality. Analytic thought has always assumed a heterosexual norm in terms of adult development. This rests from the beginning on the Oedipal complex, which assumes a gendered split between desire and identification (O'Connor and Ryan, 1993): as one cannot desire and identify with the same gender, the outcome of a healthy same-sex identification is an opposite-sex love object. Freud's liberal tolerance for other Oedipal resolutions does not remove this normative stance, which is brought into sharp relief in the situation of transgender desire. It is assumed that part of the motive for gender reassignment is a proper realignment of sexual orientation. 'My cousin asked, "If you don't want to make love to a man why did you go to all the trouble of having a sex change operation?" ... I have not changed my preference for a partner ... It is not my sexuality that was crossed, but my gender' (Spry, 1997, p. 1). The situation is further confused by the positioning of male and female as two parts of a whole, a complementary heterosexuality, enshrined in Jung's contrasexual archetype, implicitly pathologising same-sex relationships and literalising gender differences into the body, resorting to biology to capture difference.

While the solution may not be to abandon the concept of the Oedipal complex, or of archetypes, it is necessary to separate baby from bathwater, to see if 'we can drain off the accretions of post-Freudian pathologisation and meet the baby afresh' (Izzard, 1999, p. 53).

Conclusion

In some respects psychodynamic thinking about gender has come a long way. Most writers now acknowledge that there is a social context to analytic theory. Gender itself is less likely to be considered a unitary construct, but a web of difference within which individual gendered identities are formed. The category of sex itself is being challenged. Sexuality is less often confused with gender, and acceptance of fluidity in both gender and sexual roles is increasing. Things that were taken as the norm are, if not forever changed, at least up for question. Psychodynamic counselling has continued to breathe life into its theorising about gender. Sometimes the end point would seem to be the deconstruction of identity itself. Benjamin (1995) argues in response that it is not possible to live entirely free of a subjective identity, and the space for gender should be widened rather than dissolved. Gender is 'a transcendent analytic category whose truth, though false, remains central to thought' (Goldner, in Benjamin, 1995, p. 12). We cannot think entirely without categories, just as we cannot think entirely within them. We cannot do with gender, and we cannot do without it. A sense of gender is like a home – a place so imbued with mythology that it does not really exist, yet a place that is 'the point of every narrative' (Prosser, 1998, p. 205). The purpose of counselling is in part to enable people to find their own sense of belonging. By setting aside the conviction that belonging requires certainty, of aim or of outcome, perhaps there is a greater chance of finding it.

Notes

1. The first recorded use of homosexuality as a category was by Karl Kertbeny in 1869 (Wright, 1992) in relation to a proposal to repeal the German anti-sodomy legislation. His intention was to create a benign alternative to 'sodomy', with its biblical associations of wickedness and sin, without challenging the heterosexual norm. This liberal effort was transformed into a conservative one by the twentieth-century sexologist Kraft-Ebbing who brought medico-moral judgements to bear on sexual categories, so that variations from the heterosexual norm became value laden perversions rather than morally neutral differences. Foucault argued that this was inevitable: ' ... the psychological, medical category of homosexuality was constituted from the moment it was characterised' (Foucault, 1990, p. 43).
2. As well as interpreting libido as a larger life force, connected to but not consisting of sexuality alone, Jung also recognised that other instincts were as, or more, powerful in the psyche – to appease hunger, or achieve power, for example. He saw the emphasis on sex as an obsession of 'civilised societies', where other basic needs were already assured.
3. In one 1936 observational account the researchers recorded, 'The *entire village* left the next day in about 30 canoes, leaving us alone with the *women and children* in the abandoned houses.' The researchers were not aware of the implications of their account, that the only real people in the village were the men (Lévi-Strauss, cited in Conkey, 1997, p. 57, emphasis added).
4. In the event the boy, Bruce, was raised as a girl, Brenda, having his testicles removed and a vagina created, and hormone treatment to ensure the development of secondary female characteristics at puberty. Despite claims of medical success, Bruce never felt like a girl, never fitted in as a girl, and at 15 years, after finding out about his history, made the decision to return to being a boy (Colapinto, 2000).
5. Butler places the taboo against homosexuality as preceding the incest taboo and, using the premise of Freud's paper 'Mourning and melancholia', asserts the development of heterosexuality as itself a form of melancholia. The first desire is for the same-sex parent, repressed in response to the taboo, and defensively incorporated to continue as an identification. Thus 'gender identity appears primarily to be the internalisation of a prohibition that proves to be formative of identity' (Butler, 1990, p. 63).

REFERENCES

Baker Miller, J. (1978). *Towards a New Psychology of Women*. London: Pelican.

Benjamin, J. (1995). *Like Subjects, Love Objects: Essays on Recognition and Sexual Difference*. New Haven, CT: Yale University Press.

Brettell, C. and Sargent, C. (eds) (1997). *Gender in Cross Cultural Perspective*. Upper Saddle River, NJ: Prentice-Hall.

Butler, J. (1990). *Gender Trouble: Feminism and the Subversion of Identity*. London: Routledge.

Chodorow, N. (1989). *Feminism and Psychoanalytic Theory*. New Haven, CT: Yale University Press.

Colapinto, J. (2000). *As Nature Made Him: The Boy Who Was Raised as a Girl*. London: Quartet.

Conkey, M. (1997). 'Men and women in prehistory: an archaeological challenge'. In C. Brettell and C. Sargent (eds), *Gender in Cross-Cultural Perspective*. Upper Saddle River, NJ: Prentice-Hall.

Ehrenberg, M. (1997). 'The role of women in human evolution'. In C. Brettell and C. Sargent (eds), *Gender in Cross Cultural Perspective*. Upper Saddle River, NJ: Prentice-Hall.

Eichenbaum, L. and Orbach, S. (1984). *What Do Women Want?* London: Fontana/Collins.

Foucault, M. (1990). *The History of Sexuality, Volume 1: An Introduction*. London: Penguin.

Foucault. M. (1992). *The History of Sexuality, Volume 2: The Use of Pleasure*. London: Penguin.

Freud, S. (1905). 'Three essays on the theory of sexuality'. In J. Strachey (ed.), *The Standard Edition of the Complete Psychological Works of Sigmund Freud, Volume VII*. London: Hogarth.

Freud, S. (1923). 'The Ego and the Id'. In J. Strachey (ed.), *The Standard Edition of the Complete Psychological Works of Sigmund Freud, Volume XIX*. London: Hogarth.

Freud, S. (1925). 'Some psychical consequences of the anatomical distinction between the sexes'. In J. Strachey (ed.), *The Standard Edition of the Complete Psychological Works of Sigmund Freud, Volume XIX*. London: Hogarth.

Freud, S. (1932). 'Femininity'. In J. Strachey (ed.), *The Standard Edition of the Complete Psychological Works of Sigmund Freud, Volume XXII*. London: Hogarth.

Frosh, S., Phoenix, A. and Pattman, R. (2002). *Young Masculinities*. Basingstoke: Palgrave Macmillan.

Gilligan, C. (1993). *In a Different Voice: Psychological Theory and Women's Development*. Cambridge, MA: Harvard University Press.

Gilmore, D. (1997). 'The Manhood Puzzle'. In C. Brettell and C. Sargent (eds), *Gender in Cross Cultural Perspective*. Upper Saddle River, NJ: Prentice-Hall.

Goldner, V. (1991). 'Toward a critical relational theory of gender'. *Psychoanalytic Dialogue*, 1, 249–72.

Horney, K. (1926). 'The Flight from Womanhood: the masculinity complex in women as viewed by men and by women'. In M. Maguire (ed.) (1995), *Men, Women, Passion and Power*. London: Routledge.

Izzard, S. (1999). 'Oedipus – baby or bathwater? A review of psychoanalytic theories of homosexual development'. *British Journal of Psychotherapy*, 16: 1, 43–55.

Izzard, S. and Barden, N. (eds) (2001). *Rethinking Gender and Therapy: The Changing Identities of Women*. Buckingham: Open University Press.

Jukes, A. (1993). *Why Men Hate Women*. London: Free Association.

Jung, C. G. (1917). 'The psychology of the unconscious'. In H. Read, M. Fordham and G. Adler (eds), *The Collected Works of C. G. Jung, Volume 7*. London: Routledge and Kegan Paul.

Kaplan, L. (1993). *Female Perversions*. London: Penguin.

Lévi-Strauss, C. (1936) 'Contribution a l'étude de l'organisation sociale des Indiens Bororo', *Journal de la Société des Américainistes de Paris*, 28, 269–304.

Minsky, R. (1996). *Psychoanalysis and Gender*. London: Routledge,

O'Connor, N. and Ryan, J. (1993). *Wild Desires and Mistaken Identities: Lesbianism and Psychoanalysis*. London: Virago.

Prosser, J. (1998). *Second Skins: The Body Narratives of Transexuality*. New York: Columbia University Press.

Raphael-Leff, J. (2001). 'Emotional experiences of becoming a mother'. In S. Izzard and N. Barden (eds), *Rethinking Gender and Therapy: The Changing Identities of Women*. Buckingham: Open University Press.

Saguaro, S. (2000). *Psychoanalysis and Woman: A Reader*. Basingstoke: Palgrave Macmillan.

Salih, S. (2002). *Judith Butler*. London and New York: Routledge.

Samuels, A., Shorter, B. and Plaut, F. (eds) (1986). *A Critical Dictionary of Jungian Analysis*. London: Routledge and Kegan Paul.

Spry, J. (1997) *Orlando's Sleep: An Autobiography of Gender*. Norwich, VT: New Victoria.

Stoller, R. J. (1968). *Sex and Gender: The Development of Masculinity and Femininity*. London: Karnac.

Tatham, P. (1992). *The Making of Maleness: Men, Women and the Flight of Daedalus*. London: Karnac.

Taylor, J. M., Gilligan, C. and Sullivan, A. (1995). *Between Voice and Silence: Women and Girls, Race and Relationship*. Cambridge, MA: Harvard University Press.

Vas Dias, S. (2001). 'When do I know I'm a girl? The development of a sense of self in the early infant'. In S. Izzard and N. Barden (eds), *Rethinking Gender and Therapy: The Changing Identities of Women*. Buckingham: Open University Press.

Wehr, D. S. (1988). *Jung and Feminism: Liberating Archetypes*. London: Routledge.

Weininger, O. (1992) *Melanie Klein: From Theory to Reality*. London: Karnac.

Wright, E. (ed.) (1992). *Feminism and Psychoanalysis: A Critical Dictionary*. Oxford: Blackwell.

Psychodynamic Counselling and Sexual Orientation

David Mair

... homosexuals are essentially disagreeable people ... [displaying] a mixture of superciliousness, false aggression and whimpering ... subservient when confronted with a stronger person, merciless when in power, unscrupulous about trampling on a weaker person. (Bergler, cited in Lewes, 1995, p. 2)

The history of psychodynamic thinking about sexual minorities is, to put it mildly, not conducive to an easy relationship between therapist and patient. Some of the key figures in the development of psychodynamic theory propounded views of homosexuality which today sound archaic and heterosexist in the extreme. Klein, for instance, believed that heterosexuality was 'phylogenetically inscribed, presumably for the reproduction of the race. In the unconscious of the infant an awareness of the sexual organs of its own sex is waiting to be complemented by those of the opposite sex, because of an innate knowledge of parental intercourse' (Maguire, 1995, p. 205). Fairburn and Winnicott considered homosexuality in adults to be either a perversion or evidence of psychopathology (Fairburn, 1946; Winnicott, 1964). And although Freud's position on the criminality of homosexuality was more liberal than that of many thinkers of his day, he was ultimately unable to reconcile his Oedipal model of human development with its requirement for the adoption of a person of the opposite sex as their object choice, with his desire to be tolerant towards homosexuals. According to Lewes (1995), 'Freud's position on the legal and moral issues is clear, but his thinking on the specific issues of the pathological nature of homosexuality is not' (p. 20).

A major difficulty for psychodynamic counsellors in working with clients from a sexual minority arises from the central role of the Oedipus complex in a psychodynamic understanding of a mature psychosexual development of individuals. If gay sexuality is viewed as 'normal', then the traditional understanding of the Oedipus complex, with its insistence on opposite-sex object choice, must be wrong, or incomplete. If this aspect of the Oedipus complex is challenged, may not other concepts of psychodynamic theory also be open to question? The work of Lewes (1995), with his reworking of the Oedipal theory so that there are twelve potential outcomes, including exclusive homosexuality, reminds us that openly gay individuals had no part in the formation of fundamental psychodynamic theories. Lewes suggests that an exclusively heterosexual Oedipal outcome can just as easily be pathological as an exclusively homosexual one, when it has been adopted as a defence against split-off homosexuality:

> Since even optimal development is the result of trauma, the fact that a certain development results from a 'stunting' or 'blocking' or 'inhibition' of another possibility does not distinguish it from other developments. All results of the Oedipus complex are traumatic, and, for similar reasons all are 'normal'. Some are more pathological than others, but the reason for considering them so cannot be derived from the operations of the Oedipus complex. Those writers who think otherwise ignore the traumatic origins of even optimal results and, in effect, disguise a moral argument about what is 'natural' as a pseudo biological argument. (1995, p. 70)

Until relatively recently homosexuality was a criminal offence, punishable by imprisonment in the UK and elsewhere. Thus, heterosexuality was seen as a norm, and psychodynamic theories of human development served to reflect this 'given', with homosexuality relegated to the position of a perversion or, according to Freud, 'inversion'. As Domenici and Lesser (1995) write:

> By taking themselves as the standard (much as the makers of Crayola crayons came up with a light-coloured crayon and called it 'flesh' when we were children), dominant groups have constructed narratives of minorities which bolster their own needs, values, interests, self-esteem, and perspectives. (p. 5)

If gay clients are to be heard and valued as equals, it is important that heterosexual therapists (and gay ones too) have the opportunity to appreciate how a dominant group mentality pervades psychodynamic theory in almost every aspect of its understanding of homosexuality.

The first challenge for a modern psychodynamic counsellor who is working with lesbian, gay or bisexual clients is to appraise and evaluate the validity of psychodynamic theory as it applies to sexual development. Merely to espouse theory as propounded by the founding analysts will lead to a position towards sexual minority clients which pathologises a fundamental part of their self-identity, and seriously undermines the therapeutic relationship from the outset.

A secondary challenge for counsellors is posed by certain psychodynamic therapeutic techniques (specifically 'neutrality' or 'abstinence') that do not appear to take into account the needs of clients from sexual minorities. Where oppression of and discrimination against the individual exists in the real world, the idea of therapist 'neutrality' can appear perverse. As Cornett (1995) writes: '... these admonitions (of neutrality), which Freud did not observe ... were developed for a specific type of patient. Many groups of patients – including male homosexuals – were largely excluded from treatment' (p. 79). For a counsellor to hide his or her views on homosexuality could be seen as oppressive, as could failure to actively counter the negative messages that each gay client has encountered and internalised during their maturation. Although it might be argued that working psychodynamically does not require that all counsellors understand and interpret the significance of neutrality and abstinence in a uniform manner, Coren (2001) writes that ' ... psychodynamic trainings still tend to be profoundly ambivalent and suspicious about departing from the classic analytic stance' (p. 145).

The emergence into the open, and very gradual acceptance of gay, lesbian, bisexual and transgendered sexualities within Western culture has not been helped along by any change in psychodynamic thinking or practice. Rather, it is the result of social and political changes that have, eventually, permeated into the heart of psychiatric and psychotherapeutic ways of working. More often than not, psychodynamic theories have continued to pathologise minority sexualities, and it is not surprising that this has led to a sense of unease for some in espousing psychodynamic ways of thinking and working with gay[1] clients. In Milton's survey of British psychologists working with gay clients, 'psychoanalytic theory received the most critical comment ... there were no responses which suggested it was an approach of choice when working with lesbians and gay men' (1998, p. 23).

Thus we can see that there is a history of pathologising within the psychodynamic approach, and a danger of espousing therapeutic techniques that were not deemed appropriate for homosexual clients when first devised, and which when mishandled or applied without thinking can be damaging to clients. However, since contemporary psychodynamic practitioners no longer live in the historical environment in which the founding theorists lived, they need ways of thinking and working with sexual minority clients that are non-pathologising and anti-oppressive. In this chapter I discuss how psychodynamic ways of thinking and working may still be useful for gay clients and their therapists, embracing at least the possibility that modern psychodynamic work could be a 'treatment of choice' for gay clients.

Transference and countertransference

The phenomena of transference and countertransference are central tools to any practice of psychodynamic counselling, though how these terms are understood may differ from practitioner to practitioner. For instance, Coren (2001) distinguishes between '*transference as ubiquitous* (that is everywhere, and a normal part of life and social interaction) and *the transference neurosis* (the transfer, both conscious and unconscious, of fantasies, emotions and attitudes from the past onto the therapist, which is a specific illusion of the therapeutic setting)' (p. 85, emphasis in original). It is with the second of these definitions that we are most concerned, and to which we need to pay attention. As Jacobs (1999) writes: ' ... transference is the repetition by the client of former, often child-like patterns of relating to significant people, such as parents, but now seen in relation to the counsellor' (p. 16). One of the key points to consider when working psychody-namically with gay men, lesbians and bisexuals is how the cultural 'toxicity' towards their sexual orientation (Perlman, 2003) that they have grown up in may have affected intra and interpsychic development, and how this, in turn, may affect the transference towards their therapist; and equally important, how growing up amid this cultural toxicity may affect the countertransference of the therapist towards the gay/lesbian/bisexual client.

First we need to consider the ways in which the internalisation of homophobia is a universal experience for gay people, and how this internalised homophobia affects intrapsychic development. I have written elsewhere (Mair, 2000) about the impact of internalised homophobia on a group of gay men, but, briefly, here I suggest some of the most common manifestations of this within any member of a sexual minority group:

- shame, leading to a need to hide one's sexuality, often under the guise of a heterosexual relationship
- inability to sustain intimacy within long-term gay relationships due to lack of positive role-models
- denial of sexual orientation
- playing the fool/clown – 'camping it up' as a way of gaining some sort of acceptance
- fear
- living out a stereotype
- self-hatred
- avoidance of contact with other gay people, including reluctance to work with a gay therapist
- denouncing gay people – a need to see oneself as 'different' from other homosexuals
- restricting life-choices (for example, seeing parenthood as impossible; restricting choice of career; ghettoisation)
- remaining invisible (not talking about partners, trying to 'pass' as straight)

Societal and institutional homophobia can be overt and explicit, or subtle and implicit. If at one end of the spectrum is physical gay-bashing, at the other may be found the more common silence around homosexuality in everyday life. Gay people are acutely aware of the hostile and silencing messages that they encounter all around them as they mature – in the media, in education, in religion, in the heterosexist assumptions that abound in our culture – and easily, and inevitably, internalise these messages early in their development. Once inter-nalised, they become a means through which self-hatred and fear all too easily take root. Obviously, not all of the above features will be seen in every gay client, but some will. As therapists, we need to be prepared for the impact of such realities. In my own work, I have experienced gay men who found it difficult to sustain the level of intimacy in the work that developed with me as another gay man, and who felt that they needed to see a woman instead because they could not trust themselves or me to contain their feelings. More typically, shame is a predominant issue which affects not only the disclosure of being gay, but which then prevents an exploration of what it means to the client to have felt trapped for so long in a world where their sexuality needed to be hidden. Shame is a powerful and corrosive emotion, and understandably, there is a reluctance to expose that about which we feel ashamed – including our feelings of shame. Instead, there can be a premature 'flight into health', where the opportunity to look at and work through internalised homophobia is denied.

Cass (1979, 1996) proposes a six-stage model (see the box below), which describes some of the movement out of internalised homophobia for gay people. She suggests that movement from stage 1 to stage 6 can take as long as 14 years to achieve.

Rather than a straightforward movement through the stages, however, it is more likely that there will be a circular movement backwards and forwards through them, depending on environmental factors and emotional stability at any given time. It is important for counsellors to ask themselves where their gay clients might be in this particular model, as the nature of the work and of the client's internal, unconscious conflicts and defences are likely to be very different depending on the answer. For those clients who appear to be nearer to the start of the process of coming out, the issue of their sexuality is likely to be much more in the foreground of the work, whilst for those who have already achieved

---

Cass's theoretical model of homosexual identity formation

Stage 1:   Identity confusion: General feelings of being different

Stage 2:   Identity comparison: Awareness of homosexual feelings, yet the person thinks that this may just be a phase or that the feelings are just towards one specific person

Stage 3:   Identity tolerance: Stronger identity of being homosexual and starting to reach out to other homosexuals

Stage 4:   Identity acceptance: Increased contact and affiliation with other homosexuals

Stage 5:   Identity pride: The 'these are my people' stage whereupon the person comes out to more and more people and often starts to feel anger toward heterosexuals and devalues many of their institutions

Stage 6:   Identity synthesis: The intense anger of stage 5 diminishes and the person comes to perceive less of a dichotomy between the heterosexual and homosexual worlds while retaining pride in gays and lesbians

more in the way of overcoming homophobia, sexuality may recede into the background where it will still be a core feature of the person's sense of identity, but not necessarily the prime focus for therapeutic work.

Internalised homophobia is not only, however, the experience of gay men, lesbians and bisexuals. Everyone is affected by it, because everyone growing up in Western or Judaeo-Christian cultures grows up surrounded by hostile or ignorant views about homosexuality. One of the greatest dangers posed by well meaning but poorly trained counsellors (of whatever sexual orientation) working with gay clients is to imagine that good intentions are enough to assist their clients. The first and most difficult step in working with gay clients for counsellors of all sexual orientations is to become aware that their own homophobia and ignorance can take many guises. To name but a few:

● indifference towards the psychic consequences of growing up gay

● denial of difference – 'we're all the same really'

● gay-bashing (physical or verbal)

● a desire to be seen as one of the good guys – no homophobia here!

● bending over backwards to support gay people – unable to be appropriately critical or challenging of damaging behaviour/attitudes

● viewing homosexuality as sinful/depraved/sad

● equation of homosexuality with paedophilia

● stereotyping ('I can always spot a gay man/lesbian when I see one')

● equating homosexuality with femininity (in males) and masculinity (in women)

● beliefs that bisexuals 'could make up their minds if they wanted to'

● silence – failing to enquire into gay relationships; refusal to acknowledge homosexuality as a normal developmental possibility for all children, and thus to create an environment where they can experience their sexuality as natural and good

● a basic assumption that heterosexuality is the only 'normal' way to express sexuality, and that everyone would want to be heterosexual if they had the choice (heterosexism)

● embarrassment

● believing that offering 'tolerance' to homosexuals is somehow generous or noble

All or any of these reactions to our internalised homophobia, or our ignorance (and ignorance can easily become homophobia when combined with an indifference stemming from a majority based position as a heterosexual) have the ability to seriously affect our ability to use our countertransference for the benefit of the clients.

Countertransference is 'classically understood as the therapist's feelings and attitudes towards his client, which may result from unresolved issues in the therapist, [or] a means of communication of affective states between client and therapist [or] as a subtle and non-verbal way in which the client seeks to control the therapist' (Coren, 2001, pp. 88–9). As counsellors, we have a professional responsibility to look long and hard at ourselves, and at our assumptions about sexual orientation. Failure to do so lays us open to mistaking our own countertransference as being a response to our clients' issues, when the reality may be that what I am experiencing is my own transference to the client – which is a very different thing. For example, I may not be able to hear my client's distress at the reaction of her family to her coming out to them, if I unconsciously sympathise with the family about the 'unwelcome news'. Unless I am able to recognise the extent and the subtlety of my own homophobia, I may prefer to imagine that my inability to empathise with my client is a reflection of her own feelings about her sexuality.

Just as Cass proposed a model which describes movement out of internalised homophobia towards gay pride, I propose a similar model (see the box on pages 64–5) which describes the various stages through which heterosexuals move in their understanding of and attitude towards difference in sexual orientation. It would be wrong to assume that every heterosexual starts at stage 1 of this model. Just as with homosexuals, heterosexuals' self-awareness and openness depends on a host of factors such as education, religious background and previous contact with gay people. Movement is unlikely to be in a one-way, forwards direction through this model of increasing self-awareness; it is more likely that individuals will move forwards and backwards through these stages, depending on various external and internal factors.

An awareness of our own feelings about homosexuality enables us to differentiate more finely between 'reactive' and 'proactive' countertransference, that is the psychotherapist's reaction to a patient and their material, or their own transference to the client. Maguire (1995) addresses the issue of counsellor countertransference: 'Many gay men ... may drop out of analytic treatment, not, as is suggested ... because they are resistant to change, but because of the countertransference difficulties of their heterosexual analysts' (p. 221). Frommer (1995) picks up the failure of psychoanalysis to address negative countertransference, arguing that the long history of pathologising and labelling homosexuals as deviant has left many counsellors unclear and therefore unwilling to address their own homophobia in an open and honest way. The implications of such attitudes for gay clients are clear. If the analyst has been unable to extricate him/herself from an internalised heterosexist bias, 'all he may be able to do is commiserate with his patient's shame and self-hatred, but he is at a loss to help him move beyond it.' Having some idea which stage we are at on the awareness model may help us to decide whether working with gay clients is, in fact, ethical at this point in our development as counsellors.

The centrality of use of transference and countertransference in a psychodynamic way of working means the effect that our heterosexist/homophobic culture has had upon us and our clients cannot be ignored. Unless we have allowed ourselves to explore the depths of the impact upon us of these beliefs

Heterosexuals' stages of awareness of difference in sexual orientation

Stage 1 Unconscious ignorance/homophobia

The individual is either unaware of issues affecting gay people or dismissive of the idea that there may be issues of which s/he needs to become aware. Alternatively, the individual has a view of homosexuality as pathological, sinful, or deviant. Homosexuals tend to be perceived as a homogenous group of people whose defining characteristic is specific sexual acts.

Stage 2 Pre-conscious ignorance/homophobia

The individual – either through personal contact with a gay person, or training – starts to become aware of issues that they had hitherto not recognised. There is still, however, a belief that they personally are not impacted by societal beliefs or prejudices about homosexuality, or there is a desire to justify homophobic views on the grounds of religion or 'natural' sexual development.

Stage 3 Increased personal awareness

The individual begins to appreciate that their view of homosexuality has been simplistic or dismissive and starts to think more about what the consequences of growing up gay in a heterosexist society might be. There may be a feeling of guilt or shame for previous ignorance/homophobia, and a feeling that gay people are very 'different' with a consequential feeling of nervousness about voicing any views to do with homosexuality for fear of appearing insensitive. There can be a tendency for political correctness to take over – knowing intellectually what views are 'approved' and 'disapproved' can become a kind of window dressing for still unresolved/unconscious homophobia or ignorance.

Stage 4 Conscious questioning of personal ignorance/homophobia

At this stage of awareness the individual has moved beyond the politically correct views previously espoused, and begins to own and explore their own homophobia and ignorance more fully. As they do so, they begin to recognise that previously held constructs about sexuality in general may be challenged or undermined. They become more able to think about their own homosexual feelings/experiences. However, homosexuals may still be seen as a homogenous group, and there is still a clear division between heterosexuality and homosexuality.

Stage 5 Dismantling of ignorance/homophobia defences

At this stage, the individual has more awareness of some of the processes involved in growing up gay, and of the oppression of heterosexism. The person may become more vocal in supporting homosexuality and in speaking out about perceived injustices.

continued

Stage 6 Integration

Here, the individual has done significant thinking about and working through of their own homophobia and through this process has come to a new understanding of how they define their own sexuality. The distinction between homosexuality and hetero-sexuality may seem less clear. Homosexuals are no longer thought of only in terms of sexual acts, but are seen as individuals. There is awareness of oppression and a willingness to challenge this, but there is no longer a need to prove political correctness either to self, others or clients.

and attitudes, and until we have been able to acknowledge the subtle and often unconscious ways they continue to affect us, we need to think very carefully about whether working with gay clients is appropriate.

Neutrality vs affirmation

Neutrality of the therapist is seen, traditionally, as a cornerstone of successful psychodynamic work, preached (though not, perhaps, always practised) by most psychoanalytic theorists.

One way of understanding therapist neutrality is to see it as a non-judgmental stance. There may be an aspiration to a neutral opinion about my client's sexual orientation, to a position where I do not feel strongly one way or another about whether my client is gay, bisexual or heterosexual. However, neutrality towards a fundamental part of a person's self-identity is, in fact, a form of denial. Given the disparaging views of homosexuality that abound today, it is disingenuous for a therapist to pretend that s/he has somehow risen above such concerns and is now 'neutral' or non-judgmental about sexual orientation. If I am accepting of gay people and understand that sexual orientation is not a choice, then I am not neutral. If I am intolerant and believe that homosexuals are perverted, I am not neutral. And if I feel that I have no strong opinion one way or the other, then this suggests a need for further reflection and understanding. One day, perhaps, if sexual orientation truly ceases to be a divisive issue in society, neutrality in this sense may be a possibility. In our current world, it is not an honest option.

Another way of thinking about neutrality is to see it as a kind of abstinence on the part of the therapist. The chief motivation for this is, as Jacobs writes, the need for the client to be

> ... as free as possible from the counsellor's influence; hopefully clients say what they think, and not what they think the counsellor wants them to say. The more neutral both the counsellor and the setting, the greater the possibility of the client's words being unadulterated by external stimuli. (1999, p. 33)

The aim of neutrality in this sense, therefore, is to avoid therapist imposition upon the client and the material that s/he wishes to talk about. Psychodynamic counselling is not a model of counselling or helping that prescribes how sessions should proceed, what issues need to be talked about and in what order. As Jacobs adds, 'psychodynamic counselling is very definitely client-centred' (1999, p. 35).

Nevertheless, this type of neutrality, however desirable in theory, is virtually impossible to achieve in practice. Pointon and Berman (2003) write that 'even where a practitioner chooses not to talk about him or herself, personal preferences will come through; clues as simple as the appearance and location of the consulting room or the subtle nuances in an interpretation will be there. And these clues ... will inevitably include pointers to the analyst's own politics' (p. 13). Yalom (2001) notes that even Freud did not achieve 'neutrality':

> Freud entered personally and boldly into the lives of his patients. He made strong suggestions to them, he intervened on their behalf with family members, he contrived to attend social functions to see his patients in other settings, he instructed a patient to visit the cemetery and meditate on the tombstone of a dead sibling. (p. 76)

Moreover, if neutrality is taken to signify withholding or austerity on the part of the therapist, Coren (2001) argues that

> therapeutic silence or reticence is just as potentially manipulative as activity – more so in the sense that it is rarely acknowledged or examined. Frustration is just as much a manipulation of the transference as activity or 'gratification'. (p. 144)

When working with clients from sexual minorities, we need to be aware that attempts to remain neutral (where this is understood either as a kind of withholding or as the adoption of an ersatz non-judgmentalism) *about the issue of their sexual orientation*, whatever the intent of the therapist, may be construed by the client as oppressive, and thus become destructive of a therapeutic relationship. Gay clients have grown up in a world where their sexuality (and thus their very self) is disparaged, belittled, condemned, ignored, criminalised, mocked and insulted. Given the reality of this context, counsellors cannot be, and should not pretend to be, 'neutral' towards their clients' sexuality. Any such attempt will be damaging to the relationship with their gay clients, and is akin to attempting to remain 'neutral' towards racism. The truth of this struck home for me in research I carried out into gay men's experiences of counselling (Mair, 2000). Those men whose therapists had not found a way to engage positively with their clients' sexual orientation were often perceived to be homophobic or unskilled and the clients were cautious about self-revelation and safety.

If neutrality as traditionally understood is not achievable or desirable, what is the alternative? One very obvious reaction against this neutrality is gay-affirmative therapy (Davies and Neal, 1996). Gay-affirmative counselling may be understood in two different ways:

> [The first of these] stances includes therapists being comfortable with their own homosexual feelings, having the explicit agenda of raising experiences of oppression to consciousness, deprogramming and undoing negative conditioning associated with negative stereotypes of lesbians and gay men. The second ... is that gay affirmative practice can be incorporated into mainstream psychotherapy theory

and practice. Where affirmative practice is considered in this way, there are likely to be differences in how easily it is incorporated into different (counselling) orientations. (Milton and Coyle, 1999, p. 45)

In essence, a gay-affirmative approach gives the counsellor responsibility for actively acknowledging and affirming their gay client's sexuality; for identifying the trauma of growing up in a homophobic world, and using the therapeutic process to begin to reverse the damage that has been done to self-esteem. There appears to be an emphasis on *doing* which does not sit easily with a psychodynamic approach; the counsellor has an agenda (raising internalised oppression to awareness, and helping the client to overcome this) that underpins the work. The counsellor is charged with being responsible for identifying this oppression, and for helping the client to articulate it: 'clients may not be able to articulate this [oppression] – indeed may not consciously feel that they have been mistreated in any way' (Dickey, 1997, p. 10). Or as Perlman (2003, p. 57) writes: 'It is our job to engage and nurture the healthy aspects of the client's life force so that they may become more fully themselves.' There is not much space for traditional counsellor neutrality here! Such an approach has obvious attractions for counsellors who feel the need to 'help' their clients, and who feel that they must be engaged in assisting their clients to counter the impact of an oppressive, internalised world.

However, there are dangers of espousing such an approach too zealously. For instance, such an approach implies that 'being gay' is something about which the counsellor should know more than the client. It also indicates that the counsellor should be involved in educating the client as to how to become 'more truly gay' (Clark, 1987, p. 34). Even as a gay counsellor myself, can I, should I, assume that I know how to be gay on behalf of my gay clients? Does this not, if taken to extremes, become a rather arrogant position to take vis-à-vis my clients? It also places a burden of responsibility on the counsellor that few may, in truth, be willing to accept. As Du Plock (1998, p. 59) writes, 'there is a danger here ... of the therapist becoming the very "expert" we all agree we do not want to be', and:

> It may be that a gay-affirmative therapist is less likely, in their wish to introduce their own view of the 'healthy homosexual', to attend fully to the individual client than a sensitive therapist from another orientation. (1998, p. 65)

Guggenbuhl-Craig (1971) argues that counsellors need to be very wary of being seduced into a powerful or 'sorcerer' role, by clients apparently anxious to receive the benefits of their wisdom. He uses the metaphor of the contrast between powerful doctor/childish patient as the dynamic that can arise when the therapist assumes too much knowledge of what is best for the client. It is, essentially, the antithesis of a client-centred approach, and is too much like a 'closing down', rather than an 'opening up' or 'uncovering' of a client's story.

So where is a psychodynamic therapist left? On the one hand, traditional positions of neutrality and abstinence could be seen as potentially abusive, and on the other hand, gay-affirmative techniques seem to be too much about the counsellor *doing to* the client and assuming a position of expertise that could lead to arrogance and a pressure to conform to a 'gay norm' that the counsellor has predetermined. These two alternatives may usefully be superseded by the concept of therapist authenticity.

The idea of counsellor authenticity is not, traditionally, given much emphasis in psychodynamic training. It is assumed that self-disclosure will contaminate the transference relationship, rendering it less powerful and less likely to provide opportunity for insights to be gained through analysis of the therapeutic relationship. However, some theorists construe this differently. Jung, for instance, believed in spontaneity, sometimes as a manifestation of using the countertransference.

The ideas of Kohut in particular, who emphasises therapist authenticity and empathic attunement as being fundamental to work with clients, may help us. His work has been largely overlooked in modern British psychodynamic trainings, possibly as a result of an unhelpful split between object relations theories and theories of motivation, development and psychopathology (Kahn, 1991, p. 97) and because of Kohut's 'advocating the need for the therapist to be empathically engaged with his patient rather than passively neutral' (Coren, 2001, p. 59). Cornett (1995, p. 39) asserts that Kohut's theories of self-development 'are very helpful in understanding many gay [men] who seek psychotherapy' because of the fresh insight they cast upon issues of narcissistic injury.

The threefold Kohutian requirements for the emergence of healthy self-esteem – Mirroring, Idealization, and especially Twinship (the sense of *being* like significant others around me) – may be missing in the lives of many gay men and women. Where these have been lacking, Cornett suggests, traditional therapist neutrality merely repeats the lack of sufficient conditions that have led to low self-esteem and self-hatred in the first place. He suggests that a warm, encouraging and empathic environment is more likely to invite a client to be more authentic.

Thus, far from being a watering down of pure technique, the ability of the counsellor working with gay men, lesbians and bisexuals to be authentic represents what Kahn (1997) refers to as

[o]ne of the greatest moments of satisfaction of this work ... [which] comes at the moment when students realise that when they enter the consulting room, they don't need to don a therapist mask, a therapist voice, a therapist posture, and a therapist vocabulary. They can discard those accoutrements because they have much, much more than that to give to their clients. (p. 163)

The notion of counsellor authenticity enabling greater client authenticity reflects, in many ways, the work of Winnicott, who described the processes leading to the emergence of what he termed a 'false self'. This 'false self' perfectly encapsulates the position of a gay man or woman who has stayed in the closet, trying to avoid attention or trying to 'pass' as straight. Cornett believes that unless the counsellor is able to respond as a parent would to a child – with spontaneous curiosity, warmth and delight – the emergence of the authentic self may be jeopardised (1995, p. 81). One of the legacies of growing up with a sexual orientation that differs from the majority can be that of a desperate need to fit in, to be accepted, to belong – whatever the cost. This can be re-enacted within therapy as the client unconsciously attempts to meet the therapist's expectations. Counsellors must understand this dynamic. The issue of client compliance – based on the need not to be rejected by the counsellor – can undermine the therapeutic relationship from the start if the counsellor is not alert to this as a possibility, and cannot work with it promptly. If therapist proactive countertransference is, however subtly, homophobic, the ability to respond to our gay clients authentically in a way that fosters a deeper sense of self-worth will be seriously compromised.

Furthermore, for psychodynamic counsellors, there is a risk of the work becoming theory driven as opposed to relationship driven. There can emerge an understanding of therapy as consisting of discrete therapeutic building blocks – transference, countertransference, interpretation, the frame – as if these were in themselves sufficient for successful therapy. As Rowan and Jacobs (2002) comment:

> The danger is that over-concern with interference of the self might lead to unhelpful abstinence or even the development of a false self in the therapist – perhaps like Winnicott's use of the term, a false self built upon *compliance with what is taught in training*. (p. 28, my emphasis)

Gray (1994) adds:

> ... it is important to acknowledge the dangers in psychodynamic theories that are used in a generalised way ... rather than from the unique relationship that is established between the individual therapist and the individual client. (p. 30)

Again, the counsellor needs to be aware that who s/he is with the client changes given the stage of therapy they are at, and the needs and expectations of the client. Elton-Wilson (1996) describes three fundamental life stages at which clients may come to us: those who are 'in crisis' (not seeking psychological change); those who are 'visiting' (testing psychological therapy); and those who are 'willing to engage' (ready to take responsibility for psychological change). The counsellor must be flexible enough to respond appropriately to the different needs of gay clients, and to be able to assess their motivation and also where they may be on Cass's model of homosexual identity formation. Simply applying learnt techniques with no awareness of client need will be unhelpful.

Nevertheless, it is important to recognise that the quest for an authentic encounter between therapist and client is not without its potential dangers too. As Kahn (1991, p. 162) comments: 'The therapist must never lose sight of the questions: "Am I making this choice for the client or to satisfy some need of mine? Am I co-creating a new and healing relationship, or am I being drawn into an old destructive one?".' He goes on to add:

> In my opinion this freedom (of authenticity) is not for beginners. As one begins to practice this craft, it seems essential to learn to be very disciplined indeed. Once

that discipline is in the therapist's marrow, once it doesn't even need to be thought about, then there will be time to explore ways of relaxing it. It's very hard to subject oneself to discipline after indulging in freedom. (1991, p. 162)

This echoes the difference and movement between what Rowan and Jacobs (2002) refer to as the 'instrumental self' – where counselling is seen as 'a set of skills that can be learned and applied' (p. 9) – and the 'authentic self', where the skills that have been learned are subsumed into the personality of the counsellor and used when appropriate, but are not the primary or sole means of relating to the client.

Working with sexual minorities and the need for an *authentic* encounter with their counsellor can bring us face to face with a reliance on theory and challenge us to consider how we can use our psychodynamic theory in the service of the therapy, rather than trying to make the therapy fit into some predetermined way in which we believe it should proceed. The dangers outlined above also point to the very real need for good supervision with a supervisor who has experience of working with sexual minorities, if we are to be able to use our authentic selves for the benefit of the client rather than to satisfy some need of our own.

How can psychodynamic counselling help gay, lesbian and bisexual clients?

When considering how, and indeed whether, psychodynamic counselling can be helpful for gay clients, clarity about the counsellor's role is required. There will be many views of what the role of counsellor is or should be, formed by individual motivation, beliefs and life experiences, which inform our reasons for doing this work. There is a fundamental distinction between being a counsellor whose aim, conscious or unconscious, is to *change or help* people, and being a counsellor whose aim is to *provide a relationship* that our clients can use, *if they choose*, to begin a process of enhancing self-understanding. In essence, this is a difference between *doing* and *being*, a difference that underlies much of the rationale for psychodynamic counselling. Lack of clarity about the role of counsellor can lead to all sorts of confusion; it is easy to be seduced into believing that it is the counsellor's role and responsibility to bring about change through interventions, interpretations or theoretical insights. This belief, however, may lead to an unhelpful and ultimately disillusioning belief in the therapist's own power and ability to effect change in another person. Psychodynamic practice is not, primarily, about changing people but is rather about providing a space within which people may gain awareness and understanding. Change is then optional, but not obligatory. In this sense, psychodynamic counselling with gay clients may be very different from gay-affirmative counselling where the latter is understood to have a part to play in reprogramming, or educating clients about their situation, and where there is an onus on the counsellor to assume responsibility for leading the client out of his or her restricted experience of life. Psychodynamic counsellors will be concerned to facilitate a client to gain greater insight into processes that have previously been unconscious, whilst being careful to avoid communicating pressure to conform to a new therapist imposed 'norm'.

Of course, many clients come to us ostensibly because they feel they want things to be different in their lives. But this is not necessarily the same as wanting to change. They are unhappy or distressed, and they want ways out of situations that are preventing them from achieving personal fulfilment. Spinelli (2001, pp. 10–20) presents a case for reassessing the purpose of counselling and therapy from an existential perspective, and for steering it back from the edge of manualised treatments towards which it appears to be moving in certain settings. He proposes 'a focus [for counselling] that acknowledges the likelihood of sometimes significant, sometimes subtle, ameliorative outcomes *but which does not seek to make such outcomes its primary aim or goal*' (p. 7). He adds, 'if a person has a calling to help another, then that person is selling him or herself – and the world – somewhat short by seeking to become a psychotherapist' (p. 10). Such a challenge is echoed by the gay writer, Cornett: 'change in the patient's life, if it occurs at all, is potentially a positive outcome of the treatment ... but is a *by-product and not the sought result*' (1995, p. 66, my emphasis).

It is this position that I start from as a psychodynamic practitioner working with gay clients. My role is not to change people, or even to help them. It is to provide a space and a relationship where they can, if they wish, think about their lives hitherto by using the relationship itself as a means of providing insight and awareness into avoided or denied aspects of experience. It is my responsibility to be aware of the social and cultural context in which my clients have developed, and to be aware also of how this context has impinged on both of us, as well as the way in which the dynamics of this impingement may be reenacted between us. It is also my responsibility to think carefully and deeply with my clients about their story, the way that they tell that story, and to use my awareness of process to offer reflections and interpretations to the client to help them deepen their felt experience. It is not my responsibility to tell the client what I think s/he needs to do, or to become, but to support him or her as s/he engages with determining for her/himself what, if any, movement s/he wishes to make.

Psychodynamic counselling can indeed be a treatment of choice for gay clients when understood in this way, and when the counsellor has been prepared to engage with and reflect hard about his/her own homophobia.

Note

1. Throughout this chapter I use the word 'gay' to include both male and female, lesbian or gay. No gender is implied in the use of the word. Bisexuality is not covered by the use of the word 'gay' and it is important to consider that clients who identify as bisexual may strongly resent being thought of as 'gay'. However, much of the material in this chapter encourages counsellors to think carefully about their attitudes towards sexuality other than their own, and this process is equally important when working with bisexual clients.

REFERENCES

Cass, V. C. (1979). 'Homosexual identity formation: A theoretical model'. *Journal of Homosexuality*, 4: 3, 219–35.

Cass, V. C. (1996). 'Sexual orientation identity formation: A Western phenomenon'. In R. Cabaj and T. Stein (eds), *Textbook of Homosexuality and Mental Health*. Washington, DC: American Psychiatric Press.

Clark, D. (1987). *The New Loving Someone Gay*. Berkeley, CA: Celestial Arts.

Coren, A. (2001). *Short-term Psychotherapy: A Psychodynamic Approach*. Basingstoke: Palgrave Macmillan.

Cornett, C. (1995). *Reclaiming the Authentic Self: Dynamic Psychotherapy with Gay Men*. Lanham, MD: Jason Aronson.

Davies, D. and Neal, C. (1996). *Pink Therapy*. Milton Keynes: Open University Press.

Dickey, J. (1997). 'Before the struggle is won'. *Counselling News*, December, 10.

Domenici, T. and Lesser, R. C. (eds) (1995). *Disorienting Sexuality*. London: Routledge.

Du Plock, S. (1998). 'Sexual misconceptions: a critique of gay-affirmative therapy and some thoughts on an existential-phenomenological theory of sexual orientation'. *Journal of the Society for Existential Analysis*, 8: 2, 56–71.

Elton-Wilson, J. (1996). *Time-conscious Psychological Therapy: A Life-stage to Go Through*. London: Routledge.

Fairburn, W. R. D (1946). 'The treatment and rehabilitation of sexual offenders'. Cited in T. Domenici and R. C. Lesser (eds) (1995), *Disorienting Sexuality*. London: Routledge.

Frommer, M. S. (1995). 'Countertransference'. In T. Domenici and R. C. Lesser (eds), *Disorienting Sexuality*. London: Routledge.

Gray, A. (1994). *An Introduction to the Therapeutic Frame*. London: Routledge.

Guggenbuhl-Craig, A. (1971). *Power in the Helping Professions*. Putnam, CT: Spring.

Jacobs, M. (1999). *Psychodynamic Counselling in Action*. London: Sage.

Kahn, M. (1991). *Between Therapist and Client: The New Relationship*. New York: Freeman.

Lewes, K. (1995). *Psychoanalysis and Male Homosexuality*. Lanham, MD: Jason Aronson.

Maguire, M. (1995). *Men, Women, Passion and Power*. London: Routledge.

Mair, D. (2000). 'Internalised homophobia: the enemy within'. *Counselling*, August, 414–17.

Milton, M. (1998). 'Issues in psychotherapy with lesbians and gay men: a survey of British psychologists'. *British Psychological Society, Division of Counselling Psychology, Occasional Papers*, 4.

Milton, M. and Coyle, A. (1999). 'Lesbian and gay affirmative psychotherapy: issues in theory and practice'. *Sexual and Marital Therapy*, 14: 1, 43–59.

Perlman, P. (2003). 'Gay affirmative practice'. In C. Lago and B. Smith (eds), *Anti-discriminatory Counselling Practice*. London: Sage.

Pointon, C. and Berman, E, (2003). 'Therapists and the Israel–Palestine conflict'. *Counselling and Psychotherapy Journal*, 14: 6, 13–15.

Rowan, J. and Jacobs, M. (2002). *The Therapist's Use of Self*. Buckingham: Open University Press.

Spinelli, E. (2001). *The Mirror and the Hammer: Challenges to Therapeutic Orthodoxy*. London and New York: Continuum.

Winnicott, D. (1964). *The Child, The Family and the Outside World*. Harmondsworth: Penguin.

Yalom, I. (2001). *The Gift of Therapy*. London: Piatkus.

Female Counsellor, Male Client; Counselling across Gender

Fiona Aitken and Aileen Coupe

Introduction

This chapter is written from our experience of working with mainly white, working, middle class, heterosexual male clients in private practice, university counselling services, voluntary sector counselling centres, primary care and employee assistance schemes. It spans 20 years of long, medium and short-term focused work as practitioners, supervisors and trainers. We have some experience of working with gay men and male clients from different cultures, although this is not the main focus of our experience. It is arguably a Eurocentric, white, female perspective and is written from a sociocultural and object relations stance. The chapter also draws upon contemporary psychoanalytic writers and research on this subject.

The prime focus of the chapter is on the countertransference in the female/male dyad in therapy and how it affects the therapeutic climate and space for the male client. Female therapists have great potential to facilitate exploration of the male experience of masculinity and to widen choices for both men and women with respect to the effect that their gender has on relationships. The chapter highlights the intersubjectivity of the therapeutic relationship, how men and women impact on each other, particularly focusing on ways in which the female therapist might make use of vital communication from the male client and use the male/female dynamic for healing through therapy. The case examples demonstrate some of the challenges faced by women therapists and ways in which the therapeutic alliance may be affected by their countertransference.

The examples are written in the first person of the therapist and are drawn from the authors' clinical work from a range of male clients whose details are considerably disguised.

We have witnessed male clients struggling to integrate internal demands of masculinity with deep longing for connection with other men, their partners and their families. The conflict this creates is truly poignant, manifested in a variety of disguised 'distress signals'. These are often misconstrued as male inadequacy rather than acknowledged as deep signs of despair, harm, disconnection and ongoing loss and bereavement.

Gender sensitive female therapists

When training and supervising female counsellors and psychotherapists about gender differences and the effect on the dynamic of a therapeutic relationship, we have been surprised by the resistance, and even cynicism we have encountered in response to the suggestion that working with men warrants special attention. Resentful feelings surface when the focus is on male worldviews, female therapists sometimes experiencing men as occupying 'centre stage' with women in the wings. The feminist movement and equal opportunity legislation have contributed to redressing the power balance between men and women. For years there has been a focus on the growth and development of women, so much so that being asked to consider the social and psychological role of men is unexpected and unfamiliar for some women.

Men are often infantilised in society through humour. Attacks on the perception of masculinity, as demonstrated in popular television shows such as the sitcom *Men Behaving Badly* (BBC, 1992 onwards) are commonplace. This may be a healthy discharge of emotion and resentment built up over centuries, but it can also be persecutory and shaming. There can be a duality in the humour. Women have reconnected with their power in recent years and have sometimes resorted to patronage and humiliation of men in a shaming fashion. As supervisors, we notice that female counsellors can be judgemental of men, criticising their inability to relate on an emotional level or expressing relief when they meet male clients who do appear to be capable of expressing feelings and empathy.

Emotional self-expression is seen by some as essential to a helpful counselling experience. Men tend to intellectualise, rationalise and problem solve, which is sometimes questioned and denigrated. We talk about 'new men', those who are seen to integrate male and female roles thus redefining their experience of masculinity into one of connection and intimacy. On the other hand there are 'traditional men', who adhere to stereotypical male roles and behaviour, metaphorically and sometimes in reality, making strict divisions between male and female work. Even 'new men', who value self-expression and question traditional stereotypical roles will have had the experience of traditional fathering, just as female therapists will be the daughters of traditional men. Despite current values and beliefs, the internalised father impacts deeply for both men and women and will play a part in any therapeutic relationship. The dynamics of the therapeutic relationship between female therapist and male client are influenced by both unconscious and conscious past and present experiences of men (and women as mothers) and there are endless possibilities for these influences to surface and sabotage the work.

The therapeutic alliance between counsellor and client is essential to the outcome of therapy. Brooks (1998) suggests that psychotherapy involving a female therapist and male client is always a form of cross-cultural counselling. He describes clinical work with 'traditional men' who have masculine traits such as strength, stoicism, pain denial, restriction of emotional expression, being a provider and maintaining control over others. Considering this model, a dilemma for the female therapist immediately becomes apparent. On the one hand she has to engage with a masculine world of ideas: rationalising and problem solving, appreciating separateness and independence, respecting the 'male cave' (a space where he works things out alone (Gray, 1993, p. 41)), in order to make the alliance. On the other hand she expects to engage the more 'feminine' world of feelings, closeness and relationship, not always immediately evident in her male clients. It is often relationship failures that drive men towards counselling, but engaging with underlying causes can be anathema. Sabo and Gordon (1995, p. 16) assert that as masculinity is intrinsically damaging to men's health, it is in the health interests of men 'to change, abandon or resist aspects of masculinity'.

This dilemma is reinforced by sociocultural factors whereby men experience their value through achievement and competition, mimicking indestructible male heroes constantly represented in the media, history, comic books and folklore. Vulnerability, fallibility, intimacy and tears, experiences that are intrinsic to therapy, would be disastrous to expose in a school classroom. Such an expression invites comments such as 'sissy', 'mummy's boy' or 'wimp', synonymous with homosexuality and femininity. That legacy lives on and memories of past humiliation are difficult to overcome.

Samuels (2002) describes men in the 21st century as having 'gender role certainty', knowing what it is to be masculine and being aware of the male role. It is this 'gender role certainty' and the countertransference of the female therapist that needs careful scrutiny. Samuels also posits that challenges to this 'certainty' in men's lives, from relationship breakdown or absence of relationship, give rise to a sense of 'gender role strain', uncertainty about male behaviour and roles. Being in a close relationship with a female therapist is likely to evoke child-like feelings, echoing an earlier dependent relationship with mother. Such an experience is described by Rabinowitz and Cochran (2002, p. 118) as feeling like 'heading back to the maternal relational orbit that he had to escape earlier in his life'. They refer to the 'trepidation and shame' involved for a man when he 'wanders off the road of traditional masculinity' by entering therapy with a female therapist. The potential for regression, shame, vulnerability and humiliation is great. Gender role certainty is under threat in such an intimate relationship.

Moreover, a male client's masculinity may feel threatened by his perceptions of therapy as a feminine activity (Brooks, 1998; Rabinowitz and Cochran, 2002). Women are twice as likely to seek therapy as men; the 'femininity' of therapy makes it a more comfortable choice for women. Rose (2002, p. 9), speaking of language and gender in therapy, describes the temptation for female therapists to want 'to put their fingers in their ears' in response to male voices.

She refers to the ambivalence women have about men and masculinity. This concurs with our experience. Female therapists may be intellectually conscious of the constraints of masculinity as they are socially constructed but are not always able to recognise, acknowledge and demonstrate empathy towards such constructs when presented in the consulting room. The gender *attitudes* of the female therapist are worthy of considerable exploration if competent, truly empathic, therapeutic work with men is to take place. This concurs with Mair's assertions in Chapter 4 of this book, that therapists will be impeded in their work with lesbian, gay and bisexual clients, unless they have fully engaged with their own attitudes and social conditioning with respect to such clients.

Countertransference, power and authority

Gender sensitive female therapists are alert to their countertransference, which includes emotional, behavioural, sensory and cerebral responses to their male clients. Such countertransference will highlight the female therapist's experience of her own gender and sexuality, which can be both productive and challenging. Neutralising a male client to being a 'person' rather than a man frequently demonstrates an anxiety about sexual difference, reducing opportunities for contact and understanding. Exploration of the resistance to engaging fully with maleness can result in gender disorientation and confusion. This resembles embarking on a journey without map, compass or knowledge of the language. It is unfamiliar territory and identity as a woman can be challenged.

Mintz and O'Neil (1990) consider ways in which a female therapist may use her authority with a man. The therapist is usually invested with power in any therapeutic relationship, which some men might find difficult when the therapist is a woman. Fantasies of domination versus submission may be played out. Therapeutic engagement will be impossible if the female therapist becomes submissive, leaving the male client unable to surrender to the therapy. On the other hand being too authoritative may drive the male client away.

An essential tool of psychodynamic counselling involves interpretation of the transference between client and therapist. The transference relationship is a reflection of earlier relationships with authority figures from the client's past, and behaviour patterns and other forms of communication provide information about the nuances of past relationships. Ways of relating that were necessary in early life are not always helpful in adult life. It is generally accepted that transference relationships will be evident in therapy regardless of the sex of the therapist but Murdin (2002) questions this premise and suggests that a female therapist is more likely to evoke a 'mother' transference, with all the complications and potential for development that entails. The authority of the therapist is therefore all the more poignant as men struggle with the developmental challenge of separation from mother and identification with father.

Men often have no choice but to see a female therapist. Female therapists outnumber men by approximately 4:1 (Notes 3 and 4). There are rarely complaints about this, so much so that Murdin (2002, p. 86) speculates as to whether specific requests of male clients to see female therapists mask fears of confronting father figures, with the expectation of a female therapist providing a 'non-threatening nurturing relationship'.

What brings men to therapy?

More men are referring themselves for therapy than ever before. There is an increase in the number of male clients attending for counselling sessions compared with ten years ago, with increases of between 20 and 50 per cent in our own practices and local counselling services (Note 3). Changes in culture and society, employee assistance programmes, counselling in primary care, and access via the Internet have encouraged men to seek therapy (Millar, 2003, p. 23). Sociocultural changes such as the increase in women's participation in the workplace, men involved more in home making and child care and male characters portrayed by the media as more readily expressing feelings, seem to have created a climate in which men find therapy more acceptable.

Clare (2000) notes that men seem to be in crisis, which has forced them to seek help. He describes 'castrated men' as those experiencing the loss of traditional male employment that emphasises male strength or bravery as well as those whose male role in the family as breadwinner is displaced by women who have superior earning power. Although Samuels (2002) refers to 'gender role certainty' we would argue that this crisis might be a reflection of 'gender role strain'. The role of women has changed so dramatically that the potential of financial independence for women has usurped the male role of 'provider'. Women ask more of their male partners than purely economic support, particularly emotional intimacy. It seems that for many men the home and work landscape has changed and is less controllable and predictable, leading to a crisis in identity.

An additional crisis is reflected in men's health and available statistics give cause for concern. On average women live five years longer than men (Note 1); men aged 15–44 are nearly four times more likely to commit suicide (Note 2); suicides by young men aged 15–24 have increased by 75 per cent in the last ten years (Note 2); men under 65 are three times more at risk of coronary heart disease than women; sexually transmitted infections occur mostly in men (Note 1); particular occupational groups such as farmers are at highest risk of death from suicide and fatal injuries at work (Watson, 2000, p. 3). Such statistics provide evidence that some men are floundering in today's society.

Some men do refer themselves for counselling but their female counsellors are not always able to tune into their means of communication. Rabinowitz and Cochran (2002, p. 118) refer to 'the tendency to ask for too much emotional sharing' and the potential anger women may have towards a man for withholding connection. The following case example demonstrates this.

Case: Alan was referred for brief therapy following an injury resulting in long-term absence from work. As a paramedic he hated his inability to work in spite of being severely traumatised by events he had witnessed over the years. He struggled to voice his feelings, hinting at 'personal things' he could not yet speak about. Gentle attempts to open up these areas were met with resistance. In frustration I confronted him, asking him to make a decision to confront his fears and talk about these 'personal things'. The following session he was hesitant, resistant and unable to take it further; the therapy ended at that point. As a female, my countertransference was of anger at yet another man withholding feelings.

Reflections: On reflection, I realised that I had not recognised Alan's terror of engaging with his internal world. It became clear that not only had I abandoned him, repeating a pattern encountered with other women in his life, I had also evoked a deep sense of shame, noted in his physical discomfort, around his difficulty in expressing feelings. What I had felt to be him being unwilling and withholding was at that point an internal paralysis in his psyche, born out of a natural fear of being vulnerable. He was at a portal, described by Rabinowitz and Cochran (2002, p. 26) as 'both a way to organize thematic elements in the male client's narrative as well as an entry or key to the deeper, emotional elements of the client's inner psychological life. The portal is a constellation of images, words, thematic elements, emotional associations and bodily sensations. It is a holistic organizing principle.' The experience with Alan prompted substantial self-reflection on therapeutic relationships with men that were uncomfortable but illuminating.

Absent fathers

Men need both closeness with women *and* to feel male and separate. Chodorow (1978) describes the traditional journey for the son from close relationship with mother towards closeness and identification with the father as negotiating a 'bridge' between mother and father. It is more tortuous for a boy than a girl to make the journey towards individuation and development of gender identity as the loss of mother can be painful for mother and son. Girls remain attached to and identify with the mother and flirt with father across the divide:

> Dependency on his mother, attachment to her, and identification with her represent that which is not masculine; a boy must reject dependency and deny attachment and identification. Masculine gender role training is more rigid and emotionally demanding than the feminine equivalent. A boy represses those qualities he takes to be feminine inside him, and rejects and tends to devalue women and whatever he considers to be feminine in the social world. (Chodorow, 1978, p. 181)

There are now more single parent families than ever before, and only 40 per cent of separated fathers in Britain maintain contact with their children (Clare, 2000). In a world in which men are increasingly losing contact with their sons, the development of gender identity may not be met in the manner Chodorow suggests. Brooks (1998) describes the male need for kinship through activity, for example men and boys develop relationships through participating in gendered sports such as football or rugby. The absence of close relationships with fathers may invoke a sense of loss hence inhibiting a secure sense of masculinity rooted in love and belonging.

An absence of fathers to identify with may be one problem, but other experiences such as racism or unemployment may also exacerbate feelings of worthlessness as a man and father. Mothers seem to provide protection from the hurts of these experiences (Langley, 2003), but such help may be hard to accept as it implies dependency. This dynamic may be repeated, in therapy, if a man feels infantilised by the dependency inherent in the therapeutic relationship, particularly if the female therapist is insensitive to this.

Martin, a solicitor, came to therapy because the experience of two failed marriages had demoralised him. Both wives had left him. He felt unable to consider new relationships with women. Plagued with guilt about his poor relationship with his ageing father and confused as to how his marriages had failed, he was keen to 'sort out' what had 'gone wrong'. Martin challenged everything I said, demanding 'rational evidence'. I became irritated and unable to relate comfortably with his sense of logic and concreteness and insisted that he was defending against feelings. We became somewhat deadlocked. The relationship with his ex-wives was clearly enacted in the therapy room, as I abandoned him emotionally, just as they had.

I failed to understand his masculine world, and his shame at engaging with a female therapist. His early memories of suffocating dependency on his mother were powerfully present. The prospect of attachment was a profound threat to his masculinity. Examination of my resistance led to an awareness that I valued myself as a woman through my abilities to empathise and feel. Martin could not value this, which echoed how he devalued emotional dialogue in his marriages. Thus I experienced his resistance as an attack on my value as a woman and identity as a female therapist. Countertransference fears of being shamed and seen as inadequate, together with a terror of being overwhelmed by his intellect were evoked in me. He seemed to undermine my value as a woman and my sense of self, and I feared that he would overwhelm me as a man. As I became more aware of the process, I was able to engage with his need for cognitive problem solving activity. I slowly connected to Martin's deep sense of loss related to his father. My change of tactic gave him the impetus to explore his relationship with his father, who had assisted him with his homework as a child, giving him a positive experience of contact with his parent. We were able to build an alliance through my appreciation of his need for rational thinking as it was so intrinsically linked to his father. Later he could approach his fear of emotions and the negative connection with women. Essentially I had to recognise the threat to my own femininity and authority as a female therapist in order that the work could progress.

Erotic countertransference

Erotic countertransference is a frequent occurrence in therapeutic work (Mann, 1997). Intimate relationships evoke sexual feelings that need to be recognised and, where appropriate, interpreted for the benefit of the client. However, women may be more anxious about making sexual interpretations when working with a man through fears of being seen as seductive. Reluctance to discuss sexual feelings and sexuality may inhibit the potential to engage with the client's experience of *adult* male sexuality.

As women, we must be aware of *how* we are seductive, rather than defending against it. All relationships have an erotic element that it is crucial to discuss if progress is to be made. Harnessing such erotic transference between female therapist and male client is fraught with anxiety; there may be fears of litigation if she is seen to be seductive. Many meanings are attached to erotic transference, ranging from resistance to dependency and hostility to the need for love, growth and self-love.

Powerful erotic countertransference occurs when either counsellor or client has been a victim of sexual abuse. Acknowledgement of such feelings from the female therapist to the male client will inevitably create considerable anxiety as they take a step into unknown and feared emotions. Schaverien (1995) gives varying reasons for this anxiety, including cultural and gender inhibitions, the therapist's ego ideals, shame in the therapist, fears of acting out, being seen as seductive and feeling gratified by the eroticism.

Intense erotic transference, in which the male client is overtly sexually attracted to the therapist, can lead to resentment within women therapists if they feel used by male clients. Such feelings need to be fully explored in supervision so that they can be used creatively rather than destructively. Unfortunately research evidence suggests that sex is one of the topics most likely to be avoided in supervisory relationships (Webb and Wheeler, 1998). Schaverien (1995) refers to the potential for good therapeutic work to emanate from the experience of erotic countertransference. A symbolically 'good sex' engagement with a client may help to unravel conscious or unconscious conflicts, emanating from early life experiences.

Murdin (2002) explores the intersubjective experience of love and hate in the analytic dyad between female analyst and male patient. Using the lens of how the female cultural imagos of the Madonna-and-whore split can impact on the work, she identifies the countertransference deadlock as arising from fears in the man of his physical strength (the rapist), meeting fears in the female analyst of being seductive (asking for it). Male shame about sexual fantasies may meet countertransference needs in the female therapist for a man to be sensitive, and hence freedom to explore the client's masculine sexuality becomes stifled.

Clare (2000) refers to the lack of confidence in men about being male, in particular men feeling guilty for the abusive behaviour of other males. This echoes experiences of clients acknowledging, despairingly, that they don't know what being male *is* any more. An exploration of this often reveals anger at women and shame at having a penis. Hornby (2002), in *About a Boy*, tells how Will, the hero, goes to a female single parent support group, under the pretence of being a single dad, in order to meet women. Fellow female group members describe how the fathers of their children have betrayed them. He thinks to himself, 'God, men *are* bastards! I could cut off my *own* penis!'. These feelings of shame and fear resonate with issues of power and erotic transference, as the following case example illustrates.

David, a young teacher, entered therapy because of fears of being intimate or sexual; he was fearful of his penis as he felt it was too large and dangerous. Following a depressive episode he moved back home with his parents, who had a stormy and difficult relationship. David often sided with his mother, who complained about his father's 'lack of balls'. He managed his fears of being a 'mummy's boy' by standing up to his father 'like a man'.

David described feeling ashamed about a sexual fetish involving women's under-wear and use of Internet porn. He was secretive about both, eventually disclosing his practice. My countertransference feelings were of revulsion, dissociation and occasionally high sexual arousal. Additionally the relationship had a somewhat 'diminished' and 'used' quality to it in the room. I likened his use of me in the therapy to his use of pornography and noted that this experience of 'usage' intensified when a break of some sort was due. There was a parallel process in supervision, in which discussions of pornographic fantasies resulted in my feeling excruciating shame and a strong wish to hide these fantasies and feelings from my supervisor. This perhaps mirrored my client's wish to be secretive about the porn and how it related to me.

The work in supervision resulted in my asking whether David's use of his fetish and porn stepped up during breaks. He acknowledged, somewhat abashed, that it did. Noting a sort of voyeuristic fascination as to whether I featured in his fan-tasies, I also felt as though I was spoiling something for him in drawing his fetish use into the room. At times, David's secretiveness felt controlling and dominat-ing. This power struggle became conscious. I considered how the porn and fetish constituted support for his self-esteem, questioning whether he felt diminished if they became a more conscious part of our work together and lost their power as a secret activity. Exploring the different elements of power and shame in his fetish freed us to consider David's needs for love and fears that he would be too much for a woman.

Countertransference issues with male envy and narcissism

Brown (1990) identifies the following attributes as qualities for effective therapy: ability for empathic attunement; developing identity through relation-ship with others; ability to empower others; being able to monitor and observe the behaviour of the dominant group. She postulates that women learn these from their phenomenology of being female. These attributes can elicit male envy and give rise to power struggles in the work. Horney (1942), coun-tering Freud's concept of 'penis envy' (1920, p. 327), described 'womb envy', a male envy of women's ability to bear children. Male needs to succeed are conceptualised as compensation for not extending into the future, via bearing children. Men may manifest this envy by disparaging the work and withholding gratitude, thus spoiling the richness of what can be created with a female thera-pist. The female therapist may retaliate through a fear of male envy by reacting with hate in the countertransference (Winnicott, 1947). The potential for such a response is present in all therapeutic relationships. Female therapists, in particular, need to be aware of their response to men who exhibit power and control if the work is not to become persecutory for both parties. The man's identification with his gender role may emphasise independence, winning, achieving and showing off. These behaviours may encompass his sense of being special, particularly if his paternal relationship was distant or competitive. This can evoke countertransference feelings of worthlessness, frustration and hate in the female therapist. This will particularly be so if the therapist's personal experience is of men being dominant and all-powerful.

Real (1997) echoes these explicit and implicit expectations, from childhood through to manhood: to succeed, be strong, be invincible, show no vulnerability. Such expectations pervade and invade the psyche; to fail in this leads to a sense of shame about the male self. One defence against this failure is a narcissistic grandiosity, although the effort required in maintaining this can be demanding. Thus the defences employed to avoid shame often afford relief whilst breeding greater expectations and ultimately, more shame:

> In overt depression, the anguish of shame, of the toxic relationship to the self, is endured. In covert depression, the man desperately defends against such an onslaught. A common defence against the painful experience of deflated value is inflated value and a common compensation for shame, of feeling less than, is a subtle or flagrant flight into grandiosity, of feeling better than. (Real, 1997, p. 55)

Case: Roy, a retired member of a church group living alone, attended therapy because he felt listless and flat, finding difficulty in engaging with activities. He described situations in which he antagonised fellow male churchgoers. Roy perceived their reactions to him as their envy of his abilities to be assertive and powerful. He could only relate to women, including myself, by creating fantasies that women adored and admired him. He described himself as a 'superior provider'. He regaled me with stories that he knew what it was 'to be a woman' and seemed to need these fantasies to avoid experiencing feelings of inadequacy. He would often be scathing about any therapeutic intervention. At these times I felt resentment and robbed as a woman, which obstructed my ability to feel compassion and to be effective. The feeling of 'being robbed' alerted me to his possible envy. Envy was a foreign emotion to him; being enviable maintained his sense of self. Roy left the therapy with a parting comment that perhaps I needed to 're-train'.

Reflections: I reflected on this final comment as an unconscious envious attack delivered in order that his narcissistic wound would remain untouched, avoiding potential annihilation. Clare (2000, p. 28) describes how 'men occupy centre stage and women attend to them'. This echoes my experience as the 'handmaiden'. I perceived Roy as arrogant. I felt useless, unenviable, shameful, bored and empty. I grew angry and noted my countertransference reactions of working very hard to prove my value or of wanting to crush him. This mirrored reactions from women in his life whom he experienced as initially very 'keen' but then 'cold'. Reflecting on this in a framework of male envy suggests that I was holding the fearful parts of him that felt inadequate and shamed, which he located as female.

Countertransference and male dependency

The following is an extract from one of a number of deeply personal poems written by a male client during long-term therapy in which he had suicidal thoughts. Profound emotions could be revealed in poetry that could not be expressed in the sessions. He expresses in raw terms the hate of the female therapist and the need of her 'invisible strings' to hold him together.

Just Another Mind-fuck
Mrs Winklepicker establishes eye contact
With an unblinking gaze that exacts
Its price from my very insides
Making it impossible to hide
The thoughts roaming in my head:
The fact that I'd prefer to be dead;
I'd rather be alone,
Than run my race anymore;
My fears that this is all my fault;
My fears that it's not.
My fears that I shall lose all I own.
My fears that I don't give a damn … … ..

Alongside my cry to help
She's one of the invisible strings holding me up,
And without them I'd most likely fall
Or more probably jump.
Yet I still seem to have some dragons to slay
And, she says, we'll look at them another day.

My fault in my mind is easy to see;
I am manipulated yet don't want to be
I've been manipulated all my married life
By my loving yet manipulative wife
So, when Mrs Winklepicker turns the screw
I'm manipulated by her too … … … .

I was constantly moved by his vulnerability in the sessions, communicated through this poem and others, which revealed his intense need for me to recognise his experiences. The poem describes an experience of male dependence on the female therapist, feelings of shame, exposure and fear of her power. This power is reflected in the commonly held belief that women do more of the emotional work in the male/female relationship. Cantor (1990), echoed by Erickson (1993), notes how female therapists are more likely to nurture and take responsibility for the therapy, feeling guilty when the outcome is not positive. The danger is that in holding too much responsibility, especially during the dependent stages of therapy, she will ultimately become resentful.

Men often come for therapy because a relationship has ended. They report being mystified, not understanding what has happened. Typically they focus on external events rather than on their internal world. A rejected woman might more often experience shame, encapsulated in the feeling 'What is wrong with me?'. Rabinowitz and Cochran (2002, p. 27) refer to the narcissistic wounding experience following the death of family and friends, confrontation with ageing, physical decline or the recognition that not all dreams can come true. They suggest that 'these normative life experiences often trigger intense emotional conflict for many men and often are an important portal location … They are experienced as perceived failures to live up to his culture's masculine ideals … and as such are experienced as a wound to the ego or sense of self.'

Society is less tolerant of any apparent failure in a man and the shame of depression is to be avoided at all costs. Women internalise depression and blame themselves whilst men externalise depression by expressions of aggressive behaviour (Gjerde et al., 1988).

Women are twice as likely as men to be diagnosed with depression (Kessler et al., 1994). However men are conditioned to be less tolerant of feelings of depression and are less likely to seek help when they do. When personality disorders, drug and alcohol dependency in men are included, the incidence of depression in men and women is more equal. Real (1997, p. 23) argues that men tend to manifest depression differently. They are more likely to mask depression by a range of actions, a kind of self-flagellation, which can result in self-harm. The most obvious of these behaviours are addictions to alcohol and drugs as well as to gambling and violence. Some less obvious behaviour includes addictions to work, sport, and bodybuilding, which are often admired. When these are taken to the extreme, they are also harmful.

Conclusion

Counselling men can be a rewarding experience offering opportunities for engagement with male attributes and real dialogue with men. This elicits moving and beautiful experiences of male tenderness and desire for connection. These are all the more precious to witness because male clients inevitably struggle with internal beliefs about masculinity that conflict with therapeutic engagement. These beliefs can result in isolation, withdrawal and deep loss. It is thus necessary for the female therapist to engage with thoughts, feelings and responses to masculinity from the very beginning. Women assume a knowledge of what it is to live in the male world. Life experiences with men must be kept in perspective, and an open stance to hearing new stories must be adopted. Observing how a man relates to his masculinity involves both awareness of our wish to stereotype men and the search for an appreciation of difference.

We need to examine that which we experience as 'masculine' and 'feminine' and how this affects our countertransferential defences. Integration of aspects of masculinity that promote independence and self-reliance with interdependence, emotional literacy and intuition can be potent and healing for both practitioner and client. The ability to be available to erotic transference and countertransference can enable the longing for engagement to be explored. This presents particular challenges in both supervision and the therapeutic dyad.

There is potential for female therapists to feel emasculated if they have to adapt their way of working with a man. Arguably this can replicate the marginalisation some women feel in society. Women therapists may choose the profession because their 'female' attributes can be used and valued and female power can be exercised in ways that few other professions allow. We need to explore how the alliance can be threatened when there is a challenge to the female sense of value and use the ensuing power struggle as a means to enhance understanding. Sensitive judgement and monitoring of content and timing of intervention are vital in this struggle to preserve the therapeutic alliance. If such work is not done, there is a danger that the authority and skills of the female therapist become a source of threat to a male client, mirroring a man's feelings of inadequacy rather than encouraging his growth. In this context envy and its power to poison the dynamics need to be explored in supervision if the work is to reach its potential. Fear of male envy in the female therapist can dominate, suffocating empathy and inhibiting growth in the therapy. Persecutory or sadistic enactments can result from the ensuing hate in the countertransference leading to reinforcement of painful and familiar isolation for the male client.

The adversarial nature of the dynamics often present in the work with men can be creative. We appreciate the ability of many men to be focused and make rapid use of the work. Perhaps the fear of being drawn back into the maternal orbit can also usefully *fuel* a wish to change and differentiate in healthy ways. Since female therapists outnumber male practitioners we have a unique role to play in enabling men to reach a fresh appraisal of their masculinity. The 'cross-cultural' nature of the therapy conducted by women with male clients has the potential to bring about resolution of old conflicts and enhanced intimate relationships; it can also result in deadlock, reinforcing old patterns and inhibiting growth. Relationships fail when individuals act out their frustrations, anxieties and fantasies, rather than reflecting on their emotional world. The therapy room is the place where this can be addressed and the female therapist must tune into her own inner world to be open to all forms of communication from her male client.

Notes

1. ISD Scotland, 1998.
2. General Registrar Office for Scotland, 1996.
3. Local research into counselling services showed the following:
   - Nottingham Counselling Centre (March 2002–March 2003): 306 clients, 33 per cent male, 67 per cent female; 54 counsellors, 43 female counsellors, 11 male
   - Leicester Counselling Centre (March 2002–March 2003): 238 clients, 37 per cent male, 63 per cent female; 69 counsellors, 55 female counsellors, 14 male
4. The figures for British Association of Counselling and Psychotherapy membership by gender showed the split for August 2003 was 83 per cent female counsellors, 17 per cent male.

REFERENCES

Brooks, G. R. (1998). *A New Psychotherapy for Traditional Men.* New York: Jossey-Bass.

Brown, L. S. (1990). 'What female therapists have in common'. In D. W. Cantor (ed.), *Women as Therapists.* New York: Springer.

Cantor, D. W. (1990). *Women as Therapists.* New York: Springer.

Chodorow, N. (1978). *The Reproduction of Mothering.* Berkeley, CA: University of California Press.

Clare, A. (2000). On Men: Masculinity in Crisis. London: Chatto and Windus.

Erickson, B. (1993). Helping Men Change: The Role of the Female Therapist. London: Sage.

Freud, S. (1920). A General Introduction to Psychoanalysis: Twentieth Lecture. New York: Perma.

Gjerde, P., Block, J, and Block, J. H. (1988). 'Depressive symptoms and personality during late adolescence: gender differences in the externalization-internalization of symptom expression'. Journal of Abnormal Psychology, 99: 4, 475–86.

Gray, J. (1993). Men Are from Mars, Women Are from Venus. New York: HarperCollins.

Hornby, N. (2002). About A Boy. London: Penguin.

Horney, K. (1942). Collected Works of Karen Horney, Volume 2. New York: Norton.

Kessler, R. C., McGonagle, K. A., Zhao, S. et al. (1994). 'Lifetime and 12-month prevalence of DSM III-R psychiatric disorders in the United States: results from the National Comorbidity Survey'. Archives of General Psychiatry, 51: 1, 8–19.

Langley, M. R. (2003). Ode to Black Men: Be the Light in the Corner. www.lesley.edu/journals/jppp/1/jp3ii7.html, accessed 12 February 2005.

Mann, D. (1997). Psychotherapy: An Erotic Relationship. London: Routledge.

Mann, D. (2002). Love and Hate: Psychoanalytic Perspectives. Hove: Brunner-Routledge.

Men Behaving Badly (BBC TV, 1992 onwards). Simon Nye (writer). Fremantle International Distribution Ltd and Hartswood Films.

Millar, A. (2003). 'Men's experience of considering counselling: entering the unknown'. Counselling and Psychotherapy Research, 3: 1, 16–24.

Mintz, L. B. and O'Neil, J. M. (1990). 'Gender roles, sex, and the process of psychotherapy; many questions and a few answers'. Journal of Counselling and Development, 68, 381–7.

Murdin, L. (2002). 'Love and hate in the analytic encounter with a woman therapist'. in D. Mann (ed.), Love and Hate: Psychoanalytic Perspectives. Hove: Brunner-Routledge, Chapter 4.

Rabinowitz, F. E. and Cochran, S. V. (2002). Deepening Psychotherapy with Men. Washington, DC: American Psychological Association.

Real, T. (1997). I Don't Want to Talk About It: Overcoming the Secret Legacy of Depression. Dublin: Gill & Macmillan.

Rose, C. (2002). 'Talking gender but who's listening?'. Counselling and Psychotherapy Journal, 13: 7, 8–10.

Sabo, D. and Gordon, D. F. (1995). *Men's Health and Illness: Gender, Power and the Body*. Thousand Oaks, CA: Sage.

Samuels, A. (2002). Speech: 'Men and Therapy'. British Association of Supervision Practice and Research Conference, Twickenham, July.

Schaverien, J. (1995). *Desire and the Female Therapist: Engendered Gazes in Psychotherapy and Art Therapy*. London and New York: Routledge.

Watson, J. (2000). *Male Bodies: Health, Culture and Identity*. Buckingham: Open University Press.

Webb, A. and Wheeler, S. (1998). 'How honest do counsellors dare to be in the supervisory relationship? An exploratory study'. *British Journal of Guidance & Counselling*, 26: 4, 509–24.

Winnicott, D. (1947). 'Hate in the countertransference'. In *Collected Papers: Through Pediatrics to Psychoanalysis*. London: Tavistock.

PART III

Disability and Old Age

6

Counselling People with Disabilities and Chronic Illnesses: a Psychodynamic Approach

Julia Segal

Introduction

Illness and disability can have a significant effect on the way people feel about themselves and the way others feel about them. The actual effect depends on the individual, their beliefs and phantasies (conscious and unconscious) about themselves and the world they live in, as well as the beliefs and fantasies of those around them. Some clients come for counselling with concerns that have nothing to do with their health, but at some point disclose an illness or disability. Others bring their illness or disability as an important focus for counselling. The relative importance of an illness or disability in the client's life may be unclear to client or counsellor; there may be differences of opinion about what matters and what does not, for example. The process of counselling may uncover surprises for both client and counsellor as the role that a chronic illness or disability plays in a client's life reveals itself.

Clients with an illness or disability may be disadvantaged in many ways, not only by the practical issues surrounding their condition, but also by their effects on others. People suffering with illness or disability will sometimes have disturbing phantasies about their condition and themselves; working to uncover, address and ultimately change these phantasies can have far-reaching effects, sometimes enabling the client to live a much better life (or die a better death), whatever their state of physical health. However, the counsellor may also be affected by their own disturbing phantasies concerning ill health. Such phantasies need to be addressed if they are not to interfere with the counsellor's capacity to listen to, understand and help make sense of the client's experience.

Thinking about illness or disability can be disturbing for both counsellor and client as anxieties about dying or living with a chronic disability may be aroused. Counsellors may also have fears such as 'Is this catching?' and 'Will I make the client get worse?'. At the same time they may harbour conscious and unconscious hopes of promoting a physical recovery, as well as a psychological cure. People also often think it is better not to think about illness or disturbing symptoms for fear, for example, of 'bringing them on'. Confusion between whether symptoms are caused physically or psychically, by 'stress', for example, can add to problems for both client and counsellor. Fear of the bad effects of 'stress' can make it harder for a counsellor to challenge a client, with the result that the client receives a less effective service. In addition, many people are afraid that if others find out about a disturbing diagnosis or a hidden disability there will be serious consequences in terms of social life or employment.

Knowledge and experience of a particular illness or disability may also inhibit practice. Since no two disabilities (and no two people) are the same, this applies even if counsellors have a disability themselves. If beliefs about illness and disability are not discussed, they can remain governed by quite unrealistic phantasies. For example, if childhood experience of illness includes a parent being ill or dying, adults may have painful beliefs about their own (or other children's) ability to harm or cure. Counsellors who have not been confronted with these issues before may need time (and help) to sort out their own thoughts and to locate their own unrealistic assumptions and beliefs before they can help clients to do the same.

This chapter will address these issues from three intertwined points of view: that of the person who has the illness or disability; that of someone who lives with or loves an ill or disabled person (for example, a partner or child or sibling); and thirdly, that of the counsellor. Some of the issues which concern both clients and counsellors and their relationship with each other in these situations will be addressed.

Provision of counselling services for people with disabilities or chronic illnesses

There are many difficulties that can prevent people with certain disabilities or illnesses even finding a face-to-face counsellor. Counselling rooms may not have disability access or essential support services; transport can be problematic; so too can the effects of symptoms which interfere directly with communication, such as deafness or speech impediments or various cognitive problems which make it unclear how much a client takes in or understands. I will not dwell on these practical issues, since the focus of this book is on psychodynamics, but they can play a significant part in preventing people with disabilities from accessing counselling. Counsellors sometimes try to redress this situation by agreeing to offer counselling in the client's home or beside a hospital bed, for example. Unfortunately, such modifications to the setting have significant effects on the quality and nature of counselling offered, which need to be taken into consideration. Insisting that arrangements are made to enable a client to travel to the counsellor, like any other client, can sometimes be revealing; for example, by uncovering a reluctance in the client to participate in counselling, or, on the other hand, by opening up the possibility of arranging transport for other outings too. Many people with disabilities or chronic illnesses do not need special provision for access; they may turn up in the consulting room of any counsellor, with or without the counsellor being alerted beforehand.

The effect of illness or disability on the counsellor

Some counsellors react positively to clients' illness or disability, feeling that these are areas where they can provide a useful service and see good results. Others are more wary. From a psychodynamic point of view, it is important to consider the mental state of the counsellor as well as the client.

Conscious and unconscious phantasies about illness and disability

Counsellors can have many anxieties about counselling people with disabilities and chronic illnesses, some of which are quite disabling. Conscious and unconscious phantasies combine. Primitive infantile beliefs that 'talking about something will make it happen', or that 'distress or discomfort is dangerous', combine with anxieties about 'stress' causing illness, or a lack of significant medical knowledge. Since people are often afraid even to speak of these things, childhood phantasies concerning illness and disability may be unmodified by more adult reality testing. This applies both to client and counsellor; for example, both can be afraid of talking about issues which may distress someone who is ill or disabled; both can feel that cognitive problems or other embarrassing symptoms have to be politely ignored rather than mentioned; both can be afraid of facing the fact that an illness is terminal. The counsellor may fear talking directly about the client's bad behaviour or the possibility of the client being abandoned. They may also fear addressing a carer's death wishes towards someone with a disability or serious illness. Counsellors new to working with health issues have much to learn, but also the opportunity of rewarding experiences. When a counselling session provides a client with their first space to think about their situation and their (or another's) illness, and to discover thoughts, beliefs, phantasies and perhaps symptoms which have governed their feelings and behaviour, even one session may bring about considerable change for the client and relief from disturbing, unrealistic mind-sets. People suffering from an illness are often protected. A counsellor who can resist the desire to protect the client may be able to provide a service that the client wants, needs and can use.

One boy was afraid his sister had been born with a slight disability because, before she was born, he had mocked other children with the word 'spastic' and accompanying gestures; even as an adult he continued to feel guilty towards his sister. Another client with a disability that developed in adulthood expected his own children to hate him as he had hated his disabled brother when he was a child; his feelings, actions and behaviour were strongly influenced by this fear. A woman who was diagnosed with MS immediately rearranged her life; as she described this to her counsellor the counsellor began to think she was expecting to die within a few years. It turned out she was convinced, without realising it, that she was going to die at the same (young) age at which her mother had died; the MS diagnosis had simply 'confirmed' this for her. The fact that she consciously knew that MS did not normally shorten people's lives in this way had been split off from the conviction that she only had a few years left to live.

For many counsellors obvious conscious and unconscious phantasies like these will have been picked up in their own therapy, but some may have been missed. A childhood desire to 'make people better' that may underlie some of the motivation for becoming a counsellor or other health worker may itself have arisen from a desire to make a parent or sibling better from an illness. It is essential that a counsellor should not confuse their actual client too much with a damaged parent or sibling seen from the point of view of a child.

Symbolic implications

Disabilities often signify 'worse' in some way: incapable, useless, 'one sandwich short of a picnic' (if the disability is cognitive); 'no good' where 'good' unconsciously has a moral connotation as well as meaning 'capable'. Hunchbacks in literature tend to represent evil. 'One-eyed' is naturally followed by 'monster'. Illness can be associated with weakness of moral fibre, or with failure of some kind. In particular there can often be an ignorant assumption that someone who looks disabled necessarily has no interest in sex, or no hope of finding a sexual partner. All of these symbolic meanings, and many more, can affect the way a counsellor (as well as the population at large) greets and works with a client with a disability.

When faced with people with disabilities the defensive process of splitting often emerges. Examples include both a sense of superiority towards and excessive admiration for people with disabilities. For example, counsellors who struggle (perhaps unconsciously) with their own envy of other people may assume that if they were disabled they would be even more envious. This can lead to an assumption that all disabled people are envious of the able-bodied. This mechanism may be part of what makes people fear and avoid disabled or disfigured people. Idealisation is a common defence against persecutory fears: and a conscious, exaggerated admiration can make people with disabilities rightly uncomfortable. 'You are so brave', 'I couldn't cope like she does' can represent forms of idealisation that are no more helpful for a client than being patronised or made to feel stupid.

'Difference' evokes fear for which a sense of superiority can be a defence. The risk is that the counsellor's own ignorance and sense of insecurity and inferiority can be split off and evoked in the client. When I was a teenager it was common for the more insecure boys to split off their own anxieties about not being normal and acceptable and attribute them to 'spastics'; making fun of 'spastics' allowed them to feel for a moment in control, powerful and superior. Patronising attitudes represent an attempt to superimpose a sense of concern towards those who are seen as merely the representation of the uncontrolled, despised, disliked and feared parts of the self. Counsellors have to work at their shadow side, with those parts of themselves that they dislike and want to split off if they are not to risk attributing precisely those qualities to disabled clients.

Many counsellors have some knowledge of physical disability, whether it be a broken leg or a period in hospital, and they draw upon this knowledge. Clients can be in a similar position, and productive work can be done, disentangling the current situation from memories of past experiences or knowledge of other ill or disabled people. It is vital for counsellors to remember that knowing someone with one illness or disability does not necessarily provide knowledge that can be generalised to any client; such knowledge may help but it may also hinder if it creates assumptions that the counsellor fails to test. What matters is the capacity to understand the client's view of the world, however different from or similar to the counsellor's, with as few false assumptions as possible.

Anxieties about behaviour

Counsellors can also be anxious about their own behaviour or that of the client. They may be afraid of doing something wrong, or of not knowing what is required of them. For example, it is not obvious how to behave with a client who cannot speak clearly; whether to offer to help a client take off their coat; what to do if a client is unsteady on their feet or has breathing difficulties. Some disabilities disable the counsellor; for example, if a client cannot hear or understand normal speech. Some health conditions can disturb a counsellor. For example, a counsellor may react to a facial disfiguration or a powerful, unpleasant smell with an involuntary facial expression of horror or disgust; or may react to a distressing illness by thinking that the client would be better off dead. Being aware of and managing such reactions is crucial to the therapeutic relationship and the counsellor may need support to process their response appropriately (Segal, 1996).

In these situations the counsellor experiences something of the confusion and disempowerment that a newly disabled client may feel; suddenly the rules are different, the counsellor no longer quite knows where s/he stands. The counsellor may be in a position where assumptions about what someone can and cannot do are suddenly brought up sharp. Probing why a client (who is apparently home all day doing nothing) doesn't join a class or visit a friend may bring to light a series of totally unexpected practical difficulties as well as social/psychological/psychodynamic ones. The counsellor may feel humbled by their own ignorance. Just as someone with a new illness or disability does not know how other people will react, so the counsellor does not know how the client will react. Neither can count on previous social status; disability often means loss of status, and the counsellor may feel similar loss of status faced with a newly disabled client. People with disabilities are all different and what one invites or demands, another may reject angrily, humiliatingly, or with painful distress. Counsellors learn by mistakes, often after bruising experiences. Not only is the power relationship between counsellor and client somehow challenged by the client's knowledge of their own condition and the counsellor's ignorance, but the counsellor can also fear giving serious offence as they listen to someone with a disability describing the insults they have suffered. Hence the counsellor has a series of challenges when working with a disabled client and if disability is not the focus of the work, it may not be appropriate to spend the client's time discussing it. One of the problems of having a disability or chronic illness is the time and effort required to enable others to understand.

Managing the frame

People with illness or disabilities sometimes bring subtle or overt challenges to the therapeutic frame. The client might, for example, feel strongly that they need to know if the counsellor has experience of the particular condition under discussion. Or they might want counselling at home; or help with obtaining transport. The issue of whether to change the setting to accommodate the client is an important one. People with disabilities also often say they want to be treated 'just like anyone else'; in this sense a change is a loss of normality.

Similarly, counsellors sometimes find themselves wanting to become advocates for clients with disabilities, forgetting that if they do, the relationship is affected. Some changes might have to be made, but such changes may bring about a loss that must be acknowledged. Gaining an advocate may mean losing a counsellor. The experience of illness or disability often involves loss that the counsellor could help the client to bear. The counsellor too has to bear the reality of being unable to provide a perfectly adapted service.

Psychodynamic counselling demands a secure, predictable therapeutic frame created within a safe, predictable, protected space. Psychodynamic counsellors and psychotherapists do not normally work with clients in clients' homes, for example, because of the practical and symbolic implications. A different style of counselling is required if one is a guest in someone's home. The client, rather than the counsellor, is in control of the setting and this changes the dynamic of the relationship. A counsellor may be unable to monitor the subtle changes in his or her own state of mind clearly enough to work with significant transference dynamics if they are having to react to the distractions of a client's own setting: psychodynamic counselling may not be possible in such circumstances.

Psychodynamic counsellors cannot use many of their essential skills unless they work within a secure frame (Gray, 1994). Any adaptation of the frame will have an impact on the therapeutic relationship and on the client's sense of security and containment. This creates a dilemma when trying to implement 'equal opportunities', which can be interpreted as 'treating people as if they were the same as anyone else'. Clearly this does not work for clients with disabilities, as without special facilities they cannot access equivalent services. We modify the way we speak, depending on our assessment of someone's capacity to understand us; we keep quiet with some clients and speak more with others. We try to keep our respect for the client and their world constant. Crucially, psychodynamic counsellors are expected to work with all of their feelings and thoughts, not to ignore those which are socially unacceptable or uncomfortable.

Taking control of the setting for counselling is important for practical reasons that impinge on psychotherapeutic understanding, given the link between mind and body. A comfortable, familiar chair allows us to register discomfort, perhaps caused by unconsciously mirroring the client's posture; a different one would distract and distort this kind of communication. Listening for interruptions takes attention not only from the client and the relationship, but also from the counsellor's monitoring of their own state of mind and body.

Changes sometimes have to be made to accommodate people with disabilities. The question of who changes, and what is changed, may be a matter for negotiation and the implications need to be thought through. Counsellors can feel themselves pushed by something like 'survivor guilt'. 'I'm able-bodied, I should be the one who changes; how can I ask him to change when he has so much to cope with already?'. This smacks of pity, of an assumption of superiority in the capacity to cope. It can also lead to hidden resentment on the part of the counsellor who is aware that they are being asked to do something different, which may compromise their work.

When counselling people with MS I make hourly appointments. Some people take a long time to walk from the waiting room to my room and effectively lose some counselling time as a result. I had to decide who was going to 'pay' for this; should I make appointments with five minutes between them, which would allow for this but would mean that often the five minutes was 'wasted' time, adding up over the day to a significant loss of my work time? Or should I simply accept that clients who walk slowly take responsibility for this loss; they could use a wheelchair to move faster if they wished, or they could take the time to let me, walking alongside, understand some of the frustrations of slow walking. I choose the latter; a client has an hour in which we work within the constraints of their condition.

Making a change once may make it hard to refuse the next time, but a lot may be learned through the therapeutic relationship when considering such a request. Families often struggle with precisely these issues. 'If someone has flu you don't expect them to do the shopping, but is living with MS the same as having flu? Should I do the shopping for my mother every week now?'

Just as the counsellor has to decide where he or she stands with holding the boundaries of counselling and not allowing them to be compromised to the point of threatening the quality of the work, so family members have to decide whose needs take priority. Who is more deserving of consideration? What does it mean to be 'healthy'? Is my toothache 'nothing' compared to what he/she is going through? Is my child's grazed knee 'nothing'? If so, what does this mean for the child? And what kind of parent does that make me? What can be asked of a disabled father/husband/wife/mother/child? What should not be asked? The capacity to be a good parent and a good partner or a good child may be very important for someone whose illness has taken away other sources of satisfaction in life; counselling sometimes brings this to attention. If counsellors can be clear about their own needs, and can be firm about asserting them, clients can use this modelling to think about the power relations at home and the implications of the weight given to the needs of different family members.

Counselling can sometimes help to maintain or restore relationships which were threatened by beliefs and attitudes connected with disability or illness; this can be more significant for someone's wellbeing than a physical disability. In order to do this counsellors have to work with their own inhibitions and assumptions about what someone with an illness or disability can or cannot ask of others, including themselves. Freud (1915/17) thought that illness, like grief and mourning, tended to make people egocentric. In my experience, a long-term illness or disability may damage or destroy the capacity to think about, love and care for others, but it may not. Sometimes this capacity can be regained through counselling. Illness and disability does not always make people unbearably egocentric (though loss may do so temporarily). If they are this way there may be another reason for it which counselling can help to remove. In my experience bad relations within the family are sometimes caused by a previous loss, such as the loss of a baby or a child; in this case, grief work for the past loss can help to change the atmosphere within the family, whatever the state of health of members. Someone who feels useless because of their disability may discover that they can influence the lives of those around them for the better. A partner may discover a capacity to care they did not know they had.

Focus of counselling

Faced with a client who has an illness or disability, counsellors often worry about the level of importance to be attached to it in the counselling. Does it need addressing or not? Normally a counsellor would follow the client's lead on this, and if the client does not mention it the counsellor would hesitate too. However, countertransference is important and needs to be considered. The counsellor needs to think, observe and use their awareness in the client's best interest; not to ignore covert messages but to pick them up and work with them. Anything the counsellor notices is likely to be noticed by other people around the client, and there may be important issues which affect communication between the client and others that could be addressed.

This is not easy. On the one hand, clients can complain that the counsellor was 'only interested in my disability; I went to her for help with housing and that was all she talked about'. On the other hand they can complain, 'She knew I had MS and she never mentioned it all the time I saw her.' They can feel 'She was more bothered by my illness than I was' and be irritated; or they can be hugely relieved: 'No-one had asked me about that before, everyone else ignored it, but anyone could see it,' or 'Why has nobody told me that before? That explains so much.' When the counsellor consciously ignores an obvious problem it damages the rapport with the client, which both client and counsellor feel, though they may pretend not to.

This problem also arises when counsellors have disabilities themselves. In an interview with Virginia Hunter (1996), Hanna Segal talked about her first analyst's limp and his deformed hand. She describes approvingly how 'He never let me get away with not speaking about it. He was immediately onto what I noticed and my anxieties about it and so on, without allowing me any denial of the fact or my fantasies.' She contrasts this with other analysts she met later who denied the effect on their patients of the analysts' obvious abnormalities. However, treading the tightrope between thrusting the therapist's health problems into the forefront, and enabling the client to discover and explore their phantasies and anxieties about the therapist's own body, may not be easy.

Cognitive problems (including early signs of dementia) in clients can often be ignored because they are embarrassing or frightening to mention. Losing track of the conversation and memory problems, as shown by the client frequently repeating themselves or reporting events in a very muddled and confusing way, may be relevant to both the counselling and to everyday life. In my experience, when I have finally managed to register such a problem and to mention it, with hesitation, to a client, they have invariably responded by telling me that their family or their colleagues have often commented on it. The relief in the room, both mine and the client's, has been palpable as we have been able to discuss what is an embarrassing (and possibly serious) disability. However, this is in the context of counselling offered in a multiple sclerosis clinic and MS can cause these cognitive problems. What one chooses to mention in a session depends on the setting and on the contract with the client.

Many years ago, I was taught as a marriage guidance counsellor that it could be important to mention sex in the first session, even if the client does not, so that the client knows it is an issue that can be discussed. I think the same applies to counselling people with chronic illnesses or disabilities. Depending on the context, the counsellor may take responsibility for acknowledging the disability (and perhaps for discussing sex too in some instances) to make it clear that this is a topic that can be brought into the session. However, what happens thereafter should depend on the client's response and the (implied or overt) contract with the client.

Political issues

There can be political difficulties for counsellors working with people who are perceived as different. Whether counselling should only be offered to people with disabilities by people with disabilities is often a topic of heated debate.

One counsellor gave up counselling people with multiple sclerosis because she thought her post should be taken by someone with MS themselves. Unfortunately there was no-one with MS available to take up the post, and her action simply meant that the clients were no longer offered counselling.

Counsellors working with people who are different from themselves have a duty to make every effort to understand their clients' point of view, but part of the counselling process may involve addressing issues of difference between the client and others, including differences in the counselling room. Clients who want to see a therapist with similar disabilities may be expressing anxieties about their own separateness and differences; if this is an important part of the way they feel about their illness or disability it is likely to be a new case of an old (and perhaps troublesome) problem which needs addressing.

In my experience some clients have the opposite problem. Someone who has become ill or disabled may have had derogatory feelings towards other disabled or ill people. Some people do not want to join any self-help group because they despise people like themselves. For this reason some clients prefer to see a counsellor who does not have their condition; and if offered one would feel they were 'second class', providing a 'second class' service. Such concerns may be addressed with a counsellor, whether they belong to the same group as the client or apparently to a different one. It can be an advantage for the counsellor not to disclose which group he or she belongs to (if this is possible) in order to facilitate exploration of such attitudes.

There is another political issue that is important. People often talk nowadays of the person with the chronic illness or disability as the 'expert' on their own condition. This can be an improvement on the assumption that the patient knows nothing, but it can bring difficulties too. People have complained to me that some doctors expect them to know too much; they feel that decisions are being unfairly pushed back onto them when they do not have sufficient knowledge (of drugs or surgical procedures in particular) to make complex decisions. Where they want a partnership, with a doctor or nurse advising and helping, they sometimes feel that the professional uses 'the patient knows best' as an excuse to avoid the professional's own time-consuming responsibilities. Counsellors may need to be aware of the fear and resentment that some clients can feel, when asked to teach others (including the counsellor) about their condition yet again. Being the 'one who knows' or the 'expert' is not always appreciated.

The effect of illness or disability on the client

Explaining to clients what I do as a counsellor on a multidisciplinary team working with people who have multiple sclerosis, I preface my work with the question, 'What does MS mean to you?'. This question is answered by clients on many different levels; it often leads us straight to significant issues from the clients' past; often current and future concerns have significance as a result of anxieties which predated the MS by many years.

Practical considerations are important and may need addressing in counselling as well as by other professionals. Taking three hours to dress, painful daily injections, having to use a catheter or suffering the constant threat of incontinence are themselves distressing, and telling a counsellor about these difficulties and bearing the painful fact that they cannot be altered can be helpful to a client who normally hides their problems, or tries to pretend they do not matter or do not exist. When a client ruminates at length over more than one session on a particular issue, the counsellor may realise that they have missed something important. The therapist may be able to use their own reaction – such as boredom, disgust, curiosity or irritation (discussed with a supervisor beforehand) – to wonder about hidden, unconscious feelings the client may have that need to be explored. The counsellor feeling bored, for example, is often a sign that more lively sexual feelings are being shut out for some reason. Confusion in the counsellor may reflect unacknowledged confusion in the client, perhaps about something else entirely. A client talking about their practical difficulties may at the same time convey to the counsellor powerful feelings which they also convey to others around them; bearing this is mind may enable the counsellor to work with the client on the effect they are having on others, as well as on unconscious feelings they may have about themselves.

However, many clients do not even mention practical issues. They may be struggling with changes to their lives, but it is their emotional significance that seems to matter most. Given the chance to explore the meaning of MS to them, many people bring up issues concerning life and love, birth and death, dependence and control; family legacies; past losses and past grief.

My own experience is that illness or disability affects people according to their pre-existing state. Someone who has always been unsure of themselves will probably find an illness or disability increases their insecurity; while someone with more confidence will find ways of living well with their condition. Illness can knock people off track, but counselling can help to bring them back; in addition, counselling offered as a result of an illness can also uncover problems which needed dealing with a long time ago, leading to a better life.

Illness or disability can bring many losses. Locating the losses and exploring their full significance can be very useful. Often people try to belittle their own losses: 'I can't play badminton any more, but I know other people have it worse so I shouldn't complain.' The loss of the badminton might mean loss of an opportunity to shine, to be alone with no responsibilities or to find a sexual partner. Counselling helps to sort out the ramifications of the loss and its significance. Taking such losses seriously allows a mourning process to begin. Some losses are obviously distressing and significant: 'I lost my baby,' or 'I never married,' for example, have life-long effects which may be remembered painfully every day. Working through such unresolved losses with the counsellor can mean that the illness or disability becomes less troublesome since it is no longer taking place in the context of unacknowledged grief and anger relating to a quite different problem.

Acknowledging losses enables client and counsellor to sort out what has to be given up and what can be salvaged; what is inevitably lost as a result of the illness and what is just a reaction to the illness. Often people take time to cope with new disabilities. Frustration and anger are predictable responses to unwanted changes; they may also be a sign that work is in progress that will help to resolve the situation. Eventually the fight has to be 'lost' or 'given up' and the loss 'accepted'; people fear this process and may resist it as long as possible. Where this happens, it is often because the loss has symbolic meaning; not just being unable to use a hand but being useless; not just unable to maintain an erection but being unloved and unlovable. Initially people often react to practical losses by refusing to make changes which would make their lives better; there is often a particularly difficult period between the start of the problem (for example, losing balance) and discovering or accepting a solution (such as a Zimmer frame or a wheelchair). This period may last several years, though it may be less. A grieving process has to take place to allow acceptance of the high cost to the psyche of the 'solution'.

Some problems and losses simply have to be grieved and the counsellor can help by accompanying the person through the process. Significant losses always evoke earlier losses; so loss of a leg, for example, may bring feelings of being abandoned, alone, not understood which were experienced with a childhood loss. New losses may remind the person of the loss of a loved person, or of the loss of the closeness to their mother when she went back to work, or had a new baby; or of the loss of a father in childhood, for example. Talking about such losses with a counsellor can bring relief by separating out the real, present-day loss from much more frightening phantasies of loss such as the sense of the world falling apart, or the loss of everything worth having. Sometimes not only mood but also behaviour changes, and relationships may change for the better too.

In 'Mourning and its relation to manic-depressive states', Klein (1940) quotes Freud's 'Mourning and melancholia'. She refers to the need for reality testing as an essential part of the work of mourning for a lost object (that is, a person, or loved part of a person):

> Each single one of the memories and expectations in which the libido is bound to the object is brought up and hypercathected, and detachment of the libido is accomplished in respect of it. Why this compromise by which the command of reality is carried out piecemeal should be so extraordinarily painful is not at all easy to explain … . (Freud, 1915/17, p. 245)

Klein's 'contention is that the child goes through states of mind comparable to the mourning of the adult, or rather, that this early mourning is revived whenever grief is experienced in later life. The most important of the methods by which the child overcomes his states of mourning, is, in my view, the testing of reality; this process, however, as Freud stresses, is part of the work of mourning' (Klein, 1940, p. 344). She describes her view of the infant's state of mind at weaning:

> The object which is being mourned is the mother's breast and all that the breast and the milk have come to stand for in the infant's mind: namely, love, goodness and security. All these are felt by the baby to be lost, and lost as a result of his own uncontrollable greedy and destructive phantasies and impulses against his mother's breasts. Further distress about impending loss (this time of both parents) arises out of the Oedipus situation … The circle of loved objects who are attacked in phantasy, and whose loss is therefore feared, widens owing to the child's ambivalent relations to his brothers and sisters. The aggression against phantasy brothers and sisters … also gives rise to feelings of guilt and loss. The sorrow and concern about the feared loss of the 'good' objects … is, in my experience, the deepest source of painful conflicts … in the child's relations to people in general. (Klein, 1940, p. 345)

Loss of part of the body, or of part of the body's functioning resonates with earlier infantile losses and often brings fears of loss of 'love, goodness and security'. People often talk in terms of having 'lost everything' when that is clearly not true. Realistic assessment of the loss is an essential part of the work. In addition, when people have reacted to their losses by acting out, which they often do, acknowledging and understanding their behaviour can lead to insight and subsequent changes that reduce the risk of alienating others. People often feel that they can cope with their partner having an illness, but not with their bad moods and aggressive behaviour.

Understanding the grieving process can reduce the fear of the unavoidable frustrations that go along with the losses of a progressive condition. It can help to know that the process of mourning takes time; that each frustration is part of testing a new reality; work which does not have to be done endlessly over and over again. It can help people to know that the first year after a loss is likely to be the worst; that the second year is up and down but better, and that by the end of the second year the outlook is improved. One of the ways of fighting perception of change is by denying that time is passing; but losing a sense of time passing contributes to the sense of being trapped in a nightmare forever. Counselling can help to restore a sense of time passing, by helping clients to bear it and by uncovering and reminding them of their capacity to overcome past losses.

For grieving to take place and the person to regain contact with current reality, each element of loss or change needs to be brought to mind and the emotions attached to it experienced. They then change in their own time to fit the new reality. Without this work of mourning, people can continue to react in inappropriate ways, attempting to avoid feelings by avoiding certain thoughts, situations or triggers. Denial is part of the outward expression of this. Denial is normal as a first reaction to an unwanted change, as a way of preventing the mind being too overwhelmed by unmanageable feelings. Denial gives a certain breathing space. But gradually, denial needs to be replaced with acknowledgement and acceptance if the person is not to remain out of touch with reality. The deceit involved in denial is hard work and it can be a relief to give it up. The fears underlying denial are usually worse than reality. When they can be faced, acceptance of reality itself eventually comes as a relief. The discrepancy between phantasy and reality is brought to light with the question, 'What exactly is it that the person is denying?'. To discover 'it' is just an illness or disability that can be borne and not the Dreaded Lurgi of a childhood nightmare can be a huge relief.

Conclusion

Phantasies that are part of the psyche influence the way that an individual will manage an illness and disability, their own or another's. Exploring the significance of an illness, symptom or disability can affect wellbeing, for the person who has the condition and for those around them. People can live relatively well with disabling conditions, just as they can live unhappily in perfect physical health. Counselling can help to change the meaning of an illness or disability for all concerned. In addition, where life is made more difficult or uncomfortable by an illness or disability and there is no solution to the problems raised, counselling can help people to bear the feelings involved and may reduce blame and recriminations.

Understanding some of the underlying psychodynamics of illness and disability can help a counsellor to make sense of a client's reactions, and of their own too.

Counsellors need to work on their own attitudes, beliefs and understanding of illness and disability, preferably before being faced with affected clients. Recognising and processing their own phantasies and experiences of illness or disability in supervision and personal therapy when relevant will also enhance the counsellor's therapeutic potential.

Counselling people with chronic illnesses or disabilities can be very rewarding. One client may have thought for a long time about their condition and have a lot to teach the counsellor about it; another may not have thought much about it, particularly if the condition is new, and the counsellor can accompany the client as they open up new thoughts and discoveries about themselves and their situation. People get used to illness and to disability and they learn to tolerate even dramatic changes; particularly if the client is facing some condition which has a stigma attached, the support of a counsellor during the process of accommodation can be hugely appreciated. For the counsellor, the process can be educational as well as emotionally satisfying, providing the opportunity to discover new priorities for their own life at the same time as enhancing the lives of others.

REFERENCES

Freud, S. (1915/17). 'Mourning and melancholia.' In J. Strachey (ed.), *The Standard Edition of the Complete Psychological Works of Sigmund Freud, Volume XIV*. London: Hogarth.

Gray, A. (1994). *An Introduction to the Therapeutic Frame*. London: Brunner-Routledge.

Hunter, V. (1996). 'An interview with Hanna Segal'. *Psychoanalytic Review*, 80: 1, 1–28.

Klein, M. (1940). 'Mourning and its relation to manic-depressive states'. In *The Writings of Melanie Klein* (1975), *Love, Guilt and Reparation and Other Works (1921–45)*. London: Hogarth, pp. 344–69.

Segal, J. C. (1996). 'Whose disability? Counter-transference in work with people with disabilities'. *Psychodynamic Counselling*, 2: 2, 155–66.

No Words to Say It: Psychodynamic Counselling when Language Is Impaired

Shula Wilson

Introduction

There are many ways in which a sense of belonging is established in society. Sharing a cultural history, social values, understanding social mores, having similar physical characteristics, religion, and dress code are some of the inclusion factors that foster a sense of merger. However, the most important inclusion factor is the ability to communicate, to understand and be understood by others, to speak the same language. Without some or all of these similarities and abilities an individual is likely to experience the feeling of being 'an outsider' and indeed will be treated by others as such. This chapter will address the experience of being 'an outsider' particularly with respect to communication, through examining the experience of people disabled by speech impediments and the challenge to counsellors in working with such clients. Because counselling is mainly a 'talking cure' counsellors' expectation of the process of therapy, and use of their familiar skills, must be re-evaluated when faced with a client who cannot speak or articulate words clearly. The perception of disability as an 'eternal transitional phase' will be discussed as being a subtle form of exclusion, using an analogy of adolescence.

In order to be clear about language use, the following working definitions will be used throughout the chapter: *impairment* to mean a medical or physical condition, *disability* to mean limited functioning as a result of impairment or lack of adequate facilities, or both.

On being an outsider

Language, like clothes, is one of the most salient markers of 'the state of belonging'. The way an individual is 'wearing' a language, identifying, feeling and making use of it would indicate to self and others the degree to which they belong in any given context or time. The 'belonging' continuum stretches from full membership of the central majority group to being an outsider or even an outcast. Most of the emotional reactions to communication difficulties are closely interwoven with fear and anxieties intrinsic within the minority–majority relationship. The members of the outsider's minority group are often experienced by the majority group as a threat, triggered by the fear of the unknown and the unfamiliar (as in xenophobia). This is perpetuated by the outsider's actual limited access to sources of knowledge and information as a result of their communication difficulty.

In his well known tale 'The Ugly Duckling' the Danish author Hans Christian Andersen (1928) describes the suffering endured by a duckling that was not a duckling but a cygnet (a baby swan) that was rejected for being different. The mother duck's attempts to protect him were unsuccessful; she could not stop the aggressive hostility provoked by the 'duckling's' different appearance. He had to flee in search of his *own kind.*

The story of the 'odd' duckling illustrates a common experience endured by disabled people. But unlike the duckling in the tale, who finds respite in locating the swans, the group to which he belongs, there is no obvious group for disabled people to find. Role models within their immediate environment may be limited and there is a constant reminder of their difference. Regardless of how much they are loved and accepted by their family, being a stranger in a wider social group can hinder and damage the individual's identity and sense of self.

In writing *about* disability Olkin (1999, p. vii) describes her experience: 'I am bicultural. I live in two worlds – the non-disabled majority and my minority group's world of the disability community.' She adds that for 30 years she desperately tried to pass herself off as 'normal', part of the majority, despite the effects of childhood polio. Eventually she managed to admit to herself that she was a person with a disability and to accept her disabled identity. Discovering a peer group of other disabled people brought her great relief.

Impaired communication and the therapeutic relationship

Often, when communication is impaired, counsellors and psychotherapists find themselves questioning the relevance and the effectiveness of a 'talking treatment' such as psychotherapy. The challenge is how to develop a therapeutic relationship when the verbal dialogue is impaired. One of the concerns is whether or not the frustrations that ensue will add to the person's difficulties rather than help to resolve them.

Lorna was one of the first disabled people I met. She was a young woman in a wheelchair with a big bib to soak her dribble. Spasms and involuntary movements prevented her from controlling the use of her hands, which meant that she was dependent on others for feeding, toileting, washing, dressing and any other physical need she might have. Her speech was slurred, which made it difficult for me to understand. Feeling out of control due to my perceived inability to communicate with Lorna, I reverted to the 'demand and control mode' and started to ask questions. One such question was: 'If by magic you could be granted one thing, what would it be?'. I was expecting her to wish for the ability to walk or for the use of her hands, but she wished for clear speech. I was surprised at the time, as I had not realised then that people with multiple disabilities might consider impaired communication to be the worst aspect of their condition.

Greeley (1996), in her moving autobiography, writes: 'The part of my disability which causes me the most frustration is the way my speech and swallowing have been, and are, affected. This means that both communication through speech and socialising while having a meal are harder to carry out. In the past I have been very depressed about it' (p. 97). Being unable to communicate means isolation and frustration. Isolation is a widely used method of punishment, particularly solitary confinement. Dostoevsky's experience of penal servitude, as told by Storr, permanently influenced his view of human nature. Seeing convicts, who for years had been ruthlessly crushed, suddenly break out and assert their own personalities, often in a violent and irrational fashion, made him realise that individual self-expression or self-realisation was a basic human need (Storr, 1989, p. 59). Dostoevsky observed people who were silenced by their environment; they had the physical ability to speak, but their survival was dependent on complete suppression of self-expression. This led him to the insight that life loses its value without the capacity for self-expression.

In her autobiography, Barbars Newborn (1997), who suffered a stroke at the age of 21, describes the experience of aphasia; the impaired ability to use and understand language: 'the loss of language devastated me, obliterated my relationships with others and myself. I lost my connection with everything and everyone. In time I would forget myself, because I did not have any words to remind me who I was.' Newborn's testament reveals that lack of language not only severs communication with others, but more importantly it often damages the sense of self. Impaired speech limits the ways in which people can assert their personality.

Countertransference and the therapist's anxiety

When a client's communication is impaired, the therapist's anxiety is heightened; it leaves the therapeutic dyad exposed, bereft of the protective cover of language which, as well as being a means of exchange and interaction, also offers defensive options. It has the potential to hide thoughts and feelings as well as reveal them.

Young (1994), when discussing the problem of communicating the content of phantasies, quotes Riviere's (1952) concerns: 'they are apt to produce a strong impression of unreality and untruth' (p. 20). In his commentary, Young points out the elusive and subjective nature of the individual's inner world: 'This is because when we write or speak about phantasies we are clothing preverbal and very primitive mental processes in the language of words in dictionaries' (p. 80). Taking Young's metaphor of language as clothing a step further, the body that the clothes are supposed to protect could represent the raw internal world of both client and therapist. When a client's language is impaired, it is often therapists who may feel naked and exposed. For the verbally disabled client this is a familiar everyday experience for which they have developed some coping mechanisms, while for the therapist the loss of language as the main therapeutic tool may provoke anxiety. They are deprived of words, the protective mechanism by which they manage and express their own and their client's raw internal processes. As part of their countertransference reaction, therapists may feel vulnerable, frustrated and afraid; without language to cover and control the raw unconscious world, an eruption of phantasies and of chaos threatens. Words are the vessels that contain our thoughts and emotions. When these words-vessels are damaged or non-functioning, there is nothing to hold the potentially overwhelming or dangerous content, rendering counsellors and therapists vulnerable to unprocessed and uncontained emotions. The therapist's experience when language is missing could be compared to that of an autistic person, who feels bombarded with anxiety provoking and inexplicable messages without knowing how to process them.

Donna Williams (1992), who suffers from autism, relates her thoughts on the matter: 'for language to have any meaning one must be able to relate to it. For me, when the directness of relating is too great, the walls go up' (p. 182). At times, therapists who find themselves trying to communicate with a client without the mediation of clear language may share Williams' experience of wishing to hide behind walls, longing for the 'protective clothing' of language, as without it the interaction may feel too direct. This in turn can lead the therapist to let defences take over. When the use of language is impaired, both client and therapist grapple with the challenge to express themselves and understand each other without words to convey meaning.

Therapists or other helpers often find that managing the feelings of being deskilled and incompetent when faced with clients' impaired communication is highly stressful. It is difficult to bear such exposure for any length of time and defences inevitably emerge. One such form of defence is the perception of the disabled person as an 'unfinished human being', as if still in a transitional state, not yet fully formed or even as being unworthy of or beyond help.

The perception of the outsider as adolescent, in a transitional state

Disabled people are often infantilised. The image of the 'adult' as a whole object assumes an accomplished level of physical and mental functioning, a person who looks and performs like 'one of us'. When an individual is not performing to the level generally expected of adults, a question may arise as to whether or not this person is a 'real' adult, or more poignantly, 'Is this being really one of us?'. Observing an adult human being who has either a physical or lingual impairment may bring about confusion as to how such a person should be classified. The need to classify that may lead to inclusion or exclusion is a defensive reaction against the fear of 'the other'. It is also about the fear of contamination, of becoming like the impaired person. The disturbance created by the presence of impaired communication may also lead to a form of defensive reaction, in which basic, raw fears are projected onto those who are perceived as different. The process of 'projective identification' (Klein, 1948) is the most primitive form of unconscious interaction. It occurs when parts of the self are unconsciously projected into the other, who in turn identifies with the projected parts. The 'other' then becomes a threat, which opens the way to demonising differences, to justifying persecution and to activating predatory and existential death anxiety.

Foreign travel provides us with a direct experience of this phenomenon, when there is a language difference. The frustration and anxiety experienced by not being understood may cause regression to a less sophisticated, more primitive state of mind in which the limited opportunity for self-expression results in childlike speech or shouting to be understood. Reflecting on such experience could offer the therapist some insight into the way communication difficulties could cause most people to regress to an earlier developmental stage. Therapists' ability to identify their own frustration when feeling like outsiders can be used productively in the therapeutic interaction.

Dan lives in a care-home in a small town. He has his own room and a key worker, Nick, helps him with his daily needs. Dan is 23; he was born with cerebral palsy and has little control over his body. He operates an electric wheelchair and a specially adapted computer with his left hand. In order for Dan to operate the computer, a wrist-switch is fastened to the palm of his left hand that can be pressed with his fingers. For all other physical functions and needs he is entirely dependent on others.

Dan was referred for counselling by his key worker at the day centre. Before I met him the centre's occupational therapist approached me to say that she would set up Dan's computer in the counselling room. She explained that it is the means by which he communicates. The first session was a trial for both of us. I was anxious about communicating with a client who, as I was told, could not speak. The presence of the computer disturbed me; an inanimate object seemed to hold all the power. Dan's head was on the table; a wire linked the computer to his wrist. When he was trying to speak, Dan produced sounds that barely resembled words. He was just about able to indicate 'yes' and 'no'.

At our first session everything went wrong. It took Dan quite a while and a great deal of frustration to find the right manoeuvre that would allow the electric wheelchair into the small consulting room. The wires came off the wrist-switch. I started to feel anxious. Dan became anxious; it did not feel safe. He asked for the occupational therapist and for his key worker. My hesitation and inadequacy in communicating with him did not reassure him. I acknowledged the difficulties we were both experiencing and refrained from calling for help. Dan calmed down and presented me with a few typed pages. I was still too anxious to decode or interpret the message in Dan's action; instead I read the typed message. At last, some communication I can understand! While I was reading, Dan was trying to speak. After several attempts I thought I was hearing: 'I want to talk to you.' When I repeated the words, Dan indicated: 'Yes'. Then he typed: 'I never want to see Liz again.' The relationship with Liz was the main issue discussed in the typed pages. She had promised Dan that they would get married, but her parents did not approve. Dan was unconsciously reminded of his angry feelings about Liz by his disappointment at the way I was managing the session. Like Liz, who promised to love him but then left, I was offering to help him but was too anxious to be of much use. I said as much to Dan. At the end of the session Dan typed: 'Will you help me?'. What made Dan feel that despite my inadequacies I might be of help to him? Perhaps he was able to tolerate my bewildered reaction, because as a 'veteran' of impaired speech he is used to people struggling with the communication difficulty and reacting with some level of bewilderment.

The first step towards building trust had been to resist the temptation to call for the help of someone familiar who would act as Dan's interpreter. The next was to acknowledge my shortcomings and to focus on listening and decoding Dan's messages.

Allowing a third party, such as an interpreter, into a dyad can unbalance and disturb most relationships. It compromises privacy and confidentiality and risks the erosion of trust. When the client, the therapist, or both are unsure about the therapist's ability to function, such as at my first meeting with Dan, involving a third party can momentarily calm the tension and reduce anxiety. But the development of intimacy and trust will be impaired and the therapist will be seen as less dependable. In some instances the therapist needs support from others to enhance the therapeutic relationship, while endeavouring to develop the stamina needed to absorb and contain the impact of the client's communication difficulties. However, even if the therapist does not understand much of the client's speech, patience and perseverance will be valued.

In the case of Dan we were an unusual 'ménage à trois'; we were three in the room – Dan, the computer and I, the therapist. The computer had a big sign attached to it saying: 'WHAT I WRITE IS PRIVATE, DO NOT READ THE SCREEN.' The therapeutic relationship was triangular including the computer. The computer/interpreter created a chain of dependencies. First, the occupational therapist who provided technical support, then the client who, sensing my inadequacy, offered 'crutches' by producing ready-typed material. My 'disability' was exposed and the client reversed roles by offering support to me.

As the anxiety about the computer subsided I was able to notice that our sitting arrangement actually resembled a triangle. The computer was on the table and Dan and I sat side by side, facing it. He was typing: 'Last Friday, Nick, my key worker, went sick over the weekend; I was alone.' I replied: 'You are sorry for Nick's troubles and also for yourself, as you feel lonely without him. Perhaps you are also saying to me that you are feeling lonely here because I am paying attention to the computer, rather than to you.' Dan responded with a big smile of relief on his face and typed: 'I like Nick very much, he knows everything about me.' This positive transference response could be seen as a validation of the interpretation. A few weeks later Dan was typing: 'Next week I will have a week off.' This comment made me feel surprised and guilty at the same time. I said: 'By telling me that you will not be here next week, you are also reminding me that we discussed how we deal with breaks and missed sessions.' I was moved by Dan's clear assertion. I became aware of my protective countertransference; I perceived Dan as being in transition, not yet an adult. I had allowed his impaired speech to limit my expectations and probably projected onto him a degree of dependency, which I believe was triggered by my own sense of help-lessness (as well as my dependence on the skills of the occupational therapist to manage the technology).

At the end of each session Dan saved the text created, and produced it again at the beginning of the next session. Then one day I could not find the computer and Dan indicated that it had been left on the ambulance. This was a challenge and threat to me, not to have a third party present with us in the room. I realised that I had became accustomed to, and perhaps also dependent on, the presence of that third eye and voice. We kept the same arrangement, sitting side by side in front of the empty table, only this time we were looking at each other, rather than at the screen. I said: 'Perhaps the computer was left because you are a bit fed up with it. Although the computer helps you to be precise and accurate, it is also coming between us.' At the time I did not admit that I also was a bit 'fed up' with the computer's lengthy and tedious process. It seems likely that Dan knew that I was talking about myself as well. That session, despite Dan having to repeat each word several times before I could understand it, we did commu-nicate directly without the machine, despite a few words being lost or misun-derstood. Dan talked about his mother and sister. His sister has been busy, working too hard and Dan was worried about her. He also said he loves her. Dan's worry about his sister may also have reflected his concern about the ther-apist working too hard.

It may seem paradoxical that Dan had waited patiently for me to master the computer, only so that he could 'drop' it. From a developmental perspective the computer had been invested with the role of a transitional object (Winnicott, 1958), representing mother or therapist in their absence, thus fulfilling the adaptive function in working through the loss of the mother and the temporary loss of the therapist between sessions and during breaks. The computer provided comfort and security as Dan processed his relationship with the therapist until the internalisation of a trusting relationship served to transform dependency into self-reliance, and only then was he able to let go of the inanimate object.

Adolescence as a transitional state

Unlike people in exile who can hold on to memories and legends of their home-land, people such as Dan who have been born with impairment have no 'lost homeland' to dream about or long for. They rarely have a role model within their immediate environment to follow or draw inspiration from. Hence some speech impaired people may never have had the necessary encouragement to reach adulthood. Yet people who have experienced adulthood, like those who acquired speech impairment later in life (due to stroke or accident) may find themselves unprepared for life as adults without their familiar ability to commu-nicate. This may cause them to regress to an early developmental stage in which language has not yet fully formed.

The process of adolescence provides a way of conceptualising the transitional state imposed by impaired communication. Adolescence is a time of transition, during which the young person prepares to embrace the autonomy and responsibility of adulthood and to let go of the security, familiarity and dependency of childhood. Blos (1967) identified the following set of tasks to be completed in order for the young person to establish his or her autonomy and membership of the majority group.

The first task is to disengage from parental figures both as love objects and as authority figures

Separation difficulties are universal regardless of physical and mental ability or of being outsiders or full members of the community. However, disabled young people face an additional practical hurdle. They are rarely allowed to spend time unsupervised; therefore opportunities for experimenting and measuring their strength against that of peers, communicating, developing relationships and exploring their sexuality may be limited. Due to limited peer group contact, most people with impaired communication tend to be dependent on authority figures and paid helpers for social interaction and contact with the outside world.

Parents of disabled children may be torn between the desire to protect their child and compensate for the physical or lingual impairment and the recognition that their child needs to develop their own strength and social identity. The success or otherwise of the disengagement process depends on the extent to which parents, or professionals in a parental role such as therapists, are able to resolve their own internal conflict. When clients struggle with communication difficulties, the countertransference may come as an echo of the parental conflict between the desire to compensate and the task of enabling. Becoming aware of this parallel process can help therapists to monitor their own reactions and emotions triggered by the speech impaired, outsider-client. Recognising the parental conflict will also offer an insight into the client's world.

The second task is to let go of the wish to change the unchangeable

It is questionable whether this task can or should ever be fully completed. Who decides what is and what is not changeable? Is the wish to undergo orthopaedic or cosmetic surgery in order to improve the appearance and functioning of the body an indication of an incomplete task of adolescence? Can the wish to change the attitudes of others be included as part of this task?

Rather then letting go of the wish to change it might be better to develop the capacity to engage in ongoing evaluation of wishes and aspirations. The late Christopher Reeves, the actor who played 'Superman', who became paralysed in a riding accident, had dedicated his life to 'changing the unchangeable'. He actively challenged his prognosis and looked for treatments that would enable him to walk again. Such a reaction could indicate either an incomplete developmental process which became stuck at the second task of adolescence, or a positive survival mechanism in which holding on to hope is the only way to deal with an otherwise unbearable situation.

Clients who experience communication impairment find themselves oscillating between the need to adapt and accept their limitations and the need to assert their own identity and sense of self and strive towards change. The therapist must be tolerant of this ambivalence and accept both attempts to resolve internal conflict.

The third task is to ensure continuation with the past

There is a somewhat paradoxical element hidden in this task, which is about holding on to something that is no more. A ritualistic structure, such as mourning, can offer a useful framework for establishing and maintaining continuity with the past. Barbara Newborn (1997), who became aphasic after a stroke, shares her realisation that 'only when I gave myself permission to grieve for the loss of myself could I go on with the rest of my life. The paradox was that the old me, with all its intense wants and desires, was the means for discovering my new fuller self' (p. 81). Newborn describes how the grieving process acts as a 'rite of passage'. In order to move on to the next phase, the full extent and significance of the loss must be faced and worked through.

A difficult but essential aspect of the maturation process is a willingness to acknowledge pain and sadness while letting go of unfulfilled hopes and wishes. Developing the ability to recognise the past as part of oneself, yet living in the present and looking ahead to the future, may prove a challenge when communication is impaired. The wish for a new beginning may lead to using denial as a defence against the pain of loss by attempting to sever links with the past. Continuity with the past means keeping the links alive while moving forward. It may be difficult to find ways of bridging past and present. The onset of disability is a trauma, an event for which the psyche is unprepared. As with other traumatic experiences the unmanageable feelings are relegated to the unconscious, leaving only the psychological shell of experience.

One striking example is the self-imposed silence of many Holocaust survivors who try to live as if nothing had happened, who have never told their story. Now the second and third generations are desperately searching to find some links with their past, through piecing together untold stories of the parents and grandparents, confronting their pain and weaving it into the present.

Becoming disabled during adulthood may sever or damage the individual's sense of historical continuity, splitting the perception of self into two: the good, non-disabled past, and the bad, new present. Losing the ability to speak may deepen the past–present split. Klein (1952) describes such a reaction as an aspect of the paranoid-schizoid position that may cause a regression into an earlier developmental stage. The impairment leads to regression that may link the person to other aspects of arrested development. The therapeutic task at this stage is to gain an understanding of the way traumatic events may have affected the client. This is a necessary precursor to creating a bridge across the chasm that exists in relation to denied or shattered hopes, the reality of the present and the potential for the future. Once the gap has been recognised and acknowledged by the therapist and the client, the process of linking between present and the past can begin.

There is often a tension between the seductive, familiar passivity of the wish to remain stuck in the past, and the energy generated by the anger associated with severing links with it altogether. The attempt to forget the past is a form of denial used to defend against the unbearable pain of loss. The therapist must enable the client to connect to the past while recognising the wish for a less painful existence.

The concept of adolescence as the pathway towards maturation offers a theoretical framework that facilitates understanding of the regressive impact of impaired communication, which opens the way for thinking about the possibilities of bridging the past–present split within the self.

The fourth and last task is to consolidate gender identity and sexual preference

There is sometimes a reluctance to acknowledge disabled people as sexual beings, branding them as *a*sexual beings or oddities. However, even when sexuality is accepted, there are many practical and cultural obstacles on their way to exploring sexuality and forming sexual relationships.

Striving towards individuation and developing a sexual identity are essential components in the human struggle towards maturity. Being disabled may add more obstacles to achieving adulthood.

Gill was born with cerebral palsy that resulted in complete paralysis apart from some head movements. She had no speech at all. At the age of 20 her occupational thera- pist at the day centre provided her with a computerised speech device that enabled her to express herself in words for the first time in her life. Initially, the staff were pleased with Gill's newly acquired ability; she was usually quiet and reserved, well liked by every one. Some days later however, several staff members approached the manager demanding that the speech device be withdrawn from Gill. They complained that she was using 'dirty language' and abusive swear-words. It seemed to them that this speech device had unleashed a monster. They wanted to 'put the Genie back into the bottle'. The manager helped them to realise that what they were hearing was not the voice of a perverted adult, but an uncontrolled burst of the words, thoughts and feel- ings that had never been expressed. The words were those that children whisper to friends out of public earshot. It seemed that the Gill needed to clear away the 'sexual blockage' before she could use her device for interactive communication. Gill was not aware of the difference between language used in private and in public. She had no inhibitions, as she had never experienced the reaction of others to her verbal expres- sion. As a result, Gill was taken through an intensive language awareness develop- ment programme that helped her to reach an interaction level suited to her age.

Blackwell-Stratten et al. (1988) argue that unlike the non-disabled woman, who has societally sanctioned roles as mother and wife and even career woman, the disabled woman has no clearly identifiable adult roles. Her sexuality, potential for sexual fantasy and procreation are doubted or even scorned. Thus disabled women are perceived as having lost not only some of their ability, but also some of their womanhood.

Confused identity

The question: 'Who am I?' dominates the human quest for self-knowledge and encapsulates the focus of theoretical debate that emanates from a myriad psychoanalytic sources. Communication difficulties that erect a social barrier add considerable complexity to the process of achieving a consolidated identity. Developing a sense of individual identity involves loss. For the person with communication difficulties this could be described as a loss of fusion. McDougall (1989) describes the individuation process as a repression of the contradictory wish to be an individual while remaining an indissoluble part of the 'other'; this longing is subsequently compensated by the acquisition of an unwavering sense of individual identity.

Being different because of impairment, while in a transitional phase, is not all negative. For example, the fluidity of a transitional state could facilitate hope and optimism and encourage belief in the possibility of change. Communication difficulties have the potential to be resolved and integration may gradually become a reality. However, being different tends to provoke anxiety for self and others. Impaired communication may bring about a sense of helplessness and lack of control that promotes denial. The conscious and unconscious protective measures taken against the predatory fear of what is not understood and therefore unknown vary according to the personal history and life context of each individual. However, individuals who assume responsibility for their predicament can often bring about change. If a client struggles with speech it is tempting for the therapist to complete half-articulated sentences, accentuating their power and authority. Projective processes amplify the dependence that is intrinsic to a transitional phase and such action is better resisted in the best interest of the client, in order to promote independence rather than passivity and dependency.

Disability provokes attention from others that is not always helpful or desirable. Therefore some disabled people, or those affected by disability such as their parents, may be inclined to avoid being identified as disabled. Receiving and internalising positive attitudes and responses communicated by others form an important aspect of self-esteem. Negative introjects on the other hand may impair disabled individuals' belief in their ability. Lussier (1960) writes about the analysis of a boy, Peter, who was born with deformed and very short arms. Peter did not perceive himself as incapacitated in any way. He refused to use artificial limbs and insisted on exposing and using his 'different' arms; he accepted his physical condition as a permanent and positive state. The problem he struggled with was the need to prove to others, mainly his parents, that although he was not perfect, he was *normal*, like all other children or even better. Difference is in 'the eye of the beholder' (Lussier, 1980).

Conclusion

Counsellors and therapists need to use their familiar skills and experience when working with people who have communication difficulties that render them outsiders to some communities but with an enhanced awareness of the dynamics of difference. Countertransference responses will be powerful and wide ranging: incompetence, frustration, rage, despair and protectiveness are just a few examples. Tuning into, discussing and processing the countertransference will be an essential aspect of the work; it will provide many clues to the experience of the client, often uncomfortable and sometimes unbearable. Patience, openness and a level of courage will be essential if the client is ultimately to be heard and understood. Recognising that a newly acquired impairment, whether physical or lingual, propels the client into a transitional state, and believing that it can be transcended, is essential for creating safe-holding and to inspire confidence in the counselling relationship. Courage and support are needed to help the client re-experience a life stage like adolescence and to climb the steps towards becoming an autonomous adult. Therapists can provide that support and reap the rewards of seeing their clients mourn the past and grow towards the future.

REFERENCES

Andersen, H. C. (1928). *Andersen's Fairy Tales*. London: Shaw.

Blackwell-Stratten, M., Bestin, M. L., Mayerson, A. B. and Baily, S. (1988). 'Smashin Icons'. In M. Fine and A. Asch (eds), *Women with Disability: Essays in Psychology, Culture and Politics*. Philadelphia, PA: Temple University Press.

Blos, P. (1967). 'The second individuation process of adolescence'. *Psychoanalytic Study of the Child*, 22, 162–86.

Greeley, E. (1996). *The Unclear Path*. London: Hodder & Stoughton.

Klein, M. (1948). *Contributions to Psychoanalysis*. London: Hogarth.

Klein, M. (1952). 'The origins of transference'. *International Journal of Psychoanalysis*, 23, reprinted in J. Mitchell (ed.) (1986), *The Selected Melanie Klein*. Harmondsworth: Penguin.

Lussier, A. (1960) 'The analysis of a boy with congenital deformity'. *Psychoanalytic Study of the Child*, 15, 430–53.

Lussier, A. (1980). 'The physical handicap and the body ego'. *International Journal of Psychoanalysis*, 61, 179–85.

McDougall, J. (1989). *Theatres of the Body*. London: Free Association.

Newborn, B. (1997). *Return to Ithaca*. Rockport, MA: Element.

Olkin, R. (1999). *What Psychotherapists Should Know About Disability*. New York: Guildford.

Riviere, J. (1952) 'General introduction'. In M. Klein et al., *Developments in Psychoanalysis*. London: Hogarth.

Storr, A. (1989). *Solitude: A Return to the Self*. London: HarperCollins.

Williams, D. (1992). *Nobody Nowhere*. London: Bantam.

Winnicott, D. (1958). 'Metapsychological and clinical aspects of regression within the psychoanalytical set-up'. *International Journal of Psychoanalysis*, 36: 1, 6–26.

Young, R. M. (1994). *Mental Space*. London: Process.

Psychodynamic Counselling with Older People

Hilary Wellington

Introduction

This chapter will explore challenges and possibilities for working psychodynamically with older people, defined as people past statutory retirement age. This is a relatively small field, in terms of the body of literature, the number of people seeking therapy and the number of counsellors working with older people. Older clients sometimes seek bereavement counselling in settings such as Cruse, offering person-centred counselling. Some older people receive therapeutic support through clinical psychology or specialist nursing rather than through professional counselling. The 2001 census figures indicate there are over 10.8 million older people living in the United Kingdom, with projected figures for an increase in the number of people over pensionable age to 13.1 million by 2021 (www.silvesurfers.org). Older people are under-represented in the client population at present, but there is potential for growth in their demand for therapeutic services. This is reinforced by suggestions that people now reaching older age are more likely than their predecessors to explore alternatives to mainstream biomedical and social services support, and less likely to accept state help at face value.

The generations aged over 60 in Western Europe today include people who have experienced particular hardships such as two world wars, related separation and loss, the Holocaust, or first-generation migration from the West Indies, Asia, East Africa and Eastern Europe. Major life experiences such as miscarriage, stillbirth, adoption, child abuse, domestic violence, homosexuality and suicide were dealt with differently when today's older generations were young. Attitudes towards managing personal trauma have changed. It may be only in recent years that older people have begun to recognise the need to seek counselling to resolve the effects of past experiences. Older people in an ageing society face fears about becoming dependent again, being seen to be a burden on the state or on their family, and of elder abuse or neglect. In addition, threats to physical and psychological wellbeing such as bereavement, chronic pain, and fear of death are all as real as they have ever been. There is much that has the potential to cause older people to seek counselling.

The term 'older people' is somewhat problematic. Older than whom? By incorporating the word 'people', thereby acknowledging their personhood, it is considered to be preferable to terms such as 'the elderly'. Grouping people over 60 together is also problematic in that a very long age span is represented. Within this age group, approximately 5 per cent of people will experience some form of dementia. As this is a significant number of individuals it is essential to include a discussion of this topic. Some meanings, interpretations and therapeutic processes for dementia will therefore be explored within a psychodynamic context. The purpose of this is not to pathologise old age, but to raise awareness about a complementary model for explaining dementia, and to explore psychotherapeutic possibilities which may help people with dementia.

This chapter grew out of a piece of research (Wellington, 2002) which comprised a literature review and a small-scale qualitative survey of psychodynamic counsellors' experiences of working therapeutically with older clients. The chapter is divided into sections accordingly. Firstly there is a review of the developments in psychodynamic thinking about older people and their use of counselling. Leading on from this, the research findings are presented. This is followed by discussion of techniques used in therapy with older people. Finally, key points from each of these sections will be drawn together in some suggestions for good practice with older people.

Drawing on the object relations school of psychodynamic counselling, the research focused on how attachment theory and dependency impact on psychodynamic counselling for older people. Three subquestions were formulated to help to address this core question:

- Is it possible to work therapeutically with older people; and if so, what are the specific opportunities for and challenges of this work?

- What is the significance of attachment theory, both in relation to the difficulties older people experience and in the therapeutic process with older clients?

- What kinds of problems do older people bring to counselling?

Attitudes to older people, and their influence on older people's access to therapy

The question of whether older people can make use of counselling has its roots in Greek philosophy. Aristotle indicates his contempt for older people, calling them 'irresolute, without positive opinions, pessimistic, small-minded and cowardly' (cited in Coleman, 1994, 10–11). He comments in his *Rhetoric* that older people live by memory rather than hope. But should memory and hope be so strongly dichotomised? In contrast, the Roman philosopher Cicero, in his *De Senectute*, emphasised the maturity, insight, authority and wisdom that accompanies old age, acknowledging that older people can make use of earlier experience to learn and grow (cited in Coleman, 1994).

This split is echoed in the writings of the founders of psychodynamic counselling. Freud (1905) asserted that older people would be unable to benefit from psychoanalysis as he considered people to become uneducable over the age of 50, yet Freud was 49 when he wrote this, and continued to work for another 30 years (Richards, 2001)! Indeed Freud, Jung, Erikson and Klein all continued to contribute to psychoanalytic thinking well into later life.

Jung, in contrast, saw later life as a time of consolidation and fulfilment (cited in Richards, 2001). He wrote, 'We cannot live the afternoon of life according to the program of life's morning, for what in the morning was true will at evening be a lie. Whoever carries into the afternoon the law of the morning ... must pay with damage to his soul' (Jung, 1972, 396). Jung also asserted that with the ageing process the emphasis in people's lives changes from doing to being. This aspect of changing identity sounds positive in the way Jung describes it, but identity crises provoked by loss of health, retirement, developing disabilities, caring responsibilities, structured dependency, neglect and bereavement present older people with serious challenges to their psychic health.

Erikson (1965) encompassed Freud's and Jung's views of old age in the final stage of his developmental model by identifying the last crisis as integrity versus despair. Neither of these positions is reached in isolation, but in the context of a lifetime's experience. Although the crisis is often seen in polarised terms, it could be argued that, in reality, both positions may be held within the same person about different aspects of life, or according to mood or external influence. Older people may oscillate between an integrity orientation and a despair orientation. The successful, partial or unsuccessful resolution of previous crises will all contribute towards the outcome of this final task (Coleman, 1993b), thus perhaps influencing how far an older person orients themselves to one or the other position. Erikson's concept of integrity includes three key elements:

● acceptance of life as it has been lived

● abandonment of a self-centred view of life

● acceptance of and loss of fear of death

His 'state of integrity' suggests peace, wholeness and calm. This is in contrast to Klein (1963) who argues that for some clients, integration involves the realisation that there is only oneself to rely on. Any comfort derived from hope of deep connexion or reunification with the mother or a phantasy twin figure representing the other half of the self, is finally surrendered.

Psychological and sociological theory of the 1960s further fed this dichotomy. Cumming and Henry (1961) undertook a cross-sectional study of people of different ages. They concluded that people, as they aged, become more inward-focused, concentrating more on their thoughts and memories than on social engagement and external activity. The outcome of their study, disengagement theory, compares to some extent with Jung's view. However, it may have had significant negative implications for the care and support of older people. It was misappropriated to justify a lack of engagement (Coleman, 1993a) and minimised attempts to understand the internal processes of older people, allowing policy makers to get away with offering unstimulating environments to older people in need of care. Disengagement theory is often contrasted with activity theory (Havighurst, 1963), which argues that older people should continue to act as middle-aged persons. Thus, denial of the ageing process is seen as evidence of successful ageing.

The philosophical, psychotherapeutic and sociological literature referred to here provides some indications as to why older people are frequently excluded from counselling. The influence of Freud's and Cummings and Henry's work, which portrays older people as uneducable or disengaged, is powerful. Jung's work and Erikson's model of integrity are often interpreted as being about serene, happy older people with no need of counselling. Older people who appear to take Erikson's despairing path are frequently seen as too set in their ways to grow and change; or too vulnerable to withstand the rigours of psychodynamic interpretation. As Kalus (1994) suggests, citing Gilleard et al. (1992), 'unfortunately, we live in an ageist society and, while there is little evidence to support the negative stereotype suggesting psychological growth in later life is not possible, older people are still denied access to or under-use counselling and therapy services' (Kalus, 1994, p. 36). Even when older people seek counselling, they can be subjected to censure as the vignette below illustrates.

Mr C wanted to make use of counselling, and quickly established a relationship with his counsellor from whom he derived much support. He was experiencing considerable difficulty in his marriage. After two sessions, he did not return, and shortly afterwards he contacted his counsellor to say that his family had asked him not to continue in counselling because they did not wish family matters to be discussed with a third party. Mr C's psychological growth was thus being sacrificed for the sake of family pride.

There is evidence, however, that older people can and do make use of counselling. One respondent to Wellington (2002) reported how she witnesses sheer determination in her older clients. It seems they are saying through gritted teeth, 'I'm doing this *now*,' recognising that the opportunity has not previously been available to them, and that they wish to come to a point of integration before death. Richards (2001) also offers evidence of clients making use of counselling in later life, which he assesses within an Eriksonian framework of ego integrity versus despair. His work shows how his clients struggled with multiple loss, painfully ambivalent internal processes and fear of a punishing afterlife. While Richards acknowledges that, for one client, 'my hope that the relationship itself would bring him some peace and inner security was never sufficiently fulfilled' (2001, p. 14), it is also evident that the client recalled the sessions with gratitude, like Mr C in the case example above. The vignette below demonstrates how one older client made use of counselling.

Ms M was a psychologically aware woman, who had worked in Social Services all her career. She sought counselling shortly after retirement because she had become filled with a sense of foreboding and was becoming afraid to live her life, even though she wanted to enjoy her retirement. Together she and her counsellor looked back over her life, and discovered a pattern wherein shortly after each significant previous transition such as leaving school or getting married, a personal or family tragedy had occurred. Ms M worked hard on her own in between sessions, and after a short-term contract with her counsellor, declared that now she understood her fear, she could face it, and felt she had accomplished the work she needed to do.

National Service Frameworks

Since 2000, National Service Frameworks (NSFs) have been established in England as policy documents for various user groups, including separate documents for mental health and older people. NSFs are designed to set care standards in the statutory and voluntary sectors. The NSF for Older People published in 2001 set out eight areas in which service standards apply (www.dh.gov.uk (a)). These are:

1. Rooting out discrimination

2. Person-centred care

3. Intermediate care

4. General hospital care

5. Prevention of strokes and better care for people who have suffered a stroke

6. Reduction of falls

7. Mental health in older people

8. Promotion of health and active life

This document was problematic in that, although it set as two of its targets rooting out discrimination and promoting person-centred care, the details of Standard 7 on mental health for older people revealed some critical difficulties. For instance, it focused only on depression and dementia. Drug therapy was demonstrated to be the treatment of choice for dementia. No recognition was made of the emotional impact of grief or chronic pain on older people's emotional welfare, nor of the ongoing suffering some older people experience who have long-term mental health difficulties. The National Service Framework for Mental Health was directed towards people up to the age of 65 only.

In June 2005 the Department of Health published a revised standard for older people's mental health (www.dh.gov.uk (b)). This tackles some of the problems outlined above. For instance it describes how discrimination will be addressed, and makes it clear that the person's needs within their condition, rather than their age, should be the deciding factor in how support is given. There is more acknowledgement of the range of mental health problems older people are likely to experience, and the impact of physical illness on older people's mental health. The standard addresses service provision across health, social care, housing, and voluntary and not-for-profit organisations. However, while general access to psychiatric and to psychological services are listed, specific access to counselling and psychotherapy are not.

Attachment and object relations theory and its application to working with older people

Although attachment theory and object relations theory focus on the relationship between the young child and his or her primary carer, their application to the analysis of the internal world of older people is vital to the counselling process with older clients.

Klein (1940, 1946, 1963) argued that reaching the depressive position was not just a developmental stage, but a process which could take a lifetime to achieve. In her work on mourning (1940), she observed that separation from, or loss of, significant others are serious threats to the integrity between internal and external worlds that can temporarily invoke a return to the paranoid-schizoid position. As a baby copes with persecutory phantasies by building up an internal sense of her/his primary carer, so the need, in situations of loss, is to work towards integrating the lost person within the internal world. In adult life, threats to integrity may also result in a return to the manic defences of infancy.

Bowlby (1969, 1973, 1980) also based his theory of loss on clinical observation of how children deal with attachment and separation. He believed that when attachments are threatened or break down, separation anxiety arises from the conflict between the urge to regain the loved person, and the reality of the loss. The form of attachment a child had with his/her primary carer, and how early separation is negotiated, will have a major influence on how we deal with other losses throughout our lives.

Recent applications of attachment theory to therapeutic work with older people

Terry (1997) links early childhood experience and the internal world of older people. He uses Klein's theory to interpret the internal phantasies of older clients, and focuses on the expression of manic defences and depressive anxieties to analyse reactions to loss of health, body image and mobility, and to explore links between previous experiences of bereavement and current reactions. Persecutory phantasies about death are explored. Terry sees holding and containing these painful feelings for the client as key tasks for carers and counsellors.

Daniel (1997) sees therapy with older clients as essentially similar to work with younger adults (unfinished business) and yet as qualitatively different (different business). She focuses on loss, loneliness and the high incidence of depression among older people. Daniel also analyses the therapeutic relationship. Her case studies show how Klein's theories can relate to work with older clients. She supports Erikson's and Jung's models by questioning attempts to readjust older people into a socioeconomically constructed useful life. As a black therapist working mainly with white clients, Daniel sees that, in addition to differences in age, there are also differences in colour and cultural experience between her and her clients. For clients who have experienced a cultural environment in which blackness is associated with low status, powerlessness and undesirability, Daniel notes how the colour difference is drawn out in transference where she represents the bad object, or one from whom it is difficult to accept help. In turn, her clients' age impacts on her countertransference as she finds herself letting clients get away with comments she would have regarded as politically incorrect and unacceptable in younger clients.

Martindale (1989) discusses the pain and fear of becoming dependent again as old age takes hold. Some conditions of old age will mirror childhood dependency. Needs which were not met may be revived, and the fear of not receiving the support needed in old age can be traumatising. Martindale also explores transference and countertransference in situations where the client is likely to be many years older than the counsellor. He explores the expectations and ability to accept help from a younger counsellor; and the impact of a client mirroring demands of older parents, or raising the counsellor's fears about vulnerability and dependence in old age. He suggests that powerful transference relationships develop between physically dependent older people and their professional carers, when they are longing for the care of a son or daughter who is unavailable. This resonates with the transference experienced by counsellors working with carers, as the following vignette suggests.

Anne's client was caring for his wife who had dementia. Anne would often be told of the high-achieving son living abroad, who could not possibly be expected to come and help with caring tasks. This would be said in a tone of voice which implied that Anne's support was well meaning, but neither needed nor effective. On reflection Anne felt she had become the bad object in the transference, against which her client could vent his anger, when it would have been too painful to express this towards his son. Anne found these exchanges quite harsh, until she realised that they were defences against the pain of rejection by her client's adult child, and her projective identification with his feeling of rejection.

Research: dependency and attachment as continuing or returning difficulties from early life

Arising from the literature review discussed above, Wellington (2002) surveyed psychodynamic counsellors working with older people to assess the impact of dependency and attachment, both as matters which older clients bring to counselling, and in the transferential relationship. Eighteen responses were received, and difficulties relating to early childhood experiences featured in 15 client case studies. Responses for 11 clients were analysed (those where sufficient individual detail was given). The core problems are listed below, with the numbers representing the respective clients:

1. incomplete mothering, not feeling good enough for parents in teenage years

2. unresolved Oedipal difficulties

3. early childhood trauma

4. childhood abuse – sexual, physical and emotional

5. abusive childhood history leading to poor internalisation of supportive adult

6. early in counselling relationship, but expected that childhood experiences will become significant

7. abandonment in early childhood

8. early bereavement (of father)

9. physical and emotional abuse from early childhood

10. being least preferred child in family

11. not feeling/being loved by mother; sibling rivalry so intense it felt as if both could not exist but neither could become close to mother either

Some brief case notes for two of the clients show how their early suffering affected their lives.

Client 1's counsellor reported that he had experienced low self-esteem throughout his life. As he moved into later life, the unresolved hardship of not having felt good enough for his parents re-emerged as not feeling good enough as a husband. A new, but related, theme also could be seen in his marital relationship in that he felt unable to deal with or satisfy his own needs in the marriage, becoming 'down-trodden and puppet-like'.

Client 9 had experienced physical and emotional abuse from early childhood. She now had a neurodegenerative disease, and the fear of becoming dependent again was thus strong. She found it 'hard to trust anyone to care for her when her childhood experiences had involved abuse from one carer and betrayal by the other'.

These themes echo Martindale's work (1989) in that the client about whom Martindale wrote was deeply afraid of becoming dependent again because of pain ensuing from verbal abuse of himself and physical abuse of his siblings by his father. It is suggested that fears of re-experiencing dependency in old age are especially prevalent for those older clients who have had abusive relationships in childhood.

Whilst it can be seen that the results of this research indicate a strong presence of past difficulties arising from attachment and dependency, in three of the 18 clients in the sample, no attachment and dependency problems were reported. Dependency in the current lives of the clients was significant only in six cases.

One respondent to the research saw sexuality and identity as more significant than attachment and dependency.

Transference

All of the counsellors who took part in the survey were under 60, the average age being 42. The questions of whether older clients would be able to work with parental transference with younger counsellors, and as to what kind of counter-transference would arise for the counsellors, were therefore of interest.

Counsellors for Clients 1, 5, 7, 8, 9, 10 and 11 responded to the question of transference. In five cases, the transference was parental, almost entirely 'good enough' or idealised in nature. The counsellor for Client 1 reported that she 'became the mother to him as a child. It was as if he was stuck in childhood and needed to grow psychologically through counselling.' Client 9, who had suffered abuse by one parent and betrayal by the other, related to her female counsellor as she had done to her older brother, with whom she had a caring relationship. The counsellor suggested that this was 'a way, I think, of keeping her relationship with me as a safe place'. This same counsellor also noted 'despite being older than me, clients seemed to relate to me as an older person'.

The following vignette shows how transference changed during the process.

To begin with, Client 11 related to her counsellor like her son of a similar age, who would be 'too young to understand, not having had enough life experience'. She asked at one stage to work with an older counsellor, and this request freed explo-ration of the counselling relationship that helped her insight. Later, the counsellor felt that she saw him as 'the good object' and was able to internalise self-respect from the respect he showed for her.

In the transference both clients and counsellors may take on any age. Daniel (1997) presents the reverse Oedipal relationship in which 'the client has to accept the therapist as the representative of the younger generation and the future. This requires dealing with and overcoming envy of the younger person' (p. 196). One counsellor reported a greater intensity in the way she felt her older clients related to her, compared with the attachment she experienced on the part of younger clients. This made it difficult for her to end the work with them. Richards (2001, p. 13) echoes this in his work with a client who had experienced multiple losses, from whom Richards felt he introjected a need not to face endings.

Countertransference

When asked to describe their countertransference, the counsellors' responses fell into three areas, which could be described as:

- emotions raised in the counsellor which drew out empathy
- other processes within the counselling
- feelings about their own work

For instance, two counsellors commented that they had felt sad and moved by the clients' experiences, particularly at having carried so much pain for so much of their lives. One counsellor reported that her sadness focused around the sense of loss of the good experiences absent in her clients' lives. She also found that, because all her older clients were lonely people, endings were particularly difficult for her and them to work through.

Client 1's counsellor said that she felt responsible for his growth. 'It was as if he became small in the chair opposite me, and projected feelings of neediness into me.' Client 11's counsellor had felt maternal and nurturing towards his client in the earlier stages, and then had a sense of letting her go as she grew in the process.

The tension between being perceived as the wise one to whom older people had turned for help and being chronologically younger with less life experience was expressed by one of the counsellors who said he felt less skilled and less likely to challenge when working with an older client.

A related and somewhat alarming aspect of countertransference is explored in work undertaken by Bernard and Harding Davies (2000). They outline research carried out among middle-aged women who were nurses, social workers or carers, looking after much older women. A strong outcome of the studies reviewed was that women found it harder to look after older women than they did older men; and that they found some older women particularly challenging. Evers (1981, cited in Bernard and Harding Davies, 2000) suggests that this is because caring for men is closer to their conventional experience, and older women may perceive being cared for as an assault on their identity. In the countertransference, female carers are threatened by images of what they might become. Martindale (1989, 1998) explores counsellors' own fears of ageing, and of having ageing parents, which may become conscious while working with older clients. None of the respondents to the research noted any such heightened awareness, and perhaps it is only in a particularly focused study that this could be analysed. Bernard and Harding Davies went on to explore fears about growing old which middle-aged women presented in counselling, which had been triggered by caring for older relatives or patients. The implication is that younger female counsellors will need to monitor their countertransference carefully and explore their own fear of ageing.

To echo Daniel's axis of work with older clients being essentially similar to working with younger clients and yet different too, it seems that the research has suggested themes that are as likely to be presented by clients of any age as they are by older clients. The particular poignancy is that older clients have carried their pain, particularly of childhood abuse, abandonment, neglect and bereavement for so long without resolution, and in the context of becoming dependent again these fearful experiences return to haunt them in a particularly germane way. As Richards suggests in support of Daniel's argument, the problems which older clients bring, while familiar, are 'presented within a context of growing older and the changes in role and identity that are likely to be part of this process. This significantly affects both the exploration of the material and the unfolding relationship between client and counsellor' (Richards, 2001, p. 12).

Life review therapy

There are some specific methods and models that incorporate psychodynamic ideas that can help in working creatively with older clients. Life review therapy is one way of working therapeutically with older people experiencing depression, loss, or a need to make sense of their present circumstances. It is a form of evaluative reminiscence which aims to help older people remember their achievements and to put life's disappointments into perspective. It was advocated by its founder, Butler (1963), as a form of psychodynamic psychotherapy that involves 'systematic reflections in later life with a therapist and client trying to understand a life history's implications for current coping strategies' (Garland, 1994, p. 21). In keeping with psychodynamic therapy, life review focuses on life cycle development, self-reflection and the significance of the past in understanding and evaluating the present.

Butler also described life review as 'a spontaneously occurring mental process prompted by the realisation of approaching dissolution and death, and the inability to maintain one's sense of personal invulnerability, which can result in reorganisation, including achievement, wisdom, serenity and increased self-assurance' (Garland, 1994, p. 21). Butler's ideas mirror Jung's view of the second half of life as a time of greater reflection and internal exploration; and echo the optimistic path of Erikson's model in assuming that successful ageing leads to ego integrity. However, Butler does not make clear how the realisation of approaching death and inability to remain invulnerable lead to positive outcomes. These realisations could lead instead to the despairing polarity of Erikson's model or the kind of loneliness described by Klein. Butler saw independent life review as a process which may contribute to depression among older people, whom he believed were stuck in their internal processes at a guilty or disappointing stage in their lives (Haight, 1992). The therapist must aid the process of coming to terms with past events, and the integration of events, using the review as a means from which to grow and change in the time left. Although Butler saw life review as psychodynamic therapy, he did not propose the use of a transference relationship, or interpretation of defences.

Bornat (1989) summarises views on the efficacy of life review therapy. Citing Coleman, who 'found older people who were unwilling or unhappy reminiscers' (Bornat 1989, p. 282), she argues that the status of reminiscence as a therapeutic method has yet to be proven. However, in the same article, she also acknowledges Norris' assertion (Bornat 1989, p. 286), that reminiscence has value in bereavement counselling and psychotherapeutic work.

Life review therapy continues to be used in clinical psychology and by specialist nurses of older people, though its use as a counselling technique per se is not well documented. Much has been written about its benefits and dangers. Garland (1994) provides a comprehensive review of the critiques of life review therapy. It can be liberating, offering opportunities for insight, closure and a new perspective on life. It can be a powerful motivating force to cope with remaining life through seeing the past as a series of struggles, perseverance, satisfactions and triumphs. Life review can be seen as empowering, and as a refuge against the fear of death. Possible negative factors include doubts over the accuracy of some memories, despair, depression, obsessional reminiscence and suicide.

However, life review therapy is a tool that psychodynamic counsellors and therapists could reclaim in order to support older clients who have become stuck in negative thought processes, depression or low self-esteem. It could be used within the psychodynamic framework to enable clients to develop a more integrated, less split self-view.

The technique needs to be handled sensitively, taking into account the ego strength of each client, and working with insight, support, and, if possible, interpretation. The risks listed are much the same as they would be for younger clients, and strengthen the need for thorough assessment and the use of a strong therapeutic frame.

Therapeutic work with people with dementia

In the biomedical frame, 'dementia' is a blanket term for a range of neurode-generative diseases such as Alzheimer's disease in which plaques and tangles develop in the brain, causing the breakdown in function of neurotransmitters; and multi-infarct dementia, which is caused by a series of small strokes. Characteristic symptoms include personality change, loss of short-term memory and confusion. In later stages, physical function such as continence and the ability to walk and talk can be affected. In the 1990s Kitwood (1993) posited a model of dementia in which the 'malignant social psychology' (pp. 103–5) with which older people are treated in British society plays its part. Without rejecting the biomedical frame, he suggested that the possibility that trauma such as bereave-ment, loss of health or burglary triggers the onset of dementing illness of the Alzheimer's type should be considered alongside it. Such events cause loss of efficacy and social skill which the older person themselves, and other people, observe. This leads others to offer help that, while well meant at first, causes feelings of disempowerment. Further neurological impairment occurs until the person is labelled as being in the early stages of dementia. The older person is gradually eased out of society by stigmatisation, marginalisation, invalidation and banishment to hospital or a nursing home, with further impairment and depersonalisation at each phase. Kitwood advocates instead that positive person-work, including validation of a person's feelings, and holding or containment of the person's fear, anger, grief and rage, can enable a person with dementia to remain 'a full participant in our shared humanity' (p. 105)

It is questionable whether social, material or personal losses cause neurological impairment. Anecdotal accounts in families who are caring for someone with dementia have pointed to a marked decline following a traumatic event. Received biomedical wisdom counters this by arguing that neurological impair-ment must already have been in place but that the traumatic event has drawn attention to the decline. Kitwood (1995) took his cue from much earlier writers such as Morgan (1965), who analysed dementia as a manic fear of death, and Folsom (1968), who ascribed meaning to dementia as a protest against isolation and disempowerment in later life. Questions must be raised about why these pow-erful psychodynamic interpretations of dementia have remained so marginalised.

In his later work, Kitwood (1997) argued for the reinterpretation of types of behaviour seen as problematic in people with dementia. For example, wandering could be reinterpreted as symbolic interaction about searching for an attachment figure, and, if addressed sensitively, could help carers to communicate with dementing people about their psychic pain. Miesen (1992), a psychogerontologist, applied Bowlby's theory of separation anxiety to his work with older people with dementia, arguing that their requests to go home may be interpreted as a need to feel the security of the bond they experienced with their parents in early childhood. He replicated Ainsworth's 'strange situation' experiment for older people with dementia and their visiting relatives in a nursing home to gauge attachment behaviours among the older people when told that their relatives were leaving.

However, psychosocial models of dementia can be problematic inasmuch as their application can provoke guilt among carers and family members who have already suffered by witnessing their loved ones' cognitive, intellectual and emotional change. Sadly, in some cases, impatience can slide into ridicule and abuse, all of which becomes part of the malignant social psychology of Kitwood's model. It is probably more accurate to see the malignancy as coming not so much from the private family sphere, where an older relative may well be a loved and valued member; but more from the public processes in which it is deemed acceptable to discriminate against older people, to use the word 'old' as a pejorative term, and to pathologise or ignore the emotional suffering of bereaved, lonely and frightened older people.

Moreover, the symptoms of dementia could be interpreted as having unconscious roots, linking back to early childhood experiences, unmet needs, shame and loss in earlier life stages rather than to current relationships. People with dementia who withdraw from or fail to recognise spouses or children, believing them instead to be attachment figures from their past, are responding in the transference as they would to that past object.

That kind of psychic pain is similar to that suffered by older people without dementia. Questions arise about why some people experience depression or other forms of emotional distress, and some contract dementia. Caution is needed in taking a purely psychosocial approach to mental health problems in old age. The interplay between the psychodynamic process and neurological impairment in forming individual patterns of presentation warrants attention.

Psychodynamic psychotherapy for clients with dementia

Very little is written about the practice of psychodynamic psychotherapy with people with dementia. Hausman (1992) is one therapist who has worked in this way. She perceives people with dementia as no longer being able to invest in others, unable to work through grief for past and present losses, stuck in a place which prevents them from redirecting emotional energy, fixated with past experience and events. She describes how, in old age, unresolved conflict from much earlier in a person's life is likely to re-emerge, but how people with dementia do not have the ego strength or defences to cope with these intrapsychic conflicts. She sees this as a key reason why depression or paranoia often accompany dementia, and identifies psychodynamic psychotherapy as a means of addressing the internal stresses experienced by people with dementia.

However, when Hausman lists the goals for psychodynamic psychotherapy, they read more like person-centred counselling: a relationship in which the client feels cared about, an emotional outlet, enhancement of self-esteem, development of insight, and an increase in coping skills. The only goal which appears to be specifically psychodynamic is the enhancement of the most mature defences while letting go of inappropriate ones (Hausman, 1992, pp. 184–5). The barriers she explores to successful psychotherapy with people with dementia are more clearly psychodynamic, as she discusses the way that splitting may take place for the person with dementia, seeing the therapist as the good object, and the carer as the bad object. The intrapsychic struggles for a person with dementia, between past self and present self, make this defence commonplace. The losses of the observing ego and of the ability to use transference are further difficulties. Hausman describes how carers present their own difficulties with resistance and notes that carers often need therapeutic help too, ideally with a different counsellor. When working with people with dementia, the therapist experiences him/herself in the role of caregiver.

Conclusion: suggestions for good psychodynamic practice in therapeutic work with older people

Key factors can be identified that contribute to a framework for good practice with older clients. In assessment, the 'Why now?' question should be considered with extra care. The client may see this as their final opportunity for happiness and integrity before death. The assessor might wish to consider with the client whether there is a deep-seated problem that has led to their request for counselling, or whether therapy has just been presented to them as an option. Some older clients have borne their wounds for many years, especially from early losses or trauma. These wounds may have affected the client's emotional health for a lifetime, or recent events may have triggered painful internal processes.

Helping a client to achieve integrity may involve recognition of existential loneliness or integration of life experience to achieve fulfilment. Either would be valid, but caution is needed when addressing painful areas if the client has a limited support network or a fragile ego. Careful consideration needs to be given to whether the client can sustain deep psychotherapeutic work. Empathic support for loneliness and despair can be a valid therapeutic intervention.

Transference and countertransference relationships may seem 'age inappropriate'. A younger therapist may find that their older client relates to them as a parental figure, a good enough object or a wise elder. While this can enable a safe, containing environment in which therapeutic movement can take place, the client may also respond in the transference with envy. Female therapists working with female clients may experience hostility if the client is resentful about their own need for care and support. The counsellor may feel deskilled by the older client in the countertransference, either because of their greater life experience, or because the client is perceived as being frail and vulnerable and thus less able to withstand confrontation and interpretive work. Personal fears of ageing or of having demanding ageing parents might be challenging for the therapist when working with older clients.

There needs to be an awareness that generational conventions may have caused people to deal with difficult situations differently from patterns seen among younger people. Older people are less likely to have left unhappy marriages. So bereavement may lead some people to feel released, and to become more fully themselves. They may, however, need counselling to help them work through the internalisation process and accompanying combination of freedom and guilt. Disenfranchised grief as a result of an unacknowledged gay relationship, or for an older person with learning disabilities who has experienced a lifetime of being marginalised, is another experience that can cause considerable pain.

Incorporating life review into therapeutic work can be creative in counselling older people. Older people, for instance those with depression, may have become stuck in negative reminiscences and intrapsychic conflict. Skilled life review work can be a way of offering balance and movement. Another way of offering creativity and therapeutic interpretation is in exploring the meaning of behaviour that may, particularly for people with dementia, be an attempt to communicate their psychic pain.

Grief in old age can be the result of multiple losses: home, lifelong partner, work and/or health. Discussing one may lead to another. Some losses may occur simultaneously if a cared-for person loses their carer and is removed from home in the same day. Because counsellors become empathically aware of their clients' sadness, they may find themselves more reluctant than usual to work towards ending if they perceive their client to be lonely and vulnerable. Endings may, however, also be more likely with this client group to come unexpectedly in the middle of work, due to illness or death.

Counselling older people can be a valuable and rewarding experience for both counsellor and client. Psychodynamic thinking has much to contribute to the counselling process through making links between past and present and paying close attention to transference and countertransference responses. The work can be painful and demanding for both parties and adequate supervisory support will be needed. Nonetheless, older people are worthy of respect and of receiving services appropriate to their care.

REFERENCES

Bernard, M. and Harding Davies, V. (2000). 'Our ageing selves'. In M. Bernard, J. Phillips, L. Machin and V. Harding Davies (eds), *Women Ageing*. London: Routledge.

Bond, J., Briggs, R. and Coleman, P. (1993). 'The study of ageing'. In J. Bond, P. Coleman and S. Peace (eds), *Ageing in Society*. Buckingham: Open University Press.

Bornat, J. (1989). 'Oral history as a social movement: reminiscence and older people'. In J. Johnson, and R. Slater (eds) (1993), *Ageing and Later Life*. Buckingham: Open University Press.

Bowlby, J. (1969). *Attachment and Loss*. London: Hogarth.

Bowlby, J. (1973). *Separation: Anxiety and Anger*. London: Hogarth.

Bowlby, J. (1980). *Loss, Sadness and Depression*. London: Hogarth.

Butler, R. (1963). 'The life review – an interpretation of reminiscence in the aged'. *Psychiatry*, 26, 65–76.

Coleman, P. (1993a). 'Psychological ageing'. In J. Bond, P. Coleman, and S. Peace (eds), *Ageing in Society*. Buckingham: Open University Press.

Coleman, P. (1993b). 'Adjustment in later life'. In J. Bond, P. Coleman, and S. Peace (eds), *Ageing in Society* Buckingham: Open University Press.

Coleman, P. (1994). 'Reminiscence within the study of ageing: the social significance of story'. In J. Bornat (ed.), *Reminiscence Reviewed*. Buckingham: Open University Press.

Cumming, E. and Henry, W. (1961). *Growing Old: The Process of Disengagement*. New York: Basic Books.

Daniel, B. (1997). 'Working with older women'. In M. Lawrence and M. Maguire (eds), *Psychotherapy with Women: A Feminist Perspective*. London: Macmillan (now Palgrave Macmillan).

Erikson, E. (1965). *Childhood and Society*. London: Vintage (1995 printing).

Evers, H. (1981). 'Care or custody? The experience of women patients in long-stay geriatric wards'. In B. Hutter and G. Williams (eds), *Controlling Women: The Normal and the Deviant*. London: Croom Helm.

Folsom, J. (1968). 'Reality orientation for the elderly patient'. *Journal of Geriatric Psychiatry*, 1, 291–307.

Freud, S. (1905). 'On psychotherapy'. In J. Strachey (ed.), *The Standard Edition of the Complete Psychological Works of Sigmund Freud, Volume 7*. London: Hogarth.

Garland, J. (1994). 'What splendour: It all coheres'. In J. Bornat, (ed.), *Reminiscence Reviewed*. Buckingham: Open University Press.

Gilleard, C., Leiberman, S. and Peeler, R (1992). 'Family therapy for older adults: a survey of professionals' attitudes'. *Journal of Family Therapy*, 14, 413–22.

Haight, B. (1992). 'The structured life review process: a community approach to the ageing client'. In G. Jones and B. Miesen (eds), *Caregiving in Dementia: Research and Applications, Volume 1*. London: Routledge.

Hausman, C. (1992). 'Dynamic psychotherapy with elderly demented patients'. In G. Jones and B. Miesen (eds), *Caregiving in Dementia: Research and Applications, Volume 1*. London: Routledge.

Havighurst, R. (1963). 'Successful ageing'. In R. Williams, C. Tibbitts and W. Donahue (eds), *Processes of Ageing, Volume 1*. London: Atherton.

Jung, C. G. (1972). 'The transcendent function'. In H. Read, M. Fordham, G. Adler and W. McGuire (eds), *The Structure and Dynamic of the Psyche, Volume 8 of the Collected Works of C. G. Jung*, 2nd edition. London: Routledge and Kegan Paul.

Kalus, C. (1994). 'Counselling older people'. In C. Malone (compiler), *Documents File for K256 An Ageing Society*. Buckingham: Open University Press.

Kitwood, T. (1993). 'Frames of reference for an understanding of dementia'. In J. Johnson and R. Slater (eds), *Ageing and Later Life*. Buckingham: Open University Press.

Kitwood, T. (1995). 'Some problematic aspects of dementia'. In G. Berriuf and R. Parker (eds), *The History of Clinical Psychology*. London: Athlone.

Kitwood, T. (1997). *Dementia Reconsidered*. Buckingham: Open University Press.

Klein, M. (1940). 'Mourning and its relation to manic-depressive states'. In *The Writings of Melanie Klein, Volume 1*. London: Hogarth.

Klein, M. (1946). 'Notes on some schizoid mechanisms'. In *The Writings of Melanie Klein, Volume 3*. London: Hogarth.

Klein, M. (1963). 'On the sense of loneliness'. In Klein, *Our Adult World and Other Essays*. London: Heinemann.

Martindale, B. (1989). 'Becoming dependent again: the fears of some elderly persons and their younger therapists'. *Psychoanalytic Psychotherapy*, 4: 1, 67–75.

Martindale, B. (1998). 'Ageing, dying, death and eternal life'. *Psychoanalytic Psychotherapy*, 12: 3, 259–70.

Miesen, B. (1992). 'Attachment theory and dementia'. In G. Jones and B. Miesen (eds), *Caregiving in Dementia: Research and Applications, Volume 1*. London: Routledge.

Morgan, R. (1965). 'Note on the psychopathology of senility: senescent defence against the threat of death'. *Psychological Reports*, 16, 303–6.

Richards, D. (2001). 'The remains of the day'. *Counselling and Psychotherapy Journal*, 12: 7, 10–14.

Terry, P. (1997). *Counselling the Elderly and their Carers*. Basingstoke: Palgrave (now Palgrave Macmillan).

Wellington, H. (2002). *Challenge and Change: A critical appraisal of attachment theory and dependency in psychodynamic counselling for older people*. Unpublished Diploma in Counselling dissertation, University of Leicester.

Woods, R., Portnoy, S., Head, D. and Jones, G. (1992). 'Reminiscence and life review with persons with dementia: Which way forward?'. In G. Jones and B. Miesen (eds), *Caregiving in Dementia: Research and Applications, Volume 1*. London: Routledge.

INTERNET REFERENCES

www.dh.gov.uk/PolicyAndGuidance/HealthAndSocialCareTopics/OlderPeople, accessed 19 January 2004. (a)

www.dh.gov.uk/PolicyAndGuidance/HealthAndSocialCareTopics/OlderPeopleServices, accessed 20 July 2005. (b)

www.silvesurfers.org/AgeConcern/information_426.htm, accessed 9 February 2004.

PART

IV

Race and Culture

Psychodynamic Counselling, 'Race' and Culture

Gill Tuckwell

Introduction

This chapter examines 'race' and culture in relation to psychodynamic counselling, focusing on psychodynamic ways of working, referred to here as the psychodynamic frame. It is argued that the notion of 'race' is a social construct that has no scientific basis. To highlight its invalidity, some writers use the term 'race' in quotation marks. Although the writer challenges the legitimacy of race, it should be noted that, for presentational purposes, quotation marks will not be widely used in this chapter.

The relevance of the psychodynamic frame to racial and cultural phenomena in the contemporary world has been a largely neglected area in mainstream psychodynamic and psychoanalytic literature. With its focus on the intrapsychic world of the self, the psychoanalytic tradition has generally been concerned with the individual and with interpersonal relationships as they impact on self-organisation. Comparatively little attention has been given to the social context, and there has been limited recognition of the influence of sociopolitical issues on the inner world of the individual. The changing nature of global societies, together with the increasing incidence of racial and cultural diversity, calls for a renewed application of psychodynamic principles to personal and social functioning.

This chapter is organised in three major sections. The first section explores the related concepts of race and culture from a societal and a psychological perspective. The second section explores the history of psychoanalysis and offers a critique of the psychodynamic frame in addressing race and culture. The third section discusses implications for practice with regard to race and culture, and focuses on key considerations for psychodynamic counselling.

Concepts of race and culture

The related concepts of race and culture are complex and multi-layered and, in the context of plural societies, have often been viewed synonymously. While there is undoubtedly an overlap between racial and cultural phenomena, this chapter seeks to delineate clearly between these terms and to highlight the significant historical, sociopolitical and psychological forces that have been instrumental in shaping them. Hence, major themes and perspectives with regard to race and culture will be addressed.

Race

The concept of 'race' is highly misleading, suggesting that there are well defined racial types to which each human being inexorably belongs. The process of assigning individuals to a racial group is usually made on the basis of arbitrary biological characteristics such as skin colour, hair type or eye shape. This system of classification has a long history in the Western world, and was particularly prevalent in the late 18th century when many racial theorists sought to support the hypothesis that racial types are ordained by nature, and that physical differences are an indicator of intellectual capacity (Jahoda, 1999). Significantly, this was during the period of extensive European travel to Africa, Asia and North America, when white Europeans were engaged in widespread subjugation and enslavement of indigenous peoples. Theories about race were thus formulated by white people within this political context, and their drive to prove the innate inferiority of black people on scientific grounds was intertwined with a wish to sanction imperialist policies of slavery and domination (Fryer, 1984; Heller, 1970).

The idea of specific racial types was challenged in 1859 by the publication of *The Origin of Species* by Charles Darwin, who proposed a theory of evolution by natural selection. In this revolutionary work, Darwin differentiated between a species as a self-reproducing group and the various subspecies, which evolve within each species in relation to prevailing environmental conditions. In this way, the human race (*Homo sapiens*) constitutes a single species, and any differences in appearance, intellectual ability or behavioural characteristics can be attributed to variations within the species rather than to distinct racial types. Darwin's theory has been confirmed in more recent developments in DNA testing, which identifies gradual and continuous variations between individuals rather than specific racial prototypes (Vines, 1995).

Although there is no scientific basis for identifying distinct racial groups, the use of race as a means of classifying people continues to pervade the structures and practices of political and institutional life in the Western world. The enduring nature of racial thinking, despite contrary empirical evidence, therefore requires wider consideration, as was highlighted by Malik:

> We do not define races because biological data compels us to do so. Rather, society begins with an a priori division of humanity into different races for which it subsequently finds a rationale in certain physical characteristics ... The clue to the importance of race in Western thought, therefore, lies not in biology but in society. (1996, p. 5)

The widespread reluctance to abandon racial assumptions and beliefs must be understood in relation to the function that race serves in personal and political life. In the historical context of slavery and colonisation, white Europeans invariably considered themselves to be superior to black populations, and the belief in white racial superiority and black racial inferiority became an accepted ideology that underpinned the social hierarchy. Dominant white groups who have stood to gain in terms of political and economic power have thus promoted the construct of race over the centuries. While overt racist behaviour and discriminatory practices have increasingly been vetoed by successive acts of legislation in the UK and elsewhere, the legacy of white supremacy and black subservience continues to be played out in many covert ways in society, thus perpetuating existing power differentials.

This demonstrates the multi-layered nature of racial processes, where racial attitudes may be manifested in behaviour and practices that confer privilege on some groups while discriminating against others. In discussing race, it is therefore necessary to include racism, which has been defined by Ridley (1989, p. 60) as 'any behaviour or pattern of behaviour that systematically tends to deny access to opportunities or privilege to one social group while perpetuating privilege to members of another group'. Race is thus strongly associated with power and privilege in the sociopolitical arena, wherein systems and institutions function to uphold the status quo. With an emphasis on outcome rather than intention, racism frequently occurs indirectly at an institutional level through policies and mechanisms that are subtly discriminatory. The paradoxical nature of race has been aptly summarised by Fernando (1996, p. 8) in the following way: '[r]ace, as we generally conceptualise it, is a biological myth but a social reality and as such is a very powerful signifier of individual and group behaviour.'

From their respective positions in the racial hierarchy, black populations and white populations have had radically different historical and social experiences that have impacted on collective memory. For black people, traumatic, world changing events of slavery and colonisation, as well as ongoing experiences of racism, have left a cumulative legacy of inferior status and social dislocation which impact upon life chances and self-worth. For white people, the customary position of dominance and privilege has in turn left deep-seated expectations of power and authority. These historical and sociopolitical experiences thus converge with the intrapsychic world of black people and white people, and have a profound cumulative effect on the beliefs, attitudes and feelings that each group develops about self and other at both a conscious and an unconscious level.

A number of writers have discussed the historical legacy of white superiority and black inferiority with regard to internalised racial identities. Writing in the era of colonial Algeria, the radical black psychiatrist, Fanon, drew on psychoanalytic ideas to explore the interaction between the white colonisers and the black colonised. He described a dual process in which the relative political and economic status of each group was continually reinforced through internalised fears of difference and beliefs about white superiority and black inferiority (Fanon, 1952). Fanon's argument can be summarised in the following way:

- To the white person, the black person stimulates anxiety. By projecting unacceptable parts of self onto the black person, and relating to the negative projections in the black person, the white person can continue to assume a position of racial superiority.

- To the black person, the white person symbolises the higher order and the one who can bestow worth. By identifying with the white person's negative projections, the black person plays out the lower position through self-denigration, thus perpetuating the status quo.

This process of projective and introjective identification will be discussed further in the following section.

By emphasising the interaction between historical events and internalised beliefs, and giving weight to collective experiences of black populations and white populations with regard to oppression and dominance, Fanon moved the enquiry beyond the level of the individual. Similar ideas about the psychical effects of oppression on black populations were taken up by later writers, who variously used the terms *internalised oppression* (Lipsky, 1978), *internalised colonisation* (Rose, 1988) and *internalised racism* (Rose, 1997). This notion of internalised racial identity, deriving from responses to power differentials and relative status in society, has also been instrumental in the development in the USA of black and white racial identity models (Carter, 1995; Cross, 1971, 1978; Helms, 1984, 1990, 1995). These racial identity models offer a theoretical framework for understanding the correlative processes for black people and white people. The black racial identity model represents a progression from internalised oppression to a positive, secure black identity. By contrast, the white racial identity model represents a progression from internalised white supremacy to a positive non-racist stance.

It can thus be seen that race related issues, with the interplay between sociopolitical status and internalised beliefs, have far-reaching effects. While race and culture have complementary facets that are integral to identity, the specific dynamics associated with internalised beliefs about racial oppression and dominance add a further dimension. These dynamics, with their emphasis on power differentials, inevitably impact upon counselling processes and require particular understanding and skill on the part of the counsellor in order to elucidate complex racial phenomena that may emerge in the counselling interaction.

Culture

Culture has been described (Williams, 1983, p. 87) as 'one of the two or three most complicated words in the English language'. The complexity arises from the variety of meanings associated with the concept of culture which, like that of race, is dynamic in nature and defies simple definitions. Stressing the axiom that culture is learned rather than inherited, Hofstede (1994, p. 4) referred to culture as a process of 'mental programming', in which group values and beliefs are socially transmitted to each individual and profoundly influence patterns of thinking, feeling and behaving. Culture is therefore a collective phenomenon that distinguishes the members of one group of people from another.

In exploring the idea of similarities and differences between people, several writers have drawn attention to three levels of human experience. These levels are encapsulated in Kluckhohn and Murray's (1949, p. 53) oft-quoted phrase:

Every [person] is in certain respects

a. like all other [persons],

b. like some other [persons],

c. like no other [person].

In this triadic model of human life, cultural similarity is often a means of identifying with and forming attachments to certain other human beings. From this perspective, cultural affiliation can be differentiated from human universality (characteristics of the human condition that are common to all human beings) and from individual uniqueness (personal characteristics that are unique to the individual). These concepts were cited by Speight et al. (1991, p. 32) in their illustration of the interacting influences on an individual's worldview, as shown in Figure 9.1.

Pointing out that almost everyone belongs to a number of different reference groups at the same time, Hofstede (1994, p. 10) suggested that people carry

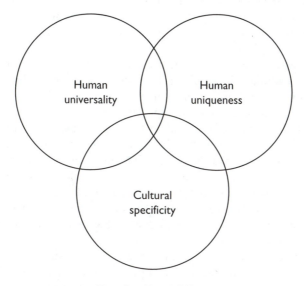

Source: Speight et al. (1991)

Figure 9.1   Influences on worldview

several layers of mental programming within themselves, corresponding to different levels of culture. He gave the following examples of these levels of culture:

- a national level according to one's country (or countries, for people who have migrated within their lifetime)

- a regional and/or ethnic and/or religious and/or linguistic affiliation level, as most nations are composed of culturally different regions and/or ethnic and/or religious and/or language groups

- a gender level, according to whether a person was born as a genitally identified girl or boy

- a generation level, which separates grandparents from parents from children

- a social class level, associated with educational opportunities and with a person's occupation or profession

At the core of any culture (whether national, regional, religious, generational, professional or whatever) is a set of values that, in turn, is manifested in attitudes, social practices and artistic expression. However, given the multiple affiliations of different group members, as well as individual preferences, no cultural group is likely to be homogeneous. This intracultural variation and cultural fluidity have accelerated over the last century through widespread migration and increasingly plural societies in which individuals are acculturated into more than one culture. Cultural boundaries have thus become more permeable, as was suggested by Fernando (1995, p. 11) who argued that 'in most parts of Britain today society is not "multicultural" as in having distinct cultural groups living side by side, but culturally hybrid with cultural overlap between groups and individuals of a complex nature, no one being culturally "pure" any more.' These complex dynamics accentuate the difficulty in identifying specific cultural characteristics.

Within any culture, the dominant values and patterns of behaviour are transmitted to young children from the earliest stages of life through a process of enculturation. In this way, culture may be seen not only as an anthropological construct pertaining to group membership but also as a psychological phenomenon that impacts upon identity and intrapsychic development. Ho (1995, p. 5) referred to this process as *internalised culture*, defined as 'the cultural influences operating within the individual that shape (not determine) personality formation and various aspects of psychological functioning'. This intrapsychic expression of culture reinforces the need to take account of within-group variations as individuals respond to normative cultural patterns in different ways. The notion of internalised culture has echoes of internalised racial identity as discussed earlier.

The complexity of culture, which operates both in intrapsychic functioning and in interpersonal encounters, clearly poses many challenges for counsellors. Intercultural differences in core values, patterns of behaviour and emotional expression give rise to much scope for misunderstanding and interpersonal conflict. It must also be noted that counselling itself is a culture specific activity that developed within the norms of Western industrialised society and continues to reflect dominant societal values. The philosophical assumptions underlying Western ideology include beliefs in individual autonomy, scientific method and the Protestant work ethic (Katz, 1985), and these vary considerably from the more spiritual, holistic and collective values that are characteristic of many African and Asian worldviews (Tuckwell, 2002). This has major implications for counselling delivery in the plural world of the 21st century where there is a need to respond to a diverse client population in culturally relevant ways.

Hence, race and culture are multi-layered concepts that embrace sociological, political and psychological perspectives. Both constructs are highly significant in the interplay between outer-world experiences and internalised beliefs about self and others, and in this way they have similar attributes in relation to social organisation and identity. At a societal level, race and culture are frequently used as a means of sociopolitical classification, which serves to differentiate various minority groups from the dominant white majority, thus upholding the existing balance of power. Despite the current climate of political correctness, racial and cultural prejudice continues to be manifested in various ways, whether unintentionally or intentionally. In this way, racial and cultural factors have similar effects in influencing social status and life chances. However, while there are some similarities between these two concepts, it is important to recognise the particular influence and dynamics of race. It has been stressed in this section that the constructs of race and culture have developed from fundamentally different origins. Whereas culture is rooted in anthropology and focuses on the shared beliefs and social practices within groups, the spurious notion of 'race' has derived from historical events and the legacy of white dominance and black oppression. Race is thus strongly associated with assumptions about white superiority and black inferiority, and these powerful images are deeply embedded in the inner world of black populations and white populations collectively. The tendency for race to be subsumed in an all-embracing concept of cultural diversity obscures the pervasive effects of race related phenomena and the multiple ways in which these may be manifested in counselling (Helms and Richardson, 1997). Using the prefixes *socio* and *psycho*, Helms and Cook (2000) offer a framework for differentiating between culture and race at both a societal and a psychological level, as shown in Table 9.1.

Table 9.1   A conceptual framework for identifying societal and psychological aspects of race and culture

Sociorace	*Psychorace*
Sociopolitical classification system based on physical characteristics used to allocate resources and ascribe positions in the social hierarchy	Internalised experiences of the sociopolitical hierarchy leading to personal beliefs about innate superiority and inferiority
Socioculture	*Psychoculture*
Sociocultural classification system based on the values, practices and rituals that define cultural group membership	Internalised attitudes, values and beliefs acquired through socialisation in a particular sociocultural group

Source: Based on Helms and Cook (2000)

Further consideration will be given to these dynamics in the remainder of this chapter, which focuses on a psychodynamic understanding of race and culture as they influence the process of counselling.

A critique of the psychodynamic frame in addressing race and culture

Rooted in the psychoanalytic tradition, the psychodynamic frame is concerned predominantly with the intrapsychic world of the individual, focusing on the formative role of early childhood and the central importance of the unconscious in shaping present reality. These key principles, which emerged from the clinical work of Freud (1856–1939) in the context of Paris, Vienna and London, formed the conceptual backdrop for later developments in the psychoanalytic movement and the various theoretical trajectories that it has spawned. While there is little direct reference to race and culture within classical psychoanalysis, the application of psychodynamic theory to counselling and psychotherapy practice reveals many underlying themes and assumptions that are pertinent to cultural and racial phenomena.

The psychoanalytic background

At the heart of the debate about the efficacy of the psychodynamic frame in the plural world of the 21st century lies the notion of universality. In classical psychoanalysis, the search for psychological meaning in human behaviour represented a quest to define universal attributes of the human condition, so as to provide a theory of normative human development. For Freud, this centred to a large extent on inner drives and unresolved conflicts, relating particularly to sexual repression and desire. By contrast, Jung took a broader approach, focusing on archetypal representations in the human psyche and the idea of a collective unconscious. Klein, in her work as a child psychoanalyst, was particularly concerned with the earliest stages of psychic development and the mechanisms by which good and bad experiences in the internal and external world are dealt with. These three foundational strands in psychoanalytic thinking, all of which focused on the intersection between unconscious processes and interpersonal relationships, were seen by the protagonists to reflect the commonality of human existence, which is sociological, psychological, and ultimately biological.

While affirming a belief in the fundamental unity of the human psyche, Freud and Jung pursued an interest in the psychology of 'primitive' peoples. Much of this work reflected contemporary attitudes of white people towards black people, often associated with notions of white intellectual superiority. Freud (1914) analysed totems and taboos and drew an analogy between the mental lives of so-called 'savages' and European neurotics. Similarly, Jung, who travelled extensively outside Europe, drew comparisons between black Africans and 'primitive' peoples, and postulated (1930) that the 'Negro' probably had a whole historical layer less in the brain. In the light of these assumptions, it has been stated (Dalal, 1987) that early psychoanalytic developments were based on a racist way of thinking. Although these racist views are reprehensible in the politically correct ideal of the 21st century, they appear to demonstrate a wish to under-stand the complex relationship between universal characteristics and other factors such as race and culture. Nevertheless, overt references to race and cul-ture in classical psychoanalysis are rare, and this lack of attention reflects a Eurocentric tendency to regard white European patterns of behaviour as universally normative for all human beings.

The debate about the validity of psychodynamic theories with a diverse client population calls for an understanding of the historical and sociopolitical context in which they were developed. Located within the ethos of modern Western civilisation, the psychodynamic tradition is rooted in notions of individualism and personal autonomy. It has been observed (Littlewood, 1992) that psycho-analytical therapy in Britain was effectively the creation of immigrants from central Europe, many of whom were Jewish and were fleeing Nazi persecution. Entering a society that was rabidly anti-Semitic, this particular immigrant group, upper middle class and cosmopolitan, formed links with the intellectual bour-geoisie of North London, from whom a considerable number of its patients were drawn. Although many of their classic papers were based on intercultural work (for example, Freud's Wolf Man was Russian), these early psychoanalytic theorists chose to focus on the development of the individual psyche rather than on cultural or intercultural factors in therapy. From this, Littlewood (1992, p. 7) has concluded that '[a] psychotherapy which was able to ignore social con-texts in favour of intrapsychic factors alone was clearly safer for the practitioner, and helped establish psychoanalysis as a universal (and thus a "scientific") process rather than as a culturally "Jewish" therapy.'

The historical backdrop of psychoanalysis and the formulation of theories on the basis of clinical work within a particular social milieu raise important issues about the relationship between universalism and interpretation, and how far these theories can be applied literally to all human beings. In a Eurocentric activity that relies on understanding and interpretation of complex psychologi-cal material, there is a fundamental question about the capacity of analysts, who are themselves products of this particular culture, to make appropriate interpre-tations with clients from a different cultural background. It was suggested in the discussion about culture earlier that cultural values and beliefs profoundly influ-ence intrapsychic development, emotional expression and social behaviour. This view was endorsed by Rose, who suggested (1988, p. 20) that cultures 'provide the vocabulary of emotions, gestures and words through which individuals embody and articulate their desires and frustrations'. The deep-seated nature of cultural and racial socialisation thus has a powerful effect on the client's presen-tation in the therapy room. In this way, cultural and racial dynamics may impact significantly on the therapeutic relationship, thereby impeding the therapist's capacity to enter the client's inner world and to understand unacknowledged aspects of the client's behaviour. Valid and meaningful interpretation of client material thus calls for therapists and counsellors to take account of the intersec-tion between universal human characteristics, culture specific variations and the influence of wider sociopolitical forces.

These questions may be considered in relation to Freud's use of the Greek Oedipus myth to explain sexual development and primary erotic attachments in the family. The Oedipal drama focuses on sexual phantasy, rivalry, favour, power, envy and loss within the context of a two-parent, patriarchal, nuclear family. However, many children in the Western world and elsewhere grow up in family situations where social arrangements and the distribution of power are radically different. Variations in family structures include single-parent families, in which children may have limited or no contact with their other parent; blended families, in which children may grow up with step-parents and step-siblings; and extended families, in which the household may comprise wider familial relations across several generations. These diverse experiences, and their impact on individual identity, call into question the significance of the Oedipus complex as a universal phenomenon.

While Freud and his contemporaries were concerned to establish universal theories, more recent developments in psychological thinking have stressed the need to pay attention to the sociocultural context. From this perspective, the central dynamics of love, power and sexual rivalry in the Oedipal triangle may be examined both in relation to the original Greek text, and in the context of 19th century Vienna, which formed the backdrop for Freud's theory. Viennese society at this time was akin to Victorian England, where there was a power imbalance between men and women, as well as repressive attitudes towards sex. In this setting, where men had greater access to power and opportunity, it would not be surprising if women were envious of their more powerful position, and hence penis envy may also be considered in relation to the sociopolitical environment. Locating Freud's Oedipal theory in the social ethos of his day enables a contextualised interpretation of major theoretical themes, which can then be applied to present-day situations. The benefits of this approach of enlarging the scope of traditional psychoanalysis have much to offer an understanding of race and culture in the therapeutic relationship.

The interaction between intrapsychic development and sociocultural conditions is also pertinent to later developments in the psychodynamic tradition. In post-Freudian thinking, attention shifted from the exclusive focus on the intrapsychic world of the self and gave greater weight to the interpersonal sphere and the emotional relationships between self and other, as was evident in the work of Klein and the object relations school. The earlier search for a definitive theory of humankind was thus intensified and challenged as divergent factions emerged within the psychoanalytical group, having opposing views. In particular, professional differences arose between the followers of Klein and the followers of Freud's daughter, Anna Freud. These differences were manifested in a series of discussions in the British Psychoanalytical Society between 1941 and 1945, later called the Controversial Discussions (King and Steiner, 1990). While this contentious climate caused considerable antagonism and distress, it also formed the backdrop for much of the creative thinking in the psychoanalytic movement.

Although Klein herself was primarily concerned with individual psychology and intrapsychic processes, her work is a product of this culture of conflict and oppression, and this is manifested in the emerging themes of identification and differentiation, and in concepts such as those of splitting and projection. This new perspective in the history of psychoanalysis thus demonstrates the interaction between interpersonal relationships and intrapsychic functioning. With the more recent emphasis on contextualisation, the central tenets of Kleinian theory provided a foundation for later writers who applied these concepts to the wider sphere of social and political relations. Kleinian psychoanalysis is accordingly of fundamental importance in understanding race and culture and elucidating complex racial and cultural dynamics at both a personal level and a societal level.

Application of psychodynamic concepts to race and culture

Race and culture operate in many complex and subtle ways in interpersonal relations. As a social construct, rooted in assumptions about white supremacy and black subservience, race is a particularly potent force in ordering the social hierarchy, and is often implicit in the structures and practices of institutional life. In the modern world of international capitalism, bureaucratic organisations, new communication technologies and global unrest, there is much scope for social dislocation, inner turmoil and mistrust of others (Elliott, 2002). In this political climate, deeply embedded racial attitudes and fears come to the fore, leading to the increasing manifestation of racist behaviours and practices.

Drawing on Klein's ideas about unconscious schizoid mechanisms for managing and displacing anxiety, some writers have discussed the paranoid nature of racism. Significant writing in this field includes that of the American political theorist, Alford (1989) and the British social scientist, Rustin (1991). In Klein's original theory (Klein, 1959) the focus is on the early months of an infant's life, which are characterised by a sense of oneness with the mother (or mother figure) and by intense anxiety about persecutory attacks from outside forces. In the paranoid-schizoid position, the infant employs unconscious defence mechanisms such as splitting, projection, introjection and projective identification in order to preserve the self from the perceived threat of annihilation. With development, the infant is able to move to the depressive position and to learn, with pain, to integrate experience and to tolerate ambivalence and the loss of the idealised mother. Applying these concepts to the sociopolitical world, Rustin (1991) explores racism as a displaced expression of persecutory anxiety and hatred, which is fuelled by splitting. Viewing the world in rigid categories of good and bad, white and black, the in-group and the out-group, the unacceptable part of the self is split off and projected onto the racial other, who may be denigrated or attacked. Similarly, guilt and anxiety about their own persecutory impulses may cause individuals to overcompensate for the unacceptable part of self by idealising the feared other. Rustin stresses the interactive nature of this process, viewing it in terms of projective identification and introjective identification, in which oppressors and victims of racial domination each play out their relative position in the racial hierarchy.

From this perspective, the Fanonist theory of white superiority and black inferiority may be seen in terms of projective identification, in which the white person evokes in the black person aspects of self that are deeply denied (the symbolic black self). The black person, who has introjected notions of white supremacy, accepts and identifies with these projections. Concurrently, the black person projects onto the white person the disowned parts of the self (the symbolic white self). Finding an opportune scapegoat in the black person's internalised notion of black subservience and shame, the white person is thus able to maintain the introjected superiority of the white self. This dual process has been summarised by Adams (1996, p. 166), who suggested that '[i]f some blacks hate themselves, it is because whites hate an inferior part of themselves and repress it and project it onto blacks. In contact with whites, blacks then internalize this shadow from the collective unconscious of whites.'

The application of Kleinian concepts to racial phenomena has much to offer in explicating complex racial dynamics. Racist behaviour and the deep-seated nature of racial socialisation profoundly influence relationships in society. While racism may be seen as an ideological formation, based on a system of distorted thinking, the tenacity of racial processes derives from the nature of schizoid mechanisms and irrational projections. This was emphasised by Rustin (1991, p. 68), who observed that '[t]he tendency to see racism as a system of ideological or false beliefs, to be banished by anti-racist teaching and propaganda, fails to see that its main power lies at an unconscious level.'

Summing up

This section has emphasised the need for contextualised understanding and application of psychodynamic concepts to the contemporary world. With increasing racial and cultural diversity in modern urban life, this approach has much to commend it in order to avoid the Eurocentric bias of traditional psychoanalysis. The growing trend of interpreting individual experiences within the context of post-modern societies challenges the idea of a single unitary theory of humankind. In post-modern thinking, the debunking of grand theories in favour of contextualised understanding makes greater links between psychological and sociopolitical processes, and places greater emphasis on the role of psychoanalysis as a critical social theory. This viewpoint was highlighted by Elliott (2002, p. 175), who suggested that 'psychoanalysis is a critical reflection on the central modes of feeling, valuing and caring in modern societies.' From this perspective, psychodynamic theory can be efficacious in drawing attention to salient themes in the contemporary social context. This approach is pertinent to psychodynamic counselling, which is itself a modification of classical psychoanalysis, reflecting the demands of present-day society. The need for relevant practice is discussed in the following section, which addresses key areas with regard to working effectively with racial and cultural dynamics in psychodynamic counselling.

Implications for practice

Whereas psychoanalysis was rooted within the discipline of psychiatry and was practised in medical settings or as a private contractual agreement between analyst and patient, its more recent counterpart, counselling, arose in response to social need and the pressure for therapeutic services to be provided in other settings. This need was particularly evident in the 1940s when members of the armed forces were returning from the war with emotional trauma. As counselling has become more readily available in the public and voluntary sectors, there is a challenge for the profession as a whole to take account of the needs of a diverse client population and to work with people in ways that make sense within their own cultural frames of reference. This section addresses considerations for counselling practice with regard to race and culture, focusing specifically on the intrapsychic world and the psychodynamic frame.

The intrapsychic world

Both sociocultural values and sociopolitical assumptions about race are deeply embedded in the internalised beliefs, attitudes and feelings that cultural and racial groups develop about self and other. These views have been built up over the course of several centuries, leaving a cumulative legacy in the collective memory. In the light of the traumatic history of oppression of black populations by white populations, the emotional reactions and ideas associated with race are particularly potent. These ideas were highlighted by Adams (1996), who explored racial fantasies about blackness and whiteness:

> We need to analyse the 'racial' fantasies of the self in relation to the other – and of the other in relation to the self. These include fantasies about whiteness and blackness; white supremacy and purity; black pride and power; white and black separatism; separation and integration; sex, violence, and intelligence; difference, similarity, and identity; superiority and inferiority; Eurocentrism and Afrocentrism; Europe and Africa – and perhaps most importantly, the 'civilised' and the 'primitive'. (1996, p. 49)

Attitudes and beliefs about race and culture are thus implicit in the intrapsychic world of both the counsellor and the client, and these impact on counselling interactions in various ways, whether in homogeneous dyads or racially and culturally mixed dyads.

In psychodynamic counselling, which focuses to a large extent on the intrapsychic world, it is crucially important that consideration be given to the effects of racial and cultural dynamics on unconscious processes. The traditional dyadic representations of psychodynamic concepts are most likely suffused with wider historical and sociopolitical influences. In this way, racial and cultural issues may intensify schizoid mechanisms and unconscious projections in the counselling dyad. Similarly, transference and countertransference reactions are heightened by the chequered history of racial and cultural relations. Stressing the impact of historical events on the relationship between a white counsellor and an ethnic minority client, Wheeler and Izzard (1997, pp. 412–13) suggested that 'the transference is charged by history, that which relates not only to the client's story but also to the history of oppressed minorities.'

From this perspective, transferential processes are viewed in a collective sense, having grown out of accumulated experiences and reactions of generations of black people and white people towards each other – experiences which are continually reinforced by social structures and a myriad images and stereotypes.

As psychodynamic counselling is generally concerned with underlying beliefs and feelings, the racially different counsellor or client may become the recipient of many of these internalised ways of viewing members of a different racial group. Describing this process in the context of a therapeutic relationship with a white client and a black therapist, Curry (1964) used the term *pre-transference* to refer to the beliefs, fantasies and myths about black people in general held by the white client before meeting the black therapist in the therapy room. Brought up in a society that reinforces negative views about black people, the white client ascribes these values and beliefs to the black therapist in the therapeutic process where they are often powerfully enacted. Whereas Curry discussed this transferential process solely from the perspective of a white client and a black counsellor, other writers (Comas-Díaz and Jacobsen 1991; Thomas 1992) have examined the dynamics that arise in black/white, white/black and black/black counsellor/client dyads. Transferences arising in these therapeutic pairings have been variously described as *cultural transference* and *cultural countertransference* (Ridley, 1995), *ethnocultural transference* and *ethnocultural countertransference* (Comas-Díaz and Jacobsen, 1991), and *culture specific transference* (Alleyne, 1998).

At the heart of the discussion of transferential processes applied to racial and cultural dynamics lies the notion of counselling as a social process that evokes the values and assumptions about racial and cultural difference widely held by society as a whole. Transference and countertransference relating to blackness and whiteness are therefore often associated with internalised attitudes of white superiority and black subservience, and these may be manifested in emotional reactions relating to fear, mistrust, anger, guilt, suspicion and compliance.

In view of deeply held assumptions about race and culture within intrapsychic life and interpersonal functioning, it is essential that counsellors be alert to racial and cultural dynamics that arise in the counselling process. The capacity to recognise and work with underlying racial and cultural nuances requires a willingness to explore and address internalised attitudes and beliefs about self and other. Unless counsellors have come to an awareness of themselves as racial and cultural beings, their capacity to work effectively with these dynamics will be considerably impeded.

The psychodynamic frame

Psychodynamic counselling is now conducted in a number of settings with a wide range of clients. The greatest challenge, therefore, in offering psychodynamic counselling in the plural world of the 21st century is to incorporate sufficient flexibility whilst preserving the integrity of the model. The limitations and the strengths of the psychodynamic frame in acknowledging aspects of race and culture are considered in this subsection.

One of the major difficulties in utilising a psychodynamic approach with clients from non-Western cultures is the focus on the inner world of the individual and on notions of individual autonomy. As a product of Western individualism, psychodynamic counselling seeks to discover the unconscious processes driving behaviour. Relying on highly verbal interactions, it requires personal disclosure of past experiences, dream material, fantasies and feelings, with a view to increasing insight and understanding. Little recognition is given to the external world, including the influence of racial and cultural factors on psychological functioning. In its attempt to establish a universal theory of human development, psychodynamic thinking proceeds from a Eurocentric assumption of normality in which different styles of behaviour or emotional expression have frequently been interpreted as pathological or deviant. For these reasons, the psychodynamic approach has often been criticised for its ethnocentric values and its culture bound conceptual base.

Clearly, when applied rigidly, this framework may be antithetical to many clients who adhere to a different value system. Many African and Asian world-views adopt a more holistic approach in which body, mind and spirit are regarded as one. The focus on self-disclosure and insight may not be highly valued by many culturally different clients, particularly those who belong to collective family systems that support notions of authority. Moreover, where clients are using a second language, the expectation that they will explore complex psychological material through metaphor and interpretation may be a barrier for meaningful interaction.

Limitations in the psychodynamic approach also arise with regard to issues of cultural pluralism and racial justice. Indeed, Littlewood and Lipsedge (1993, p. 54) pointed out that, in traditional psychoanalytical thinking, racism was interpreted from the position of individual pathology, deriving from childhood experience and 'father hatred'. Only latterly has there been greater recognition of racism in social institutions and awareness of how it is perpetuated at a societal level. Black clients on the receiving end of racism need sufficient containment in the counselling room and a framework for acknowledging racial forces in the external world if they are to feel free enough to explore the psychological trauma of racism. Counsellors also need an understanding of the sociopolitical context and their own position in the racial hierarchy if they are to work effectively with internalised racism and dominance.

Despite the limitations of the psychodynamic approach with regard to race and culture, there are also some strengths. More than any other theoretical approach, the conceptual basis of the psychodynamic approach offers a framework for examining complex dynamics related to the client's inner world, including racial and cultural beliefs about self and other, and unconscious processes in racially mixed interactions. The psychodynamic frame thus has much to commend it, provided certain protocols are adhered to, including the following:

- Counsellors must have sufficient awareness of their own cultural and racial attitudes, beliefs and values, and understanding of how their cultural and racial backgrounds may impact on the psychological process.

- Counsellors must work within their levels of competence with regard to race and culture. This will include having sufficient knowledge, respect and sensitivity towards different cultural worldviews, and an appropriate range and level of skills in working with complex cultural and racial processes.

- Counsellors must have sufficient understanding of unconscious processes related to race and culture in order to work effectively with transferences and projections that occur in the counselling dyad.

- Assessment of the client's difficulties and treatment strategy must be formulated within the client's cultural frame of reference, taking account of the client's social network and belief system.

- Sufficient time must be given to the establishment and maintenance of the counselling relationship in order to overcome cultural inhibitions and differences, and promote trust.

- A clear working agreement and boundaries must be discussed with the client, taking account of practicalities such as timing and who will attend, as well as the goal of counselling and the way of working.

Summing up

This section has focused on the challenges of psychodynamic practice in the contemporary world. Stressing the benefits of psychodynamic insight and principles for exploring racial and cultural processes at an unconscious level, it has also highlighted the need for psychodynamic counsellors to take account of wider societal issues. Recognising that race and culture are dynamic psychological and sociopolitical phenomena rather than descriptive characteristics, they are integral to the identity of the counsellor and the client. The interaction between the inner world and the outer world is thus highly pertinent to the organisation and practice of psychodynamic counselling in the 21st century.

Conclusion

In discussing the relevance of the psychodynamic frame for understanding racial and cultural dynamics in the contemporary world, consideration has been given to two complementary processes:

- the influence of sociopolitical forces on internalised racial and cultural attitudes

- the effect of intrapsychic processes on racial and cultural issues in society

Despite its traditional focus on intrapsychic life, it has been seen that a wider application of psychodynamic concepts to the sociopolitical arena enables a rich understanding of this multi-faceted area.

REFERENCES

Adams, M.V. (1996). *The Multicultural Imagination: 'Race', Color and the Unconscious.* London and New York: Routledge.

Alford, C. F. (1989). *Melanie Klein and Critical Social Theory.* New Haven, CT and London: Yale University Press.

Alleyne, A. (1998). 'Which women? What feminism?'. In I. B. Seu and M. C. Heenan (eds), *Feminism and Psychotherapy.* London: Sage.

Carter, R. T. (1995). *The Influence of Race and Racial Identity in Psychotherapy: Toward a Racially Inclusive Model.* New York: Wiley.

Comas-Díaz, L. and Jacobsen, F. M. (1991). 'Ethnocultural transference and countertransference in the therapeutic dyad'. *American Journal of Orthopsychiatry,* 61: 3, 392–402.

Cross, W. E. (1971). 'The Negro-to-Black conversion experience: toward a psychology of Black liberation'. *Black World,* 20: 9, 13–27.

Cross, W. E. (1978). 'The Cross and Thomas models of psychological Nigrescence'. *Journal of Black Psychology,* 5: 1, 13–19.

Curry, A. (1964). 'Myth, transference and the black psychotherapist'. *Psychoanalytic Review,* 51, 7–14.

Dalal, F. (1988). 'The racism of Jung'. *Race and Class,* 29: 3, 1–22.

Elliott, A. (2002). *Psychoanalytic Theory: An Introduction,* 2nd edition. Basingstoke: Palgrave Macmillan.

Fanon, F. (1952). *Black Skin, White Masks.* London: Pluto.

Fernando, S. (ed.) (1995). *Mental Health in a Multi-Ethnic Society.* London: Routledge.

Fernando, S. (1996). 'Counselling minorities: aspects of race and culture'. *RACE Newsletter* (BACP), 10, 8.

Freud, S. (1914). 'Totem and taboo'. In J. Strachey (ed.), *The Standard Edition of the Complete Psychological Works of Sigmund Freud, Volume XIII.* London: Hogarth.

Fryer, P. (1984). *Staying Power: A History of Black People in Britain.* London: Pluto.

Heller, J. S. (1970). 'Concepts of race inferiority in nineteenth century anthropology'. *Journal of the History of Medicine,* 25, 40–51.

Helms, J. E. (1984). 'Toward an explanation of the influence of race in the counseling process: a black-white model'. *Counseling Psychologist,* 12, 153–65.

Helms, J. E. (ed.) (1990). *Black and White Racial Identity Theory: Theory, Research and Practice.* Westport, CT: Greenwood.

Helms, J. E. (1995). 'An update of Helms' White and People of Color racial identity models'. In J. G. Ponterotto, J. M. Casas, L. A. Suzuki and C. M. Alexander (eds), *Handbook of Multicultural Counseling.* Thousand Oaks, CA: Sage.

Helms, J. E. and Cook, D. A. (2000). *Using Race and Culture in Counseling and Psychotherapy: Theory and Process.* Fort Worth, TX: Harcourt Brace Jovanovich.

Helms, J. E. and Richardson, T. Q. (1997). 'How "multiculturalism" obscures race and culture as differential aspects of counseling competency'. In D. B. Pope-Davis and H. L. K. Coleman (eds), *Multicultural Counseling Competencies: Assessment, Education and Training, and Supervision.* Thousand Oaks, CA: Sage.

Ho, D. Y. F. (1995). 'Internalised culture, culturocentrism and transcendence'. *Counseling Psychologist,* 23: 1, 4–24.

Hofstede, G. (1994). *Cultures and Organisations: Software of the Mind.* London: HarperCollins.

Jahoda, G. (1999). *Images of Savages: Ancient Roots of Modern Prejudice in Western Culture.* London: Routledge.

Jung, C. G. (1930). 'Your Negroid and Indian behaviour'. *Forum,* 83: 4, 193–9.

Katz, J. H. (1985). 'The sociopolitical nature of counseling'. *Counseling Psychologist,* 13: 4, 615–24.

King, P. and Steiner, R. (eds) (1990). *The Freud–Klein Controversies, 1941–45.* London: Routledge.

Klein, M. (1959). 'Our adult world and its roots in infancy'. In Klein, *Envy and Gratitude and Other Works.* London: Hogarth.

Kluckhohn, C. and Murray, H. A. (1949). 'Personality formation: the determinants'. In C. Kluckhohn and H. A. Murray (eds), *Personality in Nature, Society and Culture.* New York: Knopf.

Lipsky, S. (1978). 'Internalized oppression'. In J. Duncan (ed.), *Black Reemergence, Volume 2.* Seattle, WA: Rational Island.

Littlewood, R. (1992). 'Towards an intercultural therapy'. In J. Kareem and R. Littlewood (eds), *Intercultural Therapy: Themes, Interpretations and Practice.* Oxford: Blackwell.

Littlewood, R. and Lipsedge, M. (1993). *Aliens and Alienists: Ethnic Minorities and Psychiatry,* 2nd edition. London and New York: Routledge.

Malik, K. (1996). *The Meaning of Race: Race, History and Culture in Western Society.* London: Macmillan (now Palgrave Macmillan).

Ridley, C. R. (1989). 'Racism in counseling as an adverse behavior process'. In P. B. Pedersen, J. G. Draguns, W. J. Lonner and J. E. Trimble (eds), *Counseling Across Cultures,* 3rd edition. Honolulu, HI: University of Hawaii Press.

Ridley, C. R. (1995). *Overcoming Unintentional Racism in Counseling and Therapy: A Practitioner's Guide to Intentional Action.* Newbury Park, CA: Sage.

Rose, E. (1997). 'Daring to work with internalised racism'. *Counselling,* 8: 2, 92–4.

Rose, N. (1988). 'A commentary on Dr Roland Littlewood's paper'. *Journal of Social Work Practice,* 3: 3, 20–2.

Rustin, M. (1991). *The Good Society and the Inner World: Psychoanalysis, Politics and Culture*. London: Verso.

Speight, S. L., Myers, L. J., Cox, C. I. and Highlen, P. S. (1991). 'A redefinition of multicultural counseling'. *Journal of Counseling and Development*, 70, 29–35.

Thomas, L. (1992). 'Racism and psychotherapy: working with racism in the consulting room: an analytical view'. In J. Kareem and R. Littlewood (eds), *Intercultural Therapy: Themes, Interpretations and Practice*. Oxford: Blackwell.

Tuckwell, G. (2002). *Racial Identity, White Counsellors and Therapists*. Buckingham: Open University Press.

Vines, G. (1995). 'Genes in black and white'. *New Scientist*, 147, 34–7.

Wheeler, S. and Izzard, S. (1997). 'Psychodynamic counselor training – integrating difference'. *Psychodynamic Counselling*, 3: 4, 401–17.

Williams, R. (1983). *Keywords: A Vocabulary of Culture and Society*. London: Fontana.

10

Psychodynamic Counselling and Class

Miriam Isaac

Introduction

Class is a neglected area of enquiry in counselling and psychotherapy. Gender, 'race', sexuality and other aspects of diversity have attracted and continue to attract considerable attention. However, though passing reference to class is made in a number of discourse contexts including the noted aspects of diversity, a debate equal to that associated with 'race', one that explores the potentialities of class as both a problematic and fruitful therapeutic construct, has yet to be undertaken.

In the 1970s, when racism and sexism first came to widespread attention, the initial focus in each case was in terms of equal opportunities, and the discrimination experienced by the oppressed group. The emphasis was on the group or individual experiencing oppression – what legislation/education/access is needed to ensure that they receive equal opportunities in, for instance, education, services and employment. Little attention was paid to the relationship between the person experiencing the racism or sexism and their oppressor other than in terms of the practicalities of individual discrimination and exclusion. How the subtleties and the unconscious motivations of the oppressor group and the oppressed group were experienced in relationship to one another both professionally and personally was not yet part of the agenda. A similar trajectory can be seen in the field of disability studies. However, the emphasis has shifted. Whilst not neglecting equal opportunities and access issues, the present anti-oppressive agendas associated with 'race', gender, sexual orientation and disability now emphasise how oppression is enacted as part of a relationship between black and white, male and female, straight and gay, able-bodied and disabled, and in both institutional and private encounters. The same cannot be said for class. Class remains a hidden dynamic in professional encounters, because it would appear that the discursive agenda has remained fixed in the realm of equal opportunities and access, such as the measurement of differential access to counselling by socioeconomic group, or the language, style and assumptions of therapy (Trevithick, 1988). There is recognition of structural inequality, with a great deal of evidence suggesting social class remains the single most powerful determinant of life chances (Child Poverty Action Group, 2004; Collini, 1994; Kearney, 2003; Social Dimensions of Health Institute, 2004), but discussion of the relational dynamics of class is missing. In the 'frequently incanted quartet of race, class, gender and sexual orientation there is no doubt that class has been the least fashionable' (Collini, 1994, p. 3); the add-on, the one that is referred to but remains elusive.

I would like to suggest that there are at least two reasons for this lack of articulation. The first is to do with the close association that class has with politics, and the attitudes to politics found within the psychodynamic/psychoanalytic literature. The second is related to the problematic concept of class itself. This chapter presents an exploration of these two issues and then goes on to suggest a theoretical basis for incorporating class into a practice that more fully accounts for difference.

Politics in psychodynamic theory and practice

Rustin (1991) and Frosh (1999) locate the lack of political awareness (politics used in the broad sense of the word) and claims for political neutrality in classical psychoanalysis as rooted in both the theory and the associated practice. For instance, Rustin (1991) argues that the commonly held perception within the genre is that political activity relates to defence mechanisms such as displacement, and is a projection of inner feelings. This then renders political activity and experience valid only in an individual and interpersonal sense. Frosh (1999) supports Rustin's view and gives examples of explanations in the psychoanalytic literature that posit revolutionary politics as the product of psychopathological fixations, and radical action as the product of neurosis. He also argues that effectively, these pathologising explanations invalidate the social experience of the individual. Any activity undertaken as part of a particular group or class in society is only analysed in terms of the individual's internal world. For instance, in the past the experiences of women, black and gay people, as members of an identifiable group, were denied on this basis. Disallowing group identity or experience, concentrating *wholly* on the individual at the expense of shared experience has the effect of questioning the validity of that experience precisely because

> ... it always deals with how experience with the social becomes engaged with in ways which are deeply personal and because it searches out the unrecognised forces that give pattern to our desires, dreams and neuroses. (Frosh, 1999, p. 312)

But importantly, as Frosh makes equally clear, this is also its strength. Although psychoanalytic theory betrays individualistic and conservative tendencies, it also provides for the possibility of analysing the means by which the social world and its meanings, structures and ideologies become part of the lived experience of each individual and in turn reproduces and perpetuates specific ideological practices and forms of oppression. It also provides an explanation of how individuals become positioned socially.

In addition to questioning the role of the social in psychoanalytic discourse, both Rustin and Frosh note the historical link of psychoanalysis with conservative and conformist programmes. Rustin (1991, p. 12) highlights the use that the influential functionalist sociologist Talcott Parsons (1951, 1965) made of Freud's theory of repression. According to Rustin, Parsons incorporated repression into his theory of socialisation because it supported his commitment to the conservative values of stability, tradition, differentiation and hierarchy. Rustin also locates the way in which liberal politics emphasises human needs as being intensely individualistic, oriented entirely towards instinctive and hedonistic desires at the expense of any idea of humans as social beings, as similarly situated within a conservative and conformist programme. He highlights the link between this and the underlying philosophical position of much psychoanalytic thought. Frosh (1999, pp. 311–12) further identifies the manner in which some familial ideology has been used as deeply conservative and repressive, whilst conversely there is a total neglect of how the bourgeois family inherent within the theoretical constructs of much of psychoanalytic thinking 'serves the interests of particular power groups or modes of economic organisation'. There is also detailed chronicling of the biologism, and the paternalistic, even misogynistic 'tendencies present in many psychoanalytic formulations'. He notes the various ways psychoanalytic theory has in the past participated in 'reactionary political assumptions' and agendas against dissent, for instance in supporting the oppression of women by explaining away oppressive practices, and promulgating a conformist ideology such as 'heterosexuality as the end point of sexual development'.

Instead of the neutrality it claims, it would appear that therapy has inadvertently served, either implicitly or explicitly, political agendas promoting particular ideologies.

It is now generally accepted in social, political and psychological theorising that no theory can be neutral and that claiming neutrality serves a hidden agenda. According to Frosh (1999) and Maroda (1991) the claim of neutrality in psychoanalysis has frequently been used to justify the therapist's response to their own uncomfortable feelings. In addition, as Illovsky (2002) points out, it can result in an exclusive definition of therapy that refuses to engage with the psychological impact of social and economic forces. Moreover in taking this stance, there is the added risk of lending support, albeit unintentionally, to other conservative programmes. Indeed, Yalom states that

> If we do not recognise the dangers of our attempts to be neutral we are creating the possibility that we may become an agency for social control, enabling clients only to accept the unacceptable by defending (by default or deliberately) the indefensible. (Yalom, 1980, p. 91)

Kearney (1996), one of the few to specifically address the question of class in counselling, similarly considers that no ideology can make a claim of neutrality. Moreover, she suggests that 'having no political ideology of which we are aware is not at all the same thing as not having any political ideology' (1996, p. 23), that just as we can act out of racist or sexist assumptions without being aware that we are being racist or sexist, we can act politically without being aware of that. A constant theme within the literature on counselling and therapy is the challenge to practitioners that they should examine their unconscious motivations, constructs and worldview and that of the model within which they practise. Kearney, emphasising the need for a reassessment of the effects of class in counselling, echoes this sentiment when she suggests that

> anything which we as counsellors allow to be unexamined (like our sexism, racism etc.) is much more likely to influence our relationship with a client than something we become and remain aware of. (Kearney, 1996, p. 23)

If the therapeutic community now engages with the relational nature of 'race', gender, sexual orientation and disability, reflecting on how these issues affect practitioners and how they are brought into the therapeutic relationship in general and in the transference relationship in particular, then class should also receive similar discursive consideration. The potential value of psychoanalytic/ dynamic theory for any project linking the social with the individual 'lies in its ability to provide an account of subjectivity which links the "external" structures of the social world with the internal world of each individual' (Frosh, 1999, p. 15).

What is class?

Class is anything but a straightforward concept. Generally speaking we can identify ourselves in terms of a specific gender or ethnicity, but when it comes to class, personal definitions can be confused by misconceptions, ambivalence and status. This difficulty is augmented by the debate in social theory about what class actually is. A useful starting point and one that is relevant to this discussion is the division between 'strong' and 'weak' class theory (Lee and Turner, 1996). Although a rather crude division, it does serve to illustrate a pertinent difference in analysis, one that may add to an understanding of why class has not been fully incorporated into the diversity agenda.

The 'strong' conception of class is primarily a holistic approach to class and society. Class is perceived as a 'causal factor in historical change and in the overall organisation of society and its institutions' (Lee and Turner, 1996, p. 9). Furthermore, class is seen as fundamentally affecting the lives of individuals 'even though they themselves may be unaware that their own actions contribute to its continuance' (ibid.). The foremost proponent of this conception of class was Marx (1981, 1985). He proposed that to satisfy the basic human need for food, drink, shelter, warmth and so on humans enter into social and economic relationships with others. In so doing humans, acting on and in the world, create the world. They do this in both a material sense, the homes and shelters they build, the food they grow and eat, and in a social and economic sense, the relationships they enter into to further these needs and the social structures they build to support them. Historically, these processes produced simple societies and structures that gradually became more and more complex, as the social and economic relationships that individuals entered into to meet their needs in turn recreated them. Within this view of the world social relations are not static, not a given, or essentialist in nature, but dynamic. They change with changed circumstances. Thus human action in the world at any one time creates particular forms of social and political organisation, ways of thinking about, and acting in, the world. This has both positive and negative consequences. It may provide for human physical needs, but in so doing it has produced structures based on inequality and oppression, the roots of which are now deeply embedded in society. As the roots of these constructions have become part of history and disappeared from view, the structures or oppressive practices they involve have become naturalised, for instance in hierarchy and gender relationships (see for example Delphy, 1984; Hartsock, 1983). For Marx, his theory of historical materialism, that is the economic relationship of human beings one to another acting on the world to produce their means of living, is *the* fundamental relationship, as it gave rise to all other economic, political and social forms. Humans are inextricably linked to one another within the social and economic order.

Crompton (1998), quoting Keat and Urry (1989, pp. 94–5), holds to the view that social divisions arise as a result of class: it

> refers to social entities, which are not directly observable, yet which are historically present … The existence of classes is not to be identified with the existence of inequalities of income, wealth, status or educational opportunity … class structures are taken to cause such inequalities. The meaning of the term 'class' is not given by these inequalities. Rather it is the structure of class relationships which determines the pattern of inequality. (Crompton, 1998, p. 82)

For Marx and Marxists class is relational. There cannot be one class without another. In his seminal text *The Making of the English Working Class*, E. P. Thompson expresses this succinctly:

> By class I understand a historical phenomenon, unifying a number of disparate and seemingly unconnected events, both in the raw material of experience and in consciousness. I emphasise that it is a historical phenomenon. I do not see class as a 'structure' nor even a 'category' but as something which in fact happens (and can be shown to have happened) in human relationships. More than this, the notion of class entails the notion of historical relationship. Like any other relationship, it is a fluency, which evades analysis if we attempt to stop it dead at any given moment and anatomise its structure. The finest meshed sociological net cannot give us a pure specimen of class, any more than it can give us one of deference or of love. The relationship must always be embodied in real people and in a real context. Moreover, we cannot have two distinct classes, each with an independent being, and then bring them into relationship with each other. We cannot have love without lovers, nor deference without squires and labourers. (Thompson, 1968, p. 9)

In contrast a 'weak' class explanation, following a Weberian (1978) analysis, rejects the notion 'that class may be more than the sum of its parts' or that 'classes are independent entities in any sense'. This can be summed up as a 'positional' approach to class and is most strongly associated with ideas of *social* class (Lee and Turner, 1996, p. 9). Classes are in the first place simply empirically identifiable groupings of individuals who have certain analytically significant situations (such as their possession of property or a highly paid skill) in common.

Crucially, for an account of class within therapeutic practice incorporating diversity, the 'weak' form of class analysis tends to see issues concerning class as associated with individual class position, equal opportunities, action and meaning rather than having the interdependent, relational quality present in the 'strong' account of class. As a consequence, although the 'weak' class analysis provides us with a useful means of understanding class differences, access to resources, services and so on, it does not provide the premise by which we are able to account for the social within the internal world of the individual or within the transference communications of the therapeutic dyad because it does not see class as embodied within relationships.

In contradistinction to class defined unambiguously as related to the structural position of the client, the 'strong' account stresses the relational quality of class, a fluency that embraces the therapist's worldview and identity as well as the client's. In practical terms a 'weak' class analysis means, for example, that viewing the effects of poverty as part of the client's difficulties, without recourse to consideration of the symbolic or actual role the therapist plays in this, obscures the class dimension in the therapeutic relationship and the power relationship in the transference. This is akin to the 'colour blind' approach in racism. To paraphrase Tuckwell (2002, p. 45) writing on racial identity in counselling: by concentrating on universal, cultural or individual characteristics such as 'We're all the same', 'I treat each person as an individual', 'I don't see colour [class], it's irrelevant', counsellors and therapists are able to 'disregard their own uncomfortable feelings and insecurities' about race [class]. By dismissing or ignoring the relational quality of class or 'race' the very real possibility arises that the therapist becomes part of the process of oppression by 'the inadvertent repetition of customary power imbalances and inequitable outcomes' (ibid.). Conversely, by following a relational view of class any power differential in the dyad becomes visible and therefore something which can be worked with.

The absence of a relational analysis of class results in middle class counsellors and therapists having ideas about working class clients that either hold to a deficit model of the client, or a pathologising of difference. The client either doesn't measure up in some way to the norm, or their cultural theories are overlooked, or they are pathologised, reminiscent of earlier therapeutic interventions and theory in work with other oppressed groups such as black or gay clients. In addition, failing to provide a relational explanation 'leaves the door open for underclass theories which seek to blame the poor for their welfare dependency and lack of moral fibre' (Lavalette et al., 2001, p. 51) or a 'politics of victim blaming' (Cully, 2000). Any therapeutic approach which emphasises the pathology of the client whilst holding the power to make interpretations, and to define that pathology, can under certain circumstances be open to accusations of inequality (Tuckwell, 2002), abuse of power (Guggenbuhl-Craig,

1999), as well as bypassing the need for professionals to engage with their client's subjective experience as well as their own (Cully, 2000).

The 'strong' account of class with its view of human individuality as socially constructed is clearly present in a strand of Freudian thinking. Although Freud's professed understanding of humans as instinctually driven, with society's role as functioning to repress libidinal impulses, is a deeply conservative conceptualisation (Frosh, 1999) there is also within Freud a

> ... detailed developmental analysis describing how individuals are built up in layers around internalised social forms, themselves the product of history. This approach takes as its focal assumption the idea that individuality arises through a process of social construction, for instance, as described by object relations theorists. (Frosh, 1999, p. 156)

Frosh questions the validity of building a theory and practice which neglects the structuring factors, conditioning and influencing individual relationships that are 'systematically distorted as they are under capitalism and patriarchy'. If these factors are ignored 'the orders of causality' in the world are reversed, leading to a reductionism of the 'social order as produced by the free behaviours of individuals' (Frosh, 1999, p. 267).

Making a relationship between the inner and outer world

Rustin (1991) suggests the breakthrough from the crippling antithesis of individual and social in classical psychoanalysis came with the development of object relations theory, specifically the work of Klein, Fairburn and Winnicott. Frosh (1999) concurs but considers the work of Lacan, and the feminist psychoanalytic tradition, for instance the work of Mitchell (1975), as important in developing an heuristic procedure for analysing the social in the individual.

In addition, 'culture school' theory (Eric Fromm and Karen Horney) critiques Freud's biologism to considerable effect. Briefly, their argument centres on the proposition that what Freud saw as biologically determined was in effect culturally conditioned. However, this proposition is one-dimensional in that although it speaks of how the cultural in any one society may condition the individual in any one particular way – a good example being perhaps the cultural component of gender and gender relationships – in culture theory, the dynamic component of the relationship between the inner and outer world is missing. That is, individuals, although effectively constructed by their society, are also active with others in the construction of their own personality and in the construction of their world. This is significant in developing an understanding of class from a relational point of view.

Without wishing to exaggerate the differences between Freud and object relations theorists there is nevertheless considerable divergence in their views of the relationship between the inner and outer worlds. Freud hypothesised that the individual was a separate entity to the social world, a self-contained being, notionally an essentialised identity. Because of this, the social world is only comprehensible in the terms of the energy it generates into, and out of, the individual. As a product of biological drives the individual is posited in opposition to rather than constituting the social world and therefore can only be controlled or not controlled by it. He or she can never be seen as socially constructed or constructing the world, either wholly or in part, because the relationship with the outer world is limited to this oppositional stance. Even the relationship with the parents or primary caregivers is encapsulated within the inner world, with limited reference to the social milieu within which it is framed. Guntrip (1973, p. 49), commenting on Freud's instinct theory, notes that the latter views biology as the 'machinery of personal life ... a study of the mechanisms of behaviour', not to be confused with 'the meaningful personal experience that is the essence of the personal self'. For Freud and traditional psychoanalysts, relationships are formed with others *only* as a consequence of and as an outlet for aggressive and sexual drives. Within the object relations tradition, relations are *primary*, enacted from birth or even pre-birth, rather than as a consequence of something else.

There is no way to resolve the division between the social and the individual in Freudian theory and this has been the root cause of tensions between social theorists and psychoanalytic theory. With object relations theory the position in this respect is somewhat different. In object relations, the dominant feature of human psychology is the need to form relationships with the 'other'. Libido is object seeking rather than pleasure seeking (Fairburn in Frosh, 1999). The individual is posited as a social being of the first order and although instincts and drives are accounted for, for instance in the acknowledgment of the sex drive as *initially* biological (Guntrip, 1973) or in Klein's (1940) emphasis on envy, 'object relations theory embeds each individual in a social context and suggests that there is no way of understanding the one without the other' (Frosh, 1999, p. 100). There is no individual without the social, no self without the other. In other words, the very fact of being human, being brought into the world by 'another' and cared for by 'others' with whom we relate and construct our object relations as the building blocks of our personality, means that we are essentially social beings:

> The baby, having incorporated his parents, feels them to be live people inside his body in the concrete way in which deep unconscious phantasies are experienced – they are, in his mind, 'internal' or 'inner' objects, as I have termed them. Thus an inner world is being built up in the child's unconscious mind, corresponding to his actual experiences and the impressions he gains from people and the external world, and yet altered by his own phantasies and impulses. (Klein, 1940, p. 148)

Part of what the baby incorporates within his or her unconscious is the parents' experience and impressions of the social world, their own internalised feelings, fears, oppressions and power relationships. Accordingly, deeply embedded within our unconscious there lie aspects of the social world as experienced in our primary object relations. These are manifested in our later object relating. A process of 'active striving with external objects in the service of an integrating relational urge' is how Winnicott sees the developmental process with instincts operating secondarily and in support of, rather than as the motivating factor for relationships (in Frosh, 1999, p. 101).

Although the object relations theorists Fairbairn and Winnicott provide the potential link between the inner and outer worlds and explain how social identities such as race, gender and class may be construed, such analysis was not their project. In effect the early object relations theorists treat the mother-and-child dyad as if it were outside society, with the external world only functioning as an interference, the perfect or natural scenario being the mother and child 'in no way inherently constituted by it' (Frosh, 1999, p. 117). Nevertheless, perhaps their work provides the necessary link with the so-called 'strong' concept of class. In object relations theory, humans are essentially social beings. Their first and foremost characteristic is that of interacting or relating with others. This is an echo of Marx albeit with a different purpose in mind. Marx frequently alludes to the 'necessity of intercourse with other men', suggesting that the latter is a specifically human activity permeated by the social relation of individual to individual:

> For the animal its relation to others does not exist as a relation. Consciousness is, therefore, from the very beginning a social product, and remains so as long as men exist at all. (Marx, 1985, p. 51)

For Marx, like the object relations theorists, any consideration of the individual as outside his or her social context is a false abstraction that denies the social character of being. In addition, immanent in Marx is a sense of the inner world of the individual; for example he writes in *The German Ideology*:

> Men are the producers of their conceptions, ideas etc. Real active men as they are conditioned by a definite development of their productive forces and of the intercourse corresponding to these, up to its furthest forms. Consciousness can never be anything else than conscious existence and the existence of men is their actual life process. (1985, p. 47)

Clearly for Marx, the dynamics of the inner and outer worlds are intimately related and utterly dependent on one another. Given his concentration on the outer world rather than the inner world, references to the latter are limited to an acknowledgement of its importance but are without further articulation. The dynamic process evident in Marx resonates with the work of Klein, who could be said to incidentally provide Marx's link to the inner world. The emphasis on phantasy in Klein, the means by which the individual psyche mediates the impact of the outer world, provides the internal dynamic that contrasts with Marx's external one. In the operation of phantasy 'the (real) social world is experienced through a conflicting screen of internal forces, which alter and shape it powerfully' (Frosh, 1999, p. 128).

Furthermore, Klein links the outer world with the successful internal integration of the child. The suggestion is that in the developmental stage of negotiating the paranoid-schizoid position, there needs to be 'a predominance of good over bad experiences' to which 'both internal and external factors contribute' (Segal, 1973, p. 37). External factors here are associated with the encapsulated relationship of the mother and child. However, there is increasing acceptance that the mother/child dyad is a contextualised relationship and factors such as gender, race and class impact in myriad ways on this relationship. Given that transference in the therapeutic process mirrors the early object relating, aspects of context can therefore be found within the therapeutic dyad.

Without wishing to deny the extra material difficulties with which working class individuals can be faced, and whilst accepting these need to be taken into account within the broad church of counselling and psychotherapy, there is a danger in this use of Klein, of reintroducing the 'weak' one-dimensional view of class as related to the structural position of the client only. For example, take the situation of a middle class counsellor working with a working class client. If the analysis emphasises the problematic situation that the client faces in terms of good experience over bad experience or how those experiences have been mediated through phantasy, without paying attention to how the world impinges on their relationship in the therapy, the solution is partial and misses a productive aspect. Attention must be paid to ways in which the world impinges on the middle class counsellor or therapist. According to Tuckwell (2002, p. 3), 'where people have been systematically socialized into being in a position of power and privilege' [in this instance that associated with class], 'there is little need for them to address the issue of their [middle class] identity.' To follow this path not only reinforces the power and privilege that the middle class individual takes for granted but also obscures the interpersonal dynamics of class and invalidates the latter as a potential tool of analysis. Thus it is in transference and countertransference that the class dynamic may be most apparent and therefore most fruitfully worked with.

Power, class, transference and countertransference

Transference, the object relations making up the client's inner world and derived from early experiences in relating with others, is not only individual and familial, but also contains representations of the wider social context of the client and the counsellor.

> The client's experience, the make-up of her object relationships and inner world, is a product not only of her membership of her family, but also of a particular culture, ethnic group, social class, gender, sexual orientation and such other. (Spurling, 2004, p. 109)

The most important aspect of working with class in the transference is power. In terms of identity politics, following the discourse of post-structuralism, power is usually conceived of as omnipresent; the relations between men and women, black and white people, gays and straights, able-bodied and the disabled, are 'saturated with power'. This epistemological position mirrors commonly held views of the power differentials within society: men assault and abuse women, white people are racist towards black people, able-bodied society dominates the position of the disabled, the middle class holds power in relation to the working class, and so on and so forth (Ferguson et al., 2002). The obverse of this relationship is the feeling of powerlessness, and actual powerlessness, experienced by the oppressed group in the face of domination by the 'other'.

Although a working class client may not be experiencing material deprivation or obvious inequality, unconscious frustrations, angers and desires related to the dynamics of class may lie deeply embedded within their inner world, which may be different or similar to those of the therapist. Spurling (2004) draws attention to the need to listen carefully to perceptions and experience expressed in the transference related to social similarity and difference. Using examples related to racism and homophobia, he highlights how both members of the dyad experience difference and how this informs the transference and the countertransference. Tuckwell's (2002) discussion of black/white transference may equally apply to middle class/working class transference because both racism and classism (and for that matter sexism) reflect the power relationships within society and the dominance of one group by another. I do not argue that racism is the same as oppression on the basis of class, or that all oppressions are the same: they are not. However, the manner in which oppressive practice and domination are enacted and the way in which oppression is mediated bear striking similarities, for instance in the use of denigrating language, fantasies and myths, stereotyping, fears and, crucially, the construction of difference in and by the 'other'. The 'other' is everything that 'I' am not.

Fanon's (1967) *Black Skin, White Masks* demonstrates the relational quality of oppression. He argues that white men consider themselves to be superior to black men and that the latter wish at all costs to prove themselves of equal value, but come to identify themselves with the subordinate position assigned to them by history. The 'other' defines each position, and each position would not exist without the other. The ensuing superiority/inferiority complex is evident in contact between the two groups and according to Fanon unconsciously informs all black/white relationships. Although Fanon was drawing from post-colonial experiences and it may be erroneous to generalise from the specific, he clearly chronicles the effect of superior/subordinate power positions in *a* society. It is not difficult to draw a parallel here with middle class/working class relationships, which in common with the black/white dichotomy share an historically superior/subordinate position within a class stratified society. Symbolically and in material reality they are also defined in contradistinction to one another. Fanon identified hatred, envy, anxiety and shame as emotions located within and expressed by both groups in relationship to one another. Similarly Guggenbuhl-Craig (1999) notes the 'shadow self' as having import for both parties in the therapeutic relationship.

In a society that either valorises or excludes working class groups, for instance in labels or categorisation such as 'the deserving poor' and the 'noble worker' or conversely the 'work shy' and 'the benefit scrounger', or in proscribing of particular groups such as teenage mothers, the associated images enter our consciousness at a very deep level. The same can be said of the view of the middle class from a working class perspective and although these images are not in common parlance (another demonstration of where the power to define lies) they may be associated with envy of 'having a better life', fantasies of wealth or being 'stuck up'. Described as pre-transferences (Curry in Tuckwell, 2002) the beliefs, fantasies and myths that one group has of another are present prior to the meeting of the therapist and the client and inform their impressions of one another. Furthermore, according to Comas-Díaz and Jacobsen (1991) and Alleyne (in Tuckwell, 2002, p. 64), the content of transference is collective, in the sense that it has grown out of the 'accumulated experience' of one group in relation to another and is reinforced by institutionalised social structures. 'Power relations are the means by which society enters into the consciousness of each person' (Frosh, 1999, p. 272). In addition, intentional or not, the 'emphasis on neutrality and distance' and the 'structure of the psychoanalytic situation' distinctly emphasise 'the power asymmetries present in the therapeutic dyad' (Frosh, 1999, p. 299). It follows therefore that within the transference and countertransference the client or the therapist holds powerful images related to the social structure. The power relationship and the introjected societal structure will be part of all relationships, preceding any oral communication. This has import for the parent/child transference and countertransference as these are suffused with symbolic and literal power allied to the imagined and real power of parents. In this way the therapist becomes the focus of power in the dyadic relationship.

Couple this with the normative acceptance of power associated with being middle class, and the alienated powerlessness which is the deeply embedded experience of the working class, and there is the potential, in a dyad representing these relations, for a potentially damaging re-enactment of the accepted social and familial order. Alternatively, and critically for the class dynamic, there is also a potential for the client to explore power relations in the broad sense of the word 'as they emerge in therapy and as they mimic internalised relations from the formative periods of her or his life' (Frosh, 1999, p. 273). The therapist, as the container of both social and familial power, faces the client with the paradox of being both part of the problem and the solution. This may offer one explanation as to why working class and poorer clients are more likely to prematurely terminate their counselling and be blamed for doing so (Illovsky, 2002) and why many counsellors deny being members of an elite group (Dijk, 1993). Both may be aspects of defensive reactions to intolerable emotions. Gunaratnam (1997) comments on 'the distance between safe and manageable fact files'; in other words, viewing difference through a cultural component rather than within the 'reality of power-based and emotionally charged relationships' can leave 'professionals stranded without guidance or reference points' (p. 181).

Conclusion

Class in counselling and psychotherapy is a problematic concept; not least because of the history of theorising between the different traditions associated with the individual and society, and the erstwhile defensive postures presented by those involved. 'Grand' theorising, all-encompassing theories presented and used as if providing an answer to everything, along with unchallengeable shibboleths, bear some responsibility for our inability to develop a practice that can, in addition to many other things, take account of difference constituted on the basis of class. Identity politics associated with gender, 'race', sexuality and disability have had a considerable impact on counselling and psychotherapy. Uncomfortable as it may be, perhaps there is nothing very different about class. It is constituted dynamically, one group gains at the expense of another, it is embedded in everyday relationships, it is institutional and it is about power, the power to define, exclude and dismiss. Critically, for any therapeutic project, class is evident in the transference and countertransference relationship. The implications of this are that either class is addressed and thus is transformed into a useful tool of analysis or it is ignored to the detriment of the outcome.

REFERENCES

Child Poverty Action Group (2004). *Health and Poverty*. London: CPAG.

Collini, S. (1994). 'Escape from DWEMSville'. *Times Literary Supplement*, 27 May.

Comas-Díaz, L. and Jacobsen, F. M. (1991). 'Ethnocultural transference and countertransference in the therapeutic dyad'. *American Journal of Orthopsychiatry*, 61: 3, 392–402.

Crompton, R. (1998). *Class and Stratification*, 2nd edition. Cambridge: Polity.

Cully, L. (2000). 'Working with diversity: beyond the factfile'. In C. Davies, L. Finlay and A. Bullman (eds), *Changing Practice in Health and Social Care*. London: Sage.

Delphy, C. (1984). *Close to Home: A Materialist Analysis of Women's Oppression*. London: Hutchinson.

Dijk, T. A. (1993). *Elite Discourse and Racism*. London: Sage.

Fanon, F. (1967). *Black Skin, White Masks*. London: Pluto.

Ferguson, I., Mooney, G. and Lavalette, M. (2002). *Rethinking Welfare: A Critical Perspective*. London: Sage.

Frosh, S. (1999). *The Politics of Psychoanalysis*, 2nd edition. Basingstoke: Macmillan (now Palgrave Macmillan).

Guggenbuhl-Craig, A. (1999). *Power in the Helping Professions*. Putnam, CT: Spring.

Gunaratnam, Y. (1997). 'Culture is not enough: a critique of multi-culturalism in palliative care'. In D. Field, J. Hockey and N. Small (eds), *Death, Gender and Ethnicity*. London: Routledge.

Guntrip, H. (1973). *Psychoanalytic Theory, Therapy and the Self*. New York: Basic Books.

Hartsock, N. (1983). 'The feminist standpoint: developing the ground for a specifically feminist historical materialism'. In S. Harding and M. Hintikka (eds),

Discovering Reality: Feminist Perspectives on Epistemology, Metaphysics, Methodology, and Philosophy of Science. Dordrecht, Boston, MA and London: Reidel.

Illovsky, M. (2002). *Mental Health Professionals, Minorities and the Poor.* London: Brunner-Routledge.

Kearney, A. (1996). *Counselling Class and Politics: Undeclared Influences in Therapy.* Manchester: PCCS.

Kearney, A. (2003). 'Class and counselling'. In C. Lago and B. Smith (eds), *Anti-Discriminatory Counselling Practice.* London: Sage.

Keat. R. and Urry, J. (1989). *Social Theory as Science.* London: Routledge.

Klein, M. (1940). 'Mourning and its relation to manic-depressive states'. In J. Mitchell (ed.) (1986), *The Selected Melanie Klein.* Harmondsworth: Penguin.

Lavalette, M., Mooney, G., Mynott, E., Evans, K. and Richardson, B. (2001). 'The woeful record of the House of Blair'. *International Socialism,* 90. http://pubs. socialistreviewindex.org.uk/isj90/lavalette.htm

Lee, D, and Turner, B. (1996). *Conflicts about Class: Debating Inequality in Late Industrialism.* London: Longman.

Maroda, K. (1991). *The Power of Countertransference,* Chichester: Wiley.

Marx, K. (1981). *Economic and Philosophical Manuscripts of 1844,* 6th edition. London: Lawrence and Wishart.

Marx, K. (1985). *The German Ideology* (1845). London: Lawrence and Wishart.

Mitchell, J. (1975). *Psychoanalysis and Feminism.* Harmondsworth: Penguin.

Parsons, T. (1951). *The Social System.* London: Routledge and Kegan Paul.

Parsons, T. (1964). *Social Structure and Personality.* New York: Free Press.

Rustin, M. (1991). *The Good Society and the Inner World,* London: Verso.

Segal, H. (1973). *Introduction to the Work of Melanie Klein.* London: Hogarth.

Social Dimensions of Health Institute, University of St Andrews. Conference statement 30 September 2005.

Spurling, L. (2004). *An Introduction to Psychodynamic Counselling.* Basingstoke: Palgrave Macmillan.

Thompson, E. P. (1968). *The Making of the English Working Class.* Harmondsworth: Penguin.

Trevithick, P. (1988). 'Unconsciousness raising with working class women'. In S. Krzowski and P. Land (eds), *In Our Experience: Running Workshops with Women.* London: Women's Press.

Tuckwell, G. (2002). *Racial Identity, White Counsellors and Therapists*. Buckingham: Open University Press.

Weber, M. (1978). *Economy and Society*, two volumes. Trans. G. Roth and C. Wittich. Berkeley, CA: University of California Press.

Yalom, I. D. (1980). *Existential Psychotherapy*. New York: Basic Books.

Psychodynamic Counselling, Religion and Spirituality

Alistair Ross

At a time when religious differences dominate the world stage, conflicts abound as a result of intolerance, prejudice and unresolved aggression. Often a microcosm of world tensions will be enacted in the counselling room, when there is a religious difference between counsellor and client and especially if it remains unaddressed. The challenge of this chapter is for the reader to engage with religion and all that it entails to ensure that intolerance and ignorance are not perpetuated in the therapeutic arena. Quite why this should be a challenge is linked to the history of engagement between psychoanalysis and religion. In 1994, the theme of the Freud Museum conference was 'Is Psychoanalysis Another Religion?', and the chairman, David Black, commented that such openness to religion from the side of psychoanalysis would have been unthinkable only a few short years before. In 1996 The Institute of Psychoanalysis held a similar conference, 'Competitors or Collaborators? Psychoanalysis and Religion in the 21st Century', where Ron Britton made a similar response (www.freud.org.uk/Religion.htm). The good news is that there are constructive views about religion emerging within psychoanalysis. Jacobs, surveying the previous decade, observes 'some psychoanalysts are taking a more positive view of the phenomena of religious belief' (2000, p. vii). The bad news is that 'too many still follow Freud's negative view of religion' (West, 2000, p. 15). This tension is also found in psychodynamic counselling and psychoanalytic psychotherapy, profoundly influenced by psychoanalysis and its antipathy towards religion (Wulff, 1997).

Despite a century of psychoanalytic practice, religion – illusion or not – is still alive and well and turning up in the consulting room. Spiritual experience is a common part of life and if psychodynamic counselling is to engage with the whole of clients' experiences this needs to be acknowledged in the therapeutic encounter. Yet religion is a difficult subject to deal with as it provokes so many different, often polarised reactions. These responses need exploring to help understand what happens in a counselling relationship when issues of religion or spirituality emerge.

Religion, spirituality and counselling: a research perspective

People have instinctive responses to the word 'religion' that are not always rational and that sometimes take them by surprise. In a counsellor training exercise the words 'religion' and 'spirituality' are written up and students asked to respond with the first thing that comes to mind. The resulting list shows that responses to 'religion' could be grouped under three headings, while 'spirituality' was more difficult to categorise:

RELIGION AS FEAR-PROVOKING: Punishment; hell; terrorism; Catholic schooling and physical punishment; guilt; sin; judgement

RELIGION AS BELONGING: Tradition; community; belonging; family; morality; cathedrals; awe; wonder; vital; alive

RELIGION AS IRRELEVANT: Alien; old-fashioned; patriarchal; homophobic; completely unknown; incomprehensible; men wearing frocks

SPIRITUALITY AS: Oneness; stillness; angels; wonder; energy; light; personal; weird; confusing; warm feelings; something that happens outside church; prayer

Doing this exercise over a number of years and seeing the energy and emotions this generated (often unconscious until the exercise itself) led to my initial research into religion and spirituality in counselling. The relationship between religion and spirituality is as part of a continuum; both are vitally linked despite the perception that one is different from the other. Due to the fluid nature of religion and spirituality one of the key metaphors that has emerged is that of 'landscape' (Heelas and Woodhead, 2005; Holmes, 2004). The purpose of the research was to chart the landscape of spirituality within the counselling relationship and this was done via a questionnaire. . Some 170 questionnaires were distributed at three different conferences covering a spectrum of counselling, therapeutic, faith and spiritual positions. The questionnaire contained four questions:

Question 1 gave six overarching definitions of spirituality, from which the respondents were asked to select their first, second and third choices, using categories A–F.

Question 2 asked the respondents to rate the importance of spirituality to counselling practice.

Question 3 asked the respondents to rate the importance of spirituality during their training.

Question 4 asked the respondents to rate the importance of spirituality in supervision.

Question 1 provided the following descriptive definitions of spirituality and respondents were asked to select which category best described their view. The terms 'Being' and 'Other' were used instead of 'God' to provide as generic terms as possible:

(A) A belief in an abstract power, Other or Being that influences self and others in general, non-interventionist ways

(B) A range of metaphysical experiences that communicate moments of awe and wonder that transcend normal human experience, e.g. birth of a child, spectacular scenery, or moments when time stands still

(C) A specific belief in a divine Being that can be encountered in a direct way, leading to spiritual growth or wholeness

(D) Adherence to a spiritual or religious belief system with prescribed ideas and practices

(E) The unique potential of each person and the qualities of being human provide a dimension of spirit, without reference to external factors

(F) A sense of independent self without the desire for any religious or spiritual belief system or experiences

These descriptions provide a spectrum of spiritual belief ranging from: the transcendent to the immanent; the external to the internal; the individual self to the collective self; the location of authority being beyond self and the location of authority being within self. The descriptions are generic and are drawn from Christian, Jewish, Moslem and Buddhist religions, as well as New Age, Humanistic and Transpersonal spiritualities. The results of the questionnaire (Table 11.1) highlight several areas of interest for psychodynamic counselling.

For the counsellors that responded, religious and spiritual beliefs, notably 'a specific belief in a divine Being that can be encountered in a direct way leading to spiritual growth or wholeness' (category C) forms an important facet of their personal beliefs. This implies, firstly, that belief is a specific commitment to a truth, value or Other, rather than just a general acceptance or awareness of values or spiritual experiences (Fowler, 1990). While Hay and Hunt's (2000) work on the generic spirituality of the British public emphasises the latter, it appears from this research that counsellors hold to a much more specific belief or value system. Secondly, it implies that a divine Being or Other is the focus of this belief or value system. Thirdly, there appears to be a process of direct encounter that has specific and beneficial results in terms of growth and wholeness. A significant percentage of counsellors and therapists choose a category that attests to a specific form of spiritual belief, or experience those results in growth. The nature of spiritual belief in a therapeutic context has a dynamic form.

Table 11.1   Counsellors' descriptive definitions of spirituality

% choosing one category		
Person-centred	**Psychodynamic**	**Integrative**
C 50	C 52	C 72
E 50	E 18	E 11
	B 18	B 11
	A 6	A 6
	D 6	

Those from a person-centred tradition were located at both ends of a spectrum as is seen modelled in the work of Mearns and Thorne (2000) who take very different positions on spirituality. Integrative counsellors strongly engage with spirituality encompassing the notion of a specific Being or Other, possibly because an integrative approach allows the therapist to integrate a spiritual dimension into their work. Psychodynamic counsellors exhibit the widest diversity of spiritual beliefs as expressed in the categories available. . These views about the importance and value of spirituality appear to be much stronger than expected given the decline of the established Church and other religious traditions, and may be one reason for the increasing voice spirituality is finding in the counselling world (West, 2000, 2004). These figures might support the notion of 'detraditionalization' (Woodhead and Heelas, 2000, p. 485) where there are major changes happening in a move away from formal and denominational religion. This process is marked by a move from external, transcendent religious authority to an integral, relational here-and-now spirituality (ibid.). Lynch (2002, 2003) charts significant changes happening in spirituality and contemporary culture such as a spirituality of clubbing. As such counselling and psychotherapy have become beacons that also mark this transition.

In Table 11.1 it is noticeable that psychodynamic counsellors are less consistent in their choices, possibly influenced by embedded attitudes towards religion espoused in psychoanalysis. Yet these results indicate that over 50 per cent of psychodynamic counsellors see significant value in a direct experience of god/God/divine Being/Other leading to growth as the most important expression of their spirituality. A belief in a divine Being does not appear to be antithetical to therapeutic practice (Northcut, 1999). However, what exactly is meant by the term 'divine Being' requires greater clarity.

The second research question asked how the counsellor's spirituality influences their therapeutic practice. Table 11.2 indicates those responses that scored a 4 or 5, signifying that spirituality was very important or important for their work as a therapist.

Focusing on the response from psychodynamic counsellors the research suggests that while 52 per cent (Table 11.1) of them have a definite belief and value system including reference to a divine Being, only 26 per cent (Table 11.2) view this as important for their work as therapists. There appears to be a discrepancy between the therapists' spiritual beliefs and what impacts on the therapeutic process. Yet given the psychodynamic understanding of the unconscious and

Table 11.2 How counsellors rate the importance of spirituality to their practice

Area of work	% rating 4 or 5/5			
	Person-centred	**Psychodynamic**	**Integrative**	**Overall**
For work as a counsellor/therapist	38	26	68	46
In training	13	11	47	20
In supervision (sample size small)	33	40	42	40

how this is communicated through therapeutic encounter there is an inevitable impact in the counselling room, as Lomas observes:

> The therapist's views on almost every issue involving personal relations will influence whether he [sic] interprets a particular statement, whether he remains silent, or whether he expresses agreement. It is simply not possible for him to shed his sense of values when he enters a consulting room however much he may try to do so. (1999, p. 8)

This was a pilot project and a larger sample will be required in order to move beyond the descriptive use of statistics and establish a causal link. Nonetheless, the research indicates how important spirituality is and yet how little attention is currently paid to this from a psychodynamic perspective. This is even clearer when the figures about the importance of spirituality in training are studied as they are consistently lower than those adopted by counsellors in practice. These patterns may begin to change because of a growing understanding about issues of difference.

Religion, spirituality and psychodynamic counselling: an issue of difference

Counsellors and psychotherapists cannot remain neutral about religion and spirituality as to do so is to fail the client by not attending to their whole psyche. Despite religion and spirituality being late entrants into the field of difference, dominated as it has been by attention to race, gender and sexual orientation, the rise of fundamentalism now demands that this deficit in understanding be addressed. Four generic principles for counselling clients for whom religion and/or spirituality are essential aspects of their lives are as follows:

- The counsellor must be open to hearing and responding to a worldview that may be completely alien to them.

- The counsellor must resist pathologising or negatively labelling the client's beliefs or experiences.

- The counsellor must recognise as countertransference their emotional response to a client with a religious or spiritual presence.

- The counsellor should engage with the religious or spiritual aspect of the client rather than avoid it.

There are also important differences between religions and ways in which religious beliefs lead to intolerance and persecution of minority groups. Many religious groups worldwide have failed to engage constructively with the movement towards equality in the complex areas of gender and sexual orientation. Counsellors may find themselves being called upon to be empathic to religious beliefs that are in direct conflict with many of the principles that this book on valuing difference and diversity espouses. For example, the acceptance of homosexuality and the independence of women are not promoted by many faith communities.

Since 2003 in Britain, legislation under the Employment Equality (Religion or Belief) Regulations has made it unlawful to discriminate against workers because of religion or similar belief. The Advisory and Conciliation Service stresses that anyone already familiar with principles of good practice in other areas, such as race, gender or disability, will have little difficulty in implementing the new regulations. In the wider consciousness of society, difference must be respected and equity and justice are enshrined in law. The attitudes and motivations of the counsellor, conscious and unconscious, are paramount and a degree of personal insight and self-awareness is essential if difference is to be revered and respected.

The world we live in is also changing, especially in relation to religion in Great Britain (Davie, 1994). The beliefs and patterns of worship that are assumed to be part of British life, in its most caricatured form via the Church of England, play a diminished part in contemporary culture. In many ways relentless secularisation (Bruce, 2002) combined with the eclecticism inherent in post-modernism (Eagleton, 1996) has forever changed the cultural landscape, yet this provides both an opportunity and a challenge for religious belief. Chief Rabbi Jonathan Sacks writes:

> With the transition of Britain from a strong common culture to a more fragmented, segmented and pluralized one, we suddenly find that we are all members of a minority group, practising Christians no less than practising Jews. This is not a bad thing, because it means paradoxically as we become more diverse we discover more areas of common experience. The problems of Christians, Jews, Muslims, Sikhs, Hindus and others in trying to preserve their values and hand them to their children become more, not less, alike. In the contemporary situation ... to be a minority is part of the experience. (1995, p. vii)

So the likelihood is that a client coming for counselling from a religious background or spiritual tradition will perceive themselves as part of a minority group that is often misrepresented in the wider cultural context where 'Religion in our time has become a kind of wastepaper basket for the secular intellectual's collection of undesirable knowledge' (Budd and Rusbridger, 2005, p. 2). There is an anxiety as to whether or not clients feel they will be accepted as whole persons, including their spirituality. The only other option is to leave their faith outside the door of the counselling room. Part of the solution is for the counsellor or therapist to understand the worldview that the client brings. The religious world is changing in two central ways and it is important that counsellors be aware of this. The first change is a return to fundamentalism; the second the advent of 'belief without belonging', expressed in the term 'spirituality'.

The rise of religious fundamentalism, though predicted (Kepel, 1994; Marty and Appleby, 1994), has taken a particularly ugly turn. Terrorism as a part of contemporary life has been tragically demonstrated in New York, Madrid and London. Living in Western Europe with a secularised and consumer driven worldview has inhibited the understanding of the power of fundamentalist religion on a worldwide stage (Bruce, 2000). Overtly psychoanalytic theory is of little help in understanding fundamentalism of any kind as it has avoided 'confrontation with the historical truth claims of religion, just as the abandonment of the seduction theory avoided confrontation with the historical reality of sexual abuse' (Hood, 1997, p. 42). Truth claims from a fundamental religious or spiritual source open up a chasm for psychoanalysis and challenge its belief that it has universal meaning and appeal. Hood argues that psychoanalytic theory has the potential to be able to deal with what might be construed as the delusional aspects of religion, especially fundamentalism, yet this potential has yet to be realised.

The second development has been the recognition that some people feel part of a religious community and have an active faith commitment but no longer belong to an institutional religion. Davie (1994) calls this 'belief without belonging', a phenomenon that has seen a remarkable growth in the last decade in Britain. Bergin and Richards (1997, p. 13) write about this in a therapeutic context: 'Religious expressions tend to be denominational, external, cognitive, behavioural, ritualistic, and public. Spiritual experiences tend to be universal, ecumenical, internal, affective, spontaneous and private. It is possible to be religious without being spiritual and spiritual without being religious.'

These two developments span the vast range of experience encompassed by religion and spirituality and they complicate the task of the counsellor. On one hand counsellors need to resist the desire to respond negatively through their own psychic fundamentalism evoked by experiencing religious fundamentalism. Counsellors also need to understand aspects of spiritual experience that they have not experienced. The 'spiritual is its own unique domain and cannot be subsumed by other domains such as cognitions, emotions, social systems, and so on. The spiritual is a different realm, a different reality, and one that has not been articulated well in behavioural science and practice' (Bergin and Richards, 1997, p. 13). The task required of the psychodynamic counsellor is her or his ability to understand the part that religion plays in the life of the client, whilst being able to hold their own judgements, thoughts and feelings in suspense. If 'religion' and 'spirituality' evoke powerful, countertransferential material, this is something psychodynamic counsellors are trained to be aware of and use appropriately in the interests of the client.

Religion, spirituality and psychodynamic counselling: future collaboration?

There are four strategies by which psychodynamic counselling theory can begin to address and embrace religion. The first is through a re-evaluation of what

Freud really said about religion and spirituality. Psychoanalysis was influenced by powerful materialistic and scientific paradigms that saw religion as a discredited inheritance. Science and psychoanalysis were the future, unencumbered by religious, mystical or occult practice. Critiques have been made of Freud's views on religion (Wulff, 1997), yet Freud, despite his public image, maintained a lifelong friendship with a Swiss Protestant minister, Oskar Pfister (Meng and Freud, 1963). Their correspondence reveals Freud's valuing of his Jewish heritage, lack of involvement in Jewish religious practices, and acceptance of the religious views of others, whilst disagreeing but not condemning, valuing religion as a force of social cohesion, with frequent use of biblical symbolism and imagery. Freud's views on spirituality include references to oceanic feelings or experiences (1930), occultism (1925, 1933), telepathy (1921, 1922) and mysticism. Freud the enemy of religion has been perpetuated through *The Future of an Illusion* (1927) – a book that Freud himself described as weak.

The second strategy is to apply contemporary thinking on religion and spirituality to psychoanalytic thought. Samuels and Symington are two contemporary psychoanalytic writers with much to offer the understanding of religion. Symington (1994) argues that Freud founded a natural religion when he established psychoanalysis, religion being the 'relationship between one human being and another' where this encounter links us to the true god who 'is the ultimate being of which we and the whole universe is constructed'. 'To achieve this fulfilment, we need the understanding of our inner lives that has come to us both through psychoanalysis and also through the central insights of the great religious traditions of the world' (p. vii).

Sayers (2003) comes from a parallel perspective where she focuses on being in love:

> Born of love, psychotherapy is recovering it together with religion. Once wary of talking about love, psychotherapists and psychoanalysts are talking about it … I aim to demonstrate that, like religion, psychoanalysis and psychotherapy seek to animate or reanimate the psyche or the soul of their recipients through the medium of the psychoanalyst's or psychotherapist's oneness with his or her patients. This entails the oneness that lies at the heart of mystical and religious experience, and also at the heart of falling in love … For many it may involve experiencing oneness with God or with another as divine … Far from being dead, religion is alive and well. There is also mounting evidence that religion is good for our physical and mental well-being … But is religion – or holiness – good for our quality of life, well-being, and physical or mental health? And if it is, what are the implications for therapy? (pp. 1ff.)

Symington and Sayers stress the importance of finding the points of connection to hold psychoanalysis, religion and spirituality together. Rather than adopting a hermeneutic of exclusion, they propose a hermeneutic of inclusion. They are embarking on the tasks of dealing with the idols of our worship – religious, secular or psychoanalytic, as well as listening and working with the symbols and objects that clients bring, consciously and unconsciously (Ricoeur, 1970). Such an inclusive approach provides philosophical and interpretive foundations which enhance an examination of the psyche that includes religious and spiritual dimensions.

The third strategy would be to explore ways in which psychodynamic counselling can enhance spiritual wellbeing. One potential health promoting aspect of psychodynamic counselling is adherence to the therapeutic frame. By their nature many religious and spiritual beliefs and experiences are about encountering an Other (defined by some as God) through which transformation takes place. For example, Christians believe that the Bible is the Word of God, literally the voice of God to people today and that the Holy Spirit unites the text through the words of the preacher/minister and the hearing of the worshippers. Christians are always psychologically experiencing the in-breaking of God, who is no respecter of persons or boundaries. The notion that nothing is impossible, that the miraculous is feasible and that there is life and being beyond physical death, results in a sense that life has a permeable boundary, which is both liberating and frightening. So much so, that many religious traditions attempt to control this experience through one person – a priest in the Catholic tradition – or through a fixed liturgy. Other religious traditions will have different ways of describing this in-breaking experience, using the language of transcendence and immanence. The therapeutic frame brackets the therapeutic relationship so that the therapist does not become God-like and 'break in' in the same way that religious or spiritual experience does. This allows the client to explore their projections and transferences, safe in the knowledge that the counsellor maintains a secure boundary. In Winnicottian terms the therapeutic space symbolised by the therapeutic frame provides 'transcendent space' and

> is the third part of life of a human being, a part that we cannot ignore, an intermediate area of experiencing, to which inner reality and external life both contribute ... it shall exist as a resting place for the individual engaged in the perpetual human task of keeping inner and outer reality separate yet inter-related. (Winnicott, 1975, p. 230)

Winnicott uses the term 'illusory experience' to speak of real psychic experiences created in this 'transcendent space', 'which in adult life is inherent in art and religion' (1975, p. 230). A therapeutic boundary within which illusion and disillusionment can happen (Jacobs, 2000) enhances the psychological understanding of the client and potentially deepens their faith experience.

Another health promoting aspect of psychodynamic counselling for a client with a religious faith involves facilitating a person in their 'faith development', a concept developed by James Fowler (1990, 1996). Fowler offers a model of human development that integrates a theological understanding of faith with insights drawn from psychoanalytically influenced developmental psychology. Fowler observes that people are able to grow in faith terms, at whatever stage of the developmental process they may be. Each decade of life, each with new challenges, gives rise to new beliefs and values in tandem with psychological growth. Conversely some people find their lives out of harmony with their beliefs and values, which have become static or rooted in an earlier stage of faith development. As a person's faith grows so they are able to question and handle diversity in a creative way. But the move from one stage to another can be painful as the familiar is relinquished to be replaced by something that is not yet fully formed or understood. At these points, psychodynamic counselling can encourage that growth process, especially in relation to faith and spirituality.

The fourth and final strategy is to identify maladaptive patterns that use religion and spirituality defensively. . Everyone needs defence mechanisms to protect themselves from unbearable emotional, psychic or existential pain when they are threatened in a way that is overwhelming. As Winnicott writes, 'We are unwise not to be vulnerable, and we are prudent to be hidden' (Newman, 1995, p. 129). The endurance of experiencing 'unthinkable anxieties' and 'primitive agonies' (Newman 1995, p. 424) is challenging. Yet like any system of belief, religion or spirituality can be used as a way of avoiding psychological pain or facing reality. A faith, religious or spiritual background may give a particular pattern or shape to such defences (Ross, 2003). One defence might be the use of rituals or words in an obsessive way, another the use of a sacred text, such as the Bible or the Koran, in a way that cannot be challenged or discussed. So much authority is given to the divine authorship that any questioning of this is met with 'horror and extreme defensiveness' (Jacobs, 1993, p. 175); rationalisation can be used to disguise unconscious fears. Jacobs refers to the ordination of women in the Church of England as an example; intellectual arguments against the ordination of women mask discomfort at having to deal more equally with women. Other examples include projecting on to God or other religious figures whatever the person wants to do themselves, as in 'God has told me to buy a Mercedes'; and prayer seen as a 'quick fix', while in reality being a way of avoiding difficult relationships, intrusive thoughts and uncomfortable feelings. Conversion is a real and important part of religious traditions and has an authentic role within faith communities. It can also be used defensively as a way of trying to escape a difficult past experience. Experienced counselling practitioners will become adept at seeing beyond the anxiety and the defence to the hidden impulse or feeling that should become the focus of the therapeutic work.

Religious belief and spiritual experience can also form what Rose (2002) calls 'sick paradigm syndrome': being stuck in a certain worldview that fails to do justice to the richness and breadth of other religious and spiritual traditions. Christians can 'become locked into the story of crucifixion and death without any real awareness of resurrection … Many people remain stuck at Good Friday making religion a matter of guilt, sin and self-hatred' (2002, pp. 82ff.). All practitioners need to be aware of the potential for limiting vision that any religious dogma, therapeutic system or counselling theory can have.

Conclusion

Counselling, as a discipline, has been part of the wider post-modern trend to redefine, revalue and reassess previous modernist understandings and connections including spirituality. The critical encounter between psychoanalytic theory and religion that is currently taking place will follow in the revisionary footprints left by feminist and gay affirmative thinkers to produce a more enlightened understanding that will afford respect for difference. Psychodynamic thinking has much to offer all those who seek counselling, regardless of their culture, religion, creed, gender, sexual orientation, age or disability. Their thoughts, feelings, fantasies, hopes, desires, fears and beliefs all contribute to their unique identity and self-image. The therapist must remain open to all aspects of the client and enter into their world. There will often be differences in the religious and spiritual beliefs of counsellor and client, but it behoves the therapist to both hear them and work with them.

REFERENCES

Bair, D. (2004). *Jung*. London: Little, Brown.

Bergin, A. and Richards, P. 1997). *A Spiritual Strategy for Counselling and Psychotherapy*. Washington, DC: American Psychological Association.

Bobrow, J. (1997). 'Coming to life: the creative intercourse of psychoanalysis and Zen Buddhism'. In C. Spezzano and G. Gargiulo (eds), *Soul on the Couch*. Hillsdale, NJ: Analytic Press.

Bruce, S. (2000). *Fundamentalism*. Oxford: Blackwell.

Bruce, S. (2002). *God is Dead: Secularization in the West*. Oxford: Blackwell.

Budd, S. and Rusbridger, R. (eds) (2005). *Introducing Psychoanalysis*. London: Routledge.

Coltart, N. (1993). *How to Survive as a Psychotherapist*. London: Sheldon.

Coltart, N. (1996). *The Baby and the Bathwater*. London: Karnac.

Davie, G. (1994). *Religion in Britain Since 1945: Believing without Belonging*. Oxford: Blackwell.

Eagleton, T. (1996). *The Illusions of Postmodernism*. Oxford: Blackwell.

Epstein, M. (1995). *Thoughts without a Thinker*. New York: Basic Books.

Fordham, F. (1966), *An Introduction to Jung's Psychology*, 3rd edition. Harmondsworth: Penguin.

Fowler, J. (1990). 'Faith development research' and 'Faith/Belief'. In R. Hunter (ed.), *Dictionary of Pastoral Care and Counselling*. Nashville, TN: Abingdon.

Fowler, J. (1996). *Faithful Change*. Nashville, TN: Abingdon.

Freud, S. (1921). 'Psycho-analysis and telepathy', and (1922). 'Dreams and telepathy'. In J. Strachey (ed.), *The Standard Edition of the Complete Psychological Works of Sigmund Freud, Volume XVIII*. London: Hogarth.

Freud, S. (1925). 'The occult significance of dreams'. In J. Strachey (ed.), *The Standard Edition of the Complete Psychological Works of Sigmund Freud, Volume XIX*. London: Hogarth.

Freud, S. (1927). 'The future of an illusion', and (1930). 'Civilization and its discontents'. In J. Strachey (ed.), *The Standard Edition of the Complete Psychological Works of Sigmund Freud, Volume XXI*. London: Hogarth.

Freud, S. (1933).'Dreams and occultism'. In J. Strachey (ed.), *The Standard Edition of the Complete Psychological Works of Sigmund Freud, Volume XXII*. London: Hogarth.

Gay, P. (1988). *Freud*. London: Dent.

Hay, D. and Hunt, K. (2000). *Understanding the Spirituality of People who Don't Go to Church*. Research report. Nottingham: Nottingham University.

Heelas, P. and Woodhead, L. (2005). *The Spiritual Revolution*. Oxford: Blackwell.

Holmes, P. (2004). *Becoming More Fully Human: Exploring the Ecotone of Human Spirituality, Salugenic Discipleship, and Therapeutic Faith Community*. Unpublished PhD thesis, University of Birmingham.

Hood, R. W. Jr (1997). 'Psychoanalysis and fundamentalism'. In J. Jacobs and D. Capps (eds), *Religion, Society and Psychoanalysis*. Boulder, CO: Westview.

Izzard, S. (2003). 'Holding contradictions together: an object-relational view of healthy spirituality'. *Contact: The Interdisciplinary Journal of Pastoral Studies*, 140, 2–8.

Jacobs, M. (1992). *Freud*. London: Sage.

Jacobs, M. (1993). *Still Small Voice*, 2nd edition. London: SPCK.

Jacobs, M. (2000). *Illusion: A Psychodynamic Interpretation of Thinking and Belief*. London: Whurr.

Jones, J. (1991). *Contemporary Psychoanalysis and Religion*. New Haven, CT: Yale University Press.

Jung, C. G. (1933). *Modern Man in Search of a Soul*. London: Routledge and Kegan Paul.

Jung, C. G. (1958). *Psychology and Religion: West and East. Collected Works of C. G. Jung, Volume 11*. Princeton, NJ: Princeton University Press.

Kepel, G. (1994). *The Revenge of God*. Oxford: Polity.

Lomas, P. (1999). *Doing Good? Psychotherapy Out of Its Depth*. Milton Keynes: Open University Press.

Lynch, G. (2002). *After Religion: Generation X and the Search for Meaning*. London: DLT.

Lynch, G. (2003). *Losing My Religion?* London: DLT.

Marty, M. and Appleby, S. (eds) (1994). *Accounting for Fundamentalisms*. Chicago: University of Chicago Press.

Mearns, D. and Thorne, B. (2000). *Person-centred Therapy Today*. London: Sage.

Meng, H. and Freud, E. (eds) (1963). *Psycho-Analysis and Faith*. London: Hogarth.

Murcell, G. (2001). *English Spirituality*. London: SPCK.

Newman, A. (1995). *Winnicott's Words*. London: Free Association.

Northcut, T. (1999). 'Book reviews'. *Clinical Social Work Journal*, 27: 2, 217–20.

Palmer, M. (1997). *Freud and Jung on Religion*. London: Routledge.

Peterson, E. (1996). *The Message*. Colorado Springs, CO: Navpress.

Ricoeur, P. (1970). *Freud and Philosophy*. New Haven, CT: Yale University Press.

Rizzuto, A.-M. (1979). *The Birth of the Living God*. Chicago: University of Chicago Press.

Rizzuto, A.-M. (1998). *Why Did Freud Reject God?* New Haven, CT: Yale University Press.

Randour, M. (1993). *Exploring Sacred Landscapes*. New York: Columbia University Press.

Rose, J. (2002). *Sharing Spaces? Prayer and the Counselling Relationship*. London: DLT.

Ross, A. (2003). *Counselling Skills for Church and Faith Community Workers*. Milton Keynes: Open University Press.

Sacks, J. (1995). *Faith in the Future*. London: DLT.

Sahlein, J. (2002). 'When religion enters the dialogue: a guide for practitioners'. *Clinical Social Work Journal*, 30: 4, 381–401.

Sayers, J. (2003). *Divine Therapy*. Oxford: Oxford University Press.

Stevens, A. (1990). *On Jung*. Harmondsworth: Penguin.

Symington, N. (1994). *Emotion and Spirit*. London: Cassell.

West, W. (2000). *Psychotherapy and Spirituality*. London: Sage.

West, W. (2004). *Spiritual Issues in Therapy*. Basingstoke: Palgrave Macmillan.

Winnicott, D. (1975). *Through Paediatrics to Psychoanalysis: Collected Papers*. London: Karnac.

Woodhead, L. and Heelas, P. (eds) (2000). *Religion in Modern Times*. Oxford: Blackwell.

Wulff, D. (1997). *Psychology of Religion*, 2nd edition. Chichester: Wiley.

Index